T0331988

Access, Quality, and the Global Learning Crisis

Access, Quality, and the Global Learning Crisis

Insights from Ugandan Primary Education

Sarah Kabay

OXFORD

UNIVERSITY PRESS

OXFORD

UNIVERSITY PRESS

Great Clarendon Street, Oxford, OX2 6DP,
United Kingdom

Oxford University Press is a department of the University of Oxford.
It furthers the University's objective of excellence in research, scholarship,
and education by publishing worldwide. Oxford is a registered trade mark of
Oxford University Press in the UK and in certain other countries

© Sarah Kabay 2021

The moral rights of the author have been asserted

First Edition published in 2021

Impression: 1

Published in the United States of America by Oxford University Press
198 Madison Avenue, New York, NY 10016, United States of America

British Library Cataloguing in Publication Data

Data available

Library of Congress Control Number: 2021937270

ISBN 978–0–19–289686–5

DOI: 10.1093/oso/9780192896865.001.0001

Printed and bound in Great Britain by
Clays Ltd, Elcograf S.p.A.

Acknowledgments

I owe so much to the work, ideas, and insight of others. I would like to use this opportunity to thank a few of the many.

First, I would like to recognize and thank the Ugandan schools and communities that collaborated on this research. It has been a been a privilege to work together and I am very grateful for their knowledge, perspective, and time. Insight from administrators, teachers, parents, and students has been invaluable.

I would like to thank Irene Mutumba, along with William Bamusute, Nicholas Sekitooleko, and the team at the Private Education Development Network for the incredible opportunity to learn and work together.

I would like to thank Dean Karlan for giving me my first opportunity to travel to Uganda, take part in research, and the best job I could ever have imagined, and all of IPA Uganda for the community, colleagues, and experience. In particular, I would like to thank Simon Tumusiime and Vivienne Tibaberwa for their commitment to the project over so many years.

I would like to thank a number of different initiatives at NYU for the support and community: the International Education Program, IES-PIRT Program, Global Research Initiative, Global TIES, and Additional Insights Fellowship, as well as the Spencer Foundation. I would like to thank my committee and external readers for their insight, advice, and belief in the project: Elisabeth King, David Stasavage, William Easterly, and Carol Anne Spreen.

Thank you to Sharon Wolf, Amy Jo Dowd, Gwyneth McClendon, and Hua-Yu Sebastian Cherng for your reading, feedback, and conversation. Thank you to Benjamin Piper and Andreas de Barros for your thoughts and insight.

Many many thanks to Hiro Yoshikawa, for your example and inspiration, and for the grace and care you bring to being an adviser. I owe so much to your boundless knowledge as well as to the time and attention you have devoted to me and my work. This book would simply not exist without your support and I have learned so much from your perspective, direction, and values.

Finally, thank you to my parents, Preston, and Theodore for everything, always.

Contents

List of Figures

List of Tables

1
Introduction

The Global Learning Crisis and the Access vs. Quality Paradigm

In 2011, in Uganda, 21 percent of children in third grade could not identify a single letter of the alphabet and 58 percent could not read a single word (Uwezo, 2011). Similarly, 40 percent could not add and 64 percent could not subtract. This translates to 92 percent of third graders being unable to read at a second-grade level and 88 percent being unable to perform second-grade-level division. These results were published by the East African citizen-led assessment initiative Uwezo in a report titled *Are Our Children Learning?* One interpretation of these results would be simply to answer that question "no".

Over the past decade, considerable time, resources, and attention have been directed toward changing the answer to that question, but Uganda's low learning levels appear relatively unchanged. In 2019, 49 percent of Ugandan children in third grade still could not read a single word, 78 percent could not read a simple sentence, and 50 percent could neither add nor subtract (Uwezo, 2019).

Unfortunately, these findings are not unique to Uganda. More than 50 percent of children in second grade in Ghana, Zambia, and rural India cannot read a single word of text. More than 50 percent of children in second grade in Nicaragua, Iraq, and Kenya cannot perform two-digit subtraction (World Bank, 2018). At the end of primary school, 53 percent of children in low- and middle-income countries cannot read and understand a simple story (World Bank, 2019).

The fact that millions of children around the world are unable to read, write, or perform basic arithmetic has been christened the "Global Learning Crisis" (Adams & van der Gaag, 2010). Countless actors—ministries of education, nongovernmental organizations, businesses, international donors, activists, advocacy groups, and development agencies—have all committed to addressing the situation.

This work, however, depends on the answer to another question. If children are not learning, the most pressing issue to understand is *why not?*

Access, Quality, and the Global Learning Crisis: Insights from Ugandan Primary Education. Sarah Kabay, Oxford University Press.
© Sarah Kabay 2021. DOI: 10.1093/oso/9780192896865.003.0001

One explanation for the Global Learning Crisis is particularly prevalent. It is used to both diagnose the crisis itself and explain how we got here. I will call it the "access vs. quality paradigm." It argues that over the past two decades, we have succeeded in getting children into school—the problem is that they do not learn once they are there. In other words, an overemphasis on access to education has overlooked or undermined the quality of education.

It would be hard to overstate the pervasiveness of this idea. At the launch of UNESCO's seminal research report on the crisis, for example, UNECSO's UN representative explained, "While more children are in school, it's been at the cost of quality. The issue now is to put the focus on quality" (Lederer, 2014).

Inspiring titles such as "Africa's Education Crisis: In School but not Learning" (van Fleet, 2012) and "The New Horizon in Education: From Access to Learning," (Kim, 2015) as well as statements like "Getting children into school was the easy part" (Pritchett, 2013), the access vs. quality paradigm has precipitated a marked shift in policy and practice. International education practitioners and the donors that support them have fallen in line behind the admonishment "Look beyond counting the number of children sitting in classrooms and start focusing on learning" (Watkins, 2013).

The access vs. quality paradigm has motivated remarkable advances in the Education for All (EFA) movement, the global effort to provide quality basic education to all children, youth, and adults, but it is insufficient. In emphasizing the need to move "beyond counting the number of children sitting in classrooms," the importance of counting has sometimes been forgotten. Simply pivoting from a focus on access to a focus on quality runs the risk of reproducing exactly what the paradigm critiques, just in reverse. If the problem with the first decades of the Education for All movement was that it focused exclusively on access, the solution should not be to focus exclusively on quality. We need to work on both.

This book aims to move beyond the access vs. quality paradigm; it argues that addressing the Global Learning Crisis will require something more than a transition from access to quality. The importance of learning outcomes cannot be overstated; it is absolutely critical that we recognize that sitting in a classroom does not necessarily translate into learning. But to understand learning outcomes, we must also understand who is sitting in the classroom, which classroom, when, and why. We must recognize that access and quality are interconnected.

In some cases, our understanding of quality cannot be disentangled from issues related to access. I will offer two quick examples: a recent study in Liberia evaluated the impact of allowing different private providers to manage and run government primary schools—similar to charter schools in the US. One provider had a large positive impact on children's test scores, but this provider also increased school dropout rates. In schools managed by this provider, dropout rates increased by 50 percent, which complicated any interpretation of the provider's positive impact on test scores (Romero & Sandefur, 2020). The effect on quality, accordingly, cannot be understood without at least acknowledging the negative effects on access.

The second example concerns teacher value-added calculations, an estimation method for determining a teacher's impact on students' performance. A key challenge in this work is that a teacher's impact can depend on the characteristics of the students he or she teaches, and the assignment of teachers to schools and students to teachers is often nonrandom.[1] Accordingly, estimations of teachers' impact can be biased by how children are sorted and assigned. High-achieving students, either through their parents' effort or a school's tracking, are often assigned to high-performing teachers, thus reinforcing those teachers' positive performance. A teacher's effectiveness and the quality of the education they deliver are therefore influenced by which students have access to that teacher.

Access to education and education quality are interconnected in many ways beyond these two examples, but the discourse on international education often presents them as two independent issues—we can focus on one without necessarily affecting the other. When a connection is acknowledged, the discourse describes a negative association between the two. At best, we believe access and quality are competing concerns for limited resources; at worst, we see a trade-off between efforts to improve access to education and efforts to improve education quality. According to the access vs. quality paradigm, the Global Learning Crisis is the result of either the disconnect between access and quality or their negative association.

We need better and more nuanced understanding. From the synapses that form in the brain to the dynamics of a classroom, to large networks of schools and education systems, the activity and structure of education is defined by connectivity, interaction, and interdependence. Working in the field of education, we should expect this complexity. What might our work look like if we viewed the Global Learning Crisis from this perspective?

We can start with access. The Education for All movement often presents access as a simple dichotomy—children are either in or out of school—and that at this point issues of access are relevant mostly for particularly

---

[1] There is an important debate on value-added calculations. See, e.g., Baker et al. (2010); Rothstein (2009, 2010); Chetty, Friedman, & Rockoff (2014); Rothstein (2017a). For a collected review of these papers and responses, see Rothstein (2017b).

disadvantaged populations, such as children living in situations of conflict or crisis. In this book, I argue that persistent and enduring challenges of access affect the average child's educational experience, particularly in sub-Saharan Africa, and we should think of access to education as something that is multidimensional and dynamic. Though the number of children who at some point enroll in school has increased, it can be helpful to consider access as something more than whether a child has ever set foot inside a school.

The refrain "in school but not learning" obscures the fact that many children enroll in school late, are frequently absent, transfer between schools, and drop out of school early. In Tanzania, more than 40 percent of children in first grade are already overage (Education Population and Data Center (EPDC), 2010). In Liberia, the net attendance rate in urban primary schools is only 48 percent, and in rural primary schools, only 26 percent (Ministry of Education, 2016). Even in the comparatively more affluent Ghana, on a given day, one out of every three children is absent in the country's rural primary schools (EPDC, 2008). And nearly twenty countries in sub-Saharan Africa have primary school completion rates lower than 50 percent, indicating that more than half of children drop out before completing primary school (UNESCO, 2015). The questions "Does a child have access to school?" and "Is a school accessible?" are not static or explained by a single concern.

The difference between "Schooling is not the same as learning" and "In school but not learning" might seem like insignificant semantics, but it represents a key distinction in our understanding of the status of the world's efforts to educate all children. The former highlights a critically important truth that has been overlooked for too long, while the latter misrepresents the educational experience of millions of children.

The international education community has been galvanized by the call to better understand education quality and to focus on measuring learning outcomes, but our understanding of the learning process must incorporate issues such as school choice, irregular and infrequent attendance, transfer between schools, and early school dropout, as well as children's lives outside of the classroom, just as our understanding of access should include how a poor-quality education can discourage attendance and push children out of school.

Access and quality are two fundamental dimensions of any public service: healthcare, infrastructure, and, of course, education. Though each dimension is important, the greatest, most actionable insight might come from investigating the connection and interaction between the two. The motivating premise of this book is that in a dynamic and complex system such as education, access and quality must be considered together. Addressing the

Global Learning Crisis will require us to pay attention to which children access school and when, as well as what kinds of experiences and conditions they encounter once they are there.

In this book, I conduct a case study of Uganda's Universal Primary Education and provide an example of how to consider the Global Learning Crisis in light of both access and quality. In a single sample of Ugandan primary schools and communities, I analyze grade repetition, private primary schools, and school fees, viewing each issue as an illustration of the complex association between access to education and education quality.

This strategy is based on the belief that achieving nuanced understanding of a specific context can lead to more generalizable insight. Analysis of global and macro-level trends is important, but issues such as the Global Learning Crisis are often understood in very broad terms, encompassing dramatically different populations, cultures, and settings around the world. Detailed, focused, and interdisciplinary investigation of any single context is lacking. With this book, I provide one attempt to fill that gap.

I have chosen to analyze grade repetition, privatization, and school fees because of their significance to primary education policy and practice, and for the ways in which they exemplify the complicated relationship between access and quality. Instead of focusing on either access or quality, I analyze the connection between them. And instead of analyzing any particular issue in isolation, I focus on a single sample of schools and students and explore the various issues and factors that define their educational experiences.

The primary conclusion of the book is that access and quality do not have to be competing concerns—there can be a positive association between the two. In empirical analysis of data from my sample of Uganda primary schools and communities, I find that there are dynamics where access to education and the quality of education can be mutually reinforcing, where improving access can be associated with an improvement in quality, and where addressing quality can improve access. I argue that education reform should work to identify and support these dynamics where they exist and create them where they do not.

Education quality and children's learning are of the utmost importance, but the almost exclusive focus on test scores is myopic. In order to make real gains in learning, we must recognize and work with the connections between access and issues of quality. Viewing education as a zero-sum game, with a trade-off between efforts to improve access and efforts to improve quality, is a missed opportunity. Recognizing and working toward an alliance between access and quality could be an opportunity to realize the type of revolutionary change needed in education systems around the world.

The book is accordingly structured as follows. Chapter 2 explores current understanding and definitions of education access, education quality, and the connection between them. It then describes the ways in which the access vs. quality paradigm has been used to explain the Global Learning Crisis. In Chapter 3, I briefly summarize some of the theory and research on complexity and provide some initial examples of how these ideas can apply to the study of the Global Learning Crisis. In Chapter 4, I provide information on the Ugandan context, the sample and data I use for my empirical analysis, and general research methods. I provide a more detailed description of my methods in the Technical Appendix.

Chapters 5–7 comprise the core of the book. They investigate grade repetition, privatization, and school fees, respectively. In each chapter, I review the literature on the subject and how it is understood in terms of access and quality. I then analyze specific empirical questions with my data to test the relationship between access and quality as it is expressed by each issue. The conclusions of this empirical analysis serve as the foundation for a new understanding of access and quality, as an alliance instead of a trade-off.

My case study results in several specific and concrete recommendations for the set of Ugandan primary schools that are the focus of my analysis—for example, to more clearly communicate the country's policy on school fees, to better regulate private primary schools, and to make the transition between local languages and English more gradual. Many other low-income countries and countries in sub-Saharan Africa have much in common with Uganda. They face similar challenges. It is possible that some of the recommendations in this book might be relevant for these countries.

The key conclusion of the book, though, is that primary education must be recognized as a system defined by complexity where issues of access and quality are interconnected. Though tensions between the dimensions of access and quality exist, there can also be a positive association between efforts to improve access and efforts to improve quality. In order to encourage the revolutionary change needed to improve children's learning around the world, education policy and practice should embrace the complexity of education systems, move away from single policy solutions towards unintended consequences, flexibility, and responsiveness, and work to encourage dynamics where improvements in access and quality are mutually reinforcing.

2
Defining Access and Quality in International Education

Introduction

Education is recognized not just as a fundamental human right, but as an important catalyst for and vital component of development. It has been shown to increase income, improve health, reduce poverty, promote gender equality, boost economic growth, and foster peace (Global Partnership for Education, 2015). Motivated by this impressive résumé, governments in low- and middle- income countries devote approximately US$25 billion dollars to primary education every year (Steer, 2014).

Yet 250 million children worldwide are not learning basic reading and mathematics (UNESCO, 2014). They represent almost 40 percent of the world's 650 million primary school-aged children (UNESCO, 2014). These statistics and the ability to define the magnitude of the crisis in this way are the result of almost twenty years of work by initiatives such as the Annual Status of Education Reports (ASER), Twaweza, Uwezo, and the Early Grade Reading and Math Assessments (EGRA & EGMA). These initiatives have revolutionized the field of international education by first assessing learning outcomes, and then drawing attention to the poor results.

After over a decade of using the word "shock" to describe the results of learning assessments ("As shocking as these data are" (Wetterberg & Gove, 2011: v); "a shocking 86% of primary school students in low-income countries are not proficient in mathematics" (Istance et al., 2019: 393); "In 2005, many were shocked when for the first time the nation [India] learned that half of its Grade 5 students could not read a Grade 2 level text" (Banerji, Bhattacharjea, and Wadhwa, 2013)), we have entered a new phase. The Global Learning Crisis is now a primary concern, if not *the* primary concern of the field of international education.

Work to address the Global Learning Crisis in many ways depends upon how it is understood. In this chapter, I investigate the prevailing explanation for the Global Learning Crisis: the access vs. quality paradigm. I begin by defining

Access, Quality, and the Global Learning Crisis: Insights from Ugandan Primary Education. Sarah Kabay, Oxford University Press.
© Sarah Kabay 2021. DOI: 10.1093/oso/9780192896865.003.0002

access and quality, and then explore how these constructs are used to explain the low learning levels that characterize primary education around the world. I highlight some of the problems and limitations of the access vs. quality paradigm and introduce systems thinking and research on complex adaptive systems as a way in which to rethink access to education and educational quality and to improve upon our understanding of the Global Learning Crisis and our work to address it.

Access and Quality

On Christmas Eve, 1957, during the nation's first year of independence, Ghana's President Kwame Nkrumah made a radio broadcast to the nation:

> My first objective is to abolish from Ghana poverty, ignorance, and disease. We shall measure our progress by the improvement in the health of our people; by the number of children in school and by the quality of their education; by the availability of water and electricity in our towns and villages, and by the happiness which our people take in being able to manage their own affairs.
>
> (Ghana Information Service, 1960).

President Nkrumah's words are just one example of our tendency to view education in relation to two concerns: the number of children in school and the quality of their education or, to put it more succinctly, access and quality. This is particularly true in the field of international development education, where discussion of these two issues is ubiquitous. Often, access and quality are presented as separate concerns, as in Nkrumah's speech: attention must be paid to the number of children in school *and* to the quality of their education.

Access and quality remain the two key domains through which we view international education. Efforts to achieve universal primary education are frequently described in relation to the two terms. They are the frame within which we understand primary education. The terms are present in policy reports (Khiddu Makubuya, 2002), the literature of donors and financing (GPE, 2014; DFID, 2013), research (Sifuna, 2007; Somerset, 2011), and even popular media such as newspapers (Ahimbisibwe, 2019). It would be hard to overstate the pervasiveness of these terms. Though such proliferation often results in varying definitions and usage, there seems to be a general consensus in the international education discourse as to what access and quality mean and what they represent.

"Access" is used to refer to enrollment and the ability to attend school. In international education, access has long been defined by indicators such as the Gross Enrollment and Net Enrollment Ratios. In some cases, given concerns for how many children drop out of school, the Primary Completion Rate has also been included among the indicators of access (Lewin, 2009). In many cases, the issue of access has been distilled to a simple dichotomy: in or out of school, as in, "While there has been some progress in universal access to education…there were still 121 million out of school in 2012" (UNESCO, 2015: 3). Though efforts to analyze the ways in which children might be excluded from school exist, even going so far as to include a lack of learning as a type of exclusion (see Lewin's (2007) zones of exclusion), access is almost universally equated with enrollment rates. Generally speaking, access represents "the number of children sitting in classrooms" (Watkins, 2013).

Enduring challenges of access are believed to relate to marginalization or the unique circumstances facing particularly disadvantaged populations, such as adolescent girls or refugees. For example, it is argued that "Typically it is the marginalized, the poor, remote rural populations, those affected by conflict, and ethnic, racial and linguistic minorities who are denied an opportunity for schooling" (UNESCO, 2012: 1) and that "The problem of out-of-school children is becoming increasingly concentrated in conflict-affected countries" (UNESCO, 2015: 8). Accordingly, "Accelerated progress towards universal access to education will require a far stronger focus on the most marginalized children" (Africa Progress Panel, 2012: 76). To summarize, the term "access" is used to represent children's enrollment in school, in which there has been significant progress. Persistent challenges in access refer to extreme cases rather than the average experience of children and countries around the world.

Quality is believed to be more complicated. Even in high-resourced settings such as the United States, where education quality has long been the subject of focused research, there is still significant debate over how best to define and measure quality (Mihaly et al., 2013). In early childhood education, quality is typically broken down into two interrelated constructs: structural quality (material, physical, and human resources) and process quality (curriculum, instruction, and pedagogy) (Mashburn et al., 2008; Sylva, 2010).

Research on primary education tends to focus on more singular concerns, aiming to connect inputs such as teacher characteristics or per-pupil expenditure to student performance, but progress in the field at large has been constrained by the inability to consistently identify what specific school attributes promote student learning outcomes. For example, in reviewing 276 estimates of the effect of student-teacher ratios on student performance, Hanushek (2003) finds that 14 percent of studies reported that low student-teacher ratios had positive and statistically significant effects on students' performance, but a different 14 percent of studies found that low student-teacher ratios had negative, statistically significant effects (Hanushek, 2003).

One approach to quality put forth by Bernal, Mittag, and Qureshi (2016: 2) is to theorize that "school quality produces achievement, but is latent and unobserved." Common measures such as class size and teacher education can be used as "noisy proxies for school quality" but do not necessarily have to causally relate to achievement; instead it is assumed that "school quality is something unobserved about a school that causes more or less achievement to be produced, and that this unobserved characteristic of a school is systematically but not necessarily causally related to these variables" (Bernal, Mittag, & Qureshi, 2016: 3). A more expansive view from Ladd and Loeb (2013: 3) sees the quality of education as "the investment and consumptive value of the education," and is best captured by long-term outcomes for both individuals and society. In the short term, these researchers recommend that education quality be measured by student outcomes and information on school resources and processes (Ladd & Loeb, 2013: 21).

In international education, learning outcomes are typically used to stand in for quality. Some research presents this as self-explanatory, simply stating "To evaluate education quality, the most obvious indicator is learning achievement" (Michaelowa, 2001: 1699). In other instances, more of a case is made. For example, the UK's Department for International Development (DFID), a major donor and thought leader in international education, recognizes that education quality is a multifaceted and contested concept, but "DFID's view is that adopting such a position is unlikely to help the millions of children who are either not in school or not learning foundation skills whilst there." Instead, DFID seeks to advance the use of learning as "a vital and measurable dimension of quality education" (Berry, Barnett, & Hinton, 2015: 324; see also DFID, 2013).

In using learning outcomes to define quality, they are often set apart from issues of access. For example, the 2012 Africa Progress Report titles its education section, "A Twin Crisis in Access and Learning," and recommends that in response, "First, every government needs to redouble its efforts to ensure that all children are in school by 2015. Second, far greater attention must be directed towards the quality of education and learning achievement" (Africa Progress Panel, 2012: 74). Aligning learning outcomes with quality accordingly sets off access as a separate issue.

The current mainstream consensus in international education thus uses enrollment to stand for access and learning outcomes to stand for quality and positions the two as the defining challenges for the field. This shorthand can be useful, but it belies important layers of complexity. Definitions of access and quality that convey more of the details and variety of children's experience can be helpful. Moving away from overly reductive and simplistic definitions and indicators can express and reveal more in our effort to understand these fundamental constructs. In addition—we can imagine that learning relies on both access and quality—if a child attends school only 50 percent of the time, for example, we might expect learning to be affected.

For this reason, I propose more comprehensive definitions of access to education and education quality. In this book, I use "access" to refer to children's ability to enroll in, attend, and progress through school. It is the movement of children into, out of, and between schools. I use "quality" to refer to the resources, structures, and processes within a school and, relatedly, the differences between schools. Access to education is traditionally believed to be determined by child and community characteristics such as poverty, gender, urban/rural, and disability, which, in various contexts, strongly determine children's access to and presence in school. In many ways, though, these issues also interact with the quality of education. Issues of quality typically concern issues related to the school: time on task, teacher characteristics, instructional materials, etc., which, in various contexts, influence children's learning outcomes. Similarly, many of these issues relate to access as well.

Ideally, this conceptualization of access and quality would be captured by multiple measures for each construct; in practice, it is often difficult and costly to collect data that truly reflect the multidimensional nature of either access or quality. In this study, I include age of entry into primary school, grade repetition, attendance, transfer, school choice, and dropout as measures of access, and teacher attendance, the presence of basic scholastic materials, feeding programs, and frequency of tests as measures of quality. While not ideal, these data do at least move beyond the popular use of enrollment and test scores to stand for access and quality, respectively. Further discussion of these measures, their limitations, and other challenges for the present study are discussed in Chapter 3.

A final issue to consider is equity. Often, the issue of equity is understood in relation to access and, as previously mentioned, the idea that challenges of access are relevant only for particularly marginalized and vulnerable populations. In the Sustainable Development Goals, for example, Target 4.5 is recognized as the "most explicit in its focus on equity" and is defined as "eliminate gender disparities and ensure equal access to all levels of education and vocational training for the vulnerable, including persons with disabilities, indigenous peoples and children in vulnerable situations" (UNESCO Institute for Statistics, n.d.). Accordingly, equity is sometimes used to represent access and is paired with and distinguished from the concept of quality, as in the report "Equity and Quality? Challenges for Early Childhood and Primary Education in Ethiopia, India and Peru," (Woodhead et al., 2009), the chapter, "The Twin Crises of Quality and Equality in Education" (Walker et al., 2019), or the phrase "Equal Access to Quality Education," which is the title of a 2017 Act of Congress in the United States (115th Congress, 2017).

Another good example of the alignment of equity with access is the government of India's 2015 Education for All National Review titled "Towards Quality with Equity." In this report, the "heartening facts" of India's progress are presented as "near universal access for 199 million children and an equity dividend with gender parity at elementary level education. Furthermore, of the 14.6 million children who joined elementary schools between 2007–08 and 2012–13 56% were girls 32% from disadvantaged groups of Scheduled Castes and Scheduled Tribes and 59% Muslims" (National University of Educational Planning and Administration, 2014: iii). In looking toward the future, it is argued that "learning processes and learning outcomes are the new challenges which the schooling system is facing given the sharp increase in enrolments over a short period of time and the unique challenge of bringing education to first generation learners with parental and community aspirations to ensure a good education for them" (National University of Educational Planning and Administration, 2014: iii). Equity is seen as the effort to enroll more vulnerable and marginalized children in school, while an emphasis on learning outcomes is seen as representing quality.

As the emphasis of the Education for All movement has shifted toward quality and more attention has been focused on learning outcomes, discussion of equity in some cases has reflected this shift. The 2018 UNESCO Institute for Statistics Handbook on Measuring Equity, for example, uses the term "equity in learning" (UNESCO Institute for Statistics, 2018). Similarly, the 2018 World Development Report from the World Bank, the first such report to focus on education, argues that successful education reforms are defined by their commitment to improving "learning with equity" (World Bank, 2018: 16).

In high-resourced settings, the term inclusion is often included in the discussion of equity. The OECD defines the two terms as follows: "Equity in education means that personal or social circumstances such as gender, ethnic origin or family background, are not obstacles to achieving educational potential (fairness) and that that all individuals reach at least a basic minimum level of skills (inclusion)" (OECD, 2012: 9). These definitions given an indication of the complexity of the concept of equity. Operationalizing equity into indicators and measures further demonstrates the complexity of equity, for example, the argument that "Measures of educational equity can be classified into five categories: meritocracy, minimum standards, impartiality, equality of condition and redistribution" (UNESCO, 2018: 13).

For the purposes of this book, the key takeaway is that the concept of equity can be applied to both access and quality. Children with special needs, disabled children, ethnic, religious, and linguistic minorities, orphans, children living in informal settlements, in remote areas, or in extreme poverty, refugees and internally displaced children, and nomadic children all might be more likely than other children to experience challenges related to access. Similarly, their educational experience might be more likely to be defined by quality concerns—certified teachers might be less likely to work in remote areas, curriculum might not include certain languages, whole schools and individual children might lack basic learning materials, and teachers might focus their attention on high-performing children or those that pay fees. Many of these issues will depend on the context—in some areas, girls might have more household responsibilities, are more likely to marry early and become parents, and are less likely to be seen to have academic potential; in other areas, boys might have more economic opportunities outside of the classroom and might be more likely to drop out, or instruction and pedagogy might not resonate with boys' needs, and all will vary by children's age and education level. Both the demand for and the supply of educational opportunity will be influenced by these factors. These issues also clearly demonstrate how issues of access and quality are intertwined.

From Access to Quality

A shift in focus from access to quality is a defining trend in current efforts to address the Global Learning Crisis. The United Nations serves as a key bellwether in this field, and, accordingly, the transition from the UN's second Millennium Development Goal to its fourth Sustainable Development Goal serves as a good illustration of this shift. The second Millennium Development Goal, "Achieve Universal Primary Education (UPE)" was criticized for the "commitment to achieve UPE by 2015, without specific reference to its quality" (UNESCO, 2004: 19). In response, the fourth Sustainable Development Goal is: "Quality Education: Ensure inclusive and equitable quality education and promote lifelong learning opportunities for all" (World Bank, 2018: 14).

One interpretation of the current focus on quality is to presume that the first Millennium Development Goal and access to primary education have been achieved. For example, "The Millennium Development Goal of achieving universal primary education by 2015 will be met in nearly all countries" (Birdsall, 2013: xi) and "The vast majority of countries will meet the Millennium Development Goal target of universal primary school completion and very few countries will miss it by much" (Pritchett, 2013: 15).

The problem is that "the promise of schooling—getting children into seats in a building called a school—has not translated into the reality of education" (Pritchett, 2013: 2). Education goals, policies, and systems were designed to get children into school, not necessarily to make them learn, and "Learning requires more than a student's physical presence in a classroom" (Pritchett & Banerji, 2013: 1). Achieving Universal Primary Education is accordingly a necessary prerequisite, a shortsighted goal, or a misguided assumption, but "getting children into school was the easy part" (Pritchett, 2013: 2).

This argument offers an invaluable contribution to the Education for All movement. Learning is unfortunately not guaranteed to all children who attend school. In far too many school systems, the vast majority of children are learning very little, if anything at all, despite regularly attending school. But one key component of this argument is inaccurate and misleading—the idea that Universal Primary Education or primary school completion has been achieved.

Schools and education systems cannot simply be realigned in order to move from an emphasis on access to a focus on learning, as issues of educational access are far from being solved and highly relevant to learning. For example, returning to the figures referenced in Chapter 1, because 58 percent of Ugandan third graders could not read a single word and 64 percent could not perform basic addition and subtraction, the prevailing interpretation is that after three years in a classroom, children have very little to show for it. However, an alternative explanation is that for many children, enrollment in third grade does not represent three years in a classroom. The majority of children's educational experience is far more complicated. This underexamined range of experience may be highly relevant to understanding the process of learning.

Basic statistics from Ugandan primary education offer an illustration of enduring challenges related to access. I will highlight a few here: Average annual rates of absence in Ugandan primary schools range from 12 percent in the central region to 28 percent in the north (Musisi, Kasente, & Balihuta, 2008). Overall, primary school absence rates in Uganda are around 20 percent, indicating that on any given day, one out of every five children is absent (Unicef, n.d.). Rates of absence also tend to be underreported and do not include the several weeks at the beginning of each school term that it takes for children to begin to report to school, when children drop out of and re-enter school, or periods when schools are closed for elections and other one-off holidays, which can last for months. In my sample, 15 percent of children reported that they had been absent from school for more than a month at a time; 34 percent reported that they had missed at least one day of school the previous week.

Additionally, more than 50 percent of Ugandan children are overage when they start primary school (Education Policy and Data Center (EPDC), 2012). Once there, estimates for a repetition rate in first grade are as high as 50 percent (Weatherholt et al., 2017). The combination of late enrollment and high rates of grade repetition means that more than 80 percent of children are overage by the end of primary school (EPDC, 2012). Looking at any single grade draws attention to the heterogeneity of Ugandan classrooms, as illustrated by Figure 2.1.

If children enroll in school late, infrequently attend, and drop out of school early, have they ever meaningfully accessed school? These different indicators and the connections between them provide insightful dimensionality to our understanding of access. For example, dropping out of school typically is not a single, discrete event, but often an accumulation of extended absences, a long history of infrequently accessing school, or a continuation of having never effectively engaged in school. I find in my data, for example, that late enrollment and frequent absence are the best predictors of school dropout.

Related concerns such as child labor and time use provide additional layers to the issue of access. More than 50 percent of children in Uganda are working, the vast majority of whom divide their time between work and school (Ugandan Bureau of Statistics, 2010). The fertility rate in Uganda is an

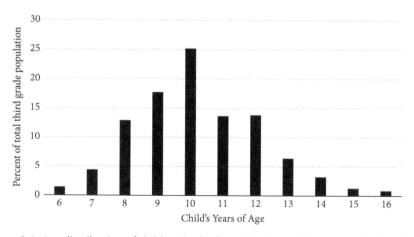

Figure 2.1 Age distribution of children in third grade in Uganda (generated using data from Uwezo (2011)

average of five births per woman, one indicator of large families, and that in addition to income-generating activities, children often take care of younger siblings and perform many unpaid work activities in the household (World Bank, 2020).

Perhaps the most dramatic challenge to the access vs. quality paradigm and its claim that "nearly every child in the world starts school, and nearly all complete primary school (as their country defines it)" (Pritchett, 2013: 2) is the fact that Uganda's primary school completion rate is estimated to be 52 percent, indicating that approximately one out of every two Ugandan children does not make it through seventh grade (World Bank, 2017). Given the rise of unregistered private primary schools and other data quality concerns, it is likely that these figures are somewhat inaccurate, but it remains clear that a significant percentage of Ugandan children do not complete primary school.

The subject of completion rates introduces an additional fault in the shift from access to quality—it assumes we have accurate data on access. In general, enrollment data are highly inaccurate. Even in high-resource settings such as the United States, high-quality, comprehensive data on enrollment and dropout are few and far between (Chapman, Laird, & Kewal Ramani, 2010).

The challenges to collecting accurate information on children are magnified in low-resource settings such as Uganda. In the sample of schools I use for this book, an average grade 5 classroom includes over eighty children, 70 percent of whom had transferred between schools at least once, 88 percent of whom have repeated at least once, and more than 10 percent have transferred and/or repeated more than three times. Such large classes with high rates of absence, repetition, and transfer make it difficult to determine where children are actually enrolled, even without the incentive of per capita funding to overstate enrollment. I have seen instances where children are enrolled in multiple schools at once and where school registers include long lists of names that could represent chronically absent children, transfers, dropouts, or so called "ghost" children. In many education systems around the world, we do not have reliable or accurate data on where children are enrolled and how often they attend.

In my sample, our team made a significant effort to generate accurate enrollment data and faced many challenges. We had an enumerator visit each classroom and work with teachers to rank each child's attendance on a scale of 1 to 5, referencing enrollment registers but also aiming to include new entrants and address any other updates or inaccuracies. A "1" indicated perfect attendance, and a "5" was reserved for children who for any reason were not actually enrolled. The goal of this protocol was to give teachers a simple and nonincriminating way to edit enrollment lists and weed out any inaccurate names. Before randomly selecting pupils to include in the research sample, I excluded those ranked 5.

Even with this procedure, our lists were highly inaccurate. When the survey teams returned to schools to conduct interviews, in 135 out of the 136 schools, at least one name on the enrollment list was false—either the child had dropped out or transferred to a different school or never existed in the first place. In Uganda, these names are typically referred to as "ghost pupils." In some cases, enrollment lists are deliberately manipulated, as schools receive funding based upon the number of children they serve. Potentially just as big a factor, though, is the fact that large class sizes and the frequent movement of children in, out of, and between schools make it difficult for many schools to maintain accurate enrollment registers. On average, of the thirty-five children randomly selected per school, 6.5 of the originally selected names were false; accordingly, 18.5 percent of our already edited enrollment lists were false.

Much of the research on the Global Learning Crisis uses administrative data, which in most contexts do not include any quality checks and are known to be highly inaccurate. Independent research also often fails to resolve concerns for accuracy in enrollment data. Many studies simply select children from those present on a given day. This misses a significant population of children who are frequently absent.

The claim that universal enrollment has been achieved and that "nearly every schooling system in the world can track enrollment over time, across space, and by grade with high frequency (annually, at worst) and with some precision" (Pritchett, 2015: 8–9) thus does not apply to Uganda. Unfortunately, Uganda's experience appears closer to the rule rather than the exception: of the 207 countries included in the Global Monitoring Report, sixty-two, or one out of every three countries, did not have sufficient enrollment data for primary education (UNESCO, 2015). And that is just for basic administrative data—not any quality checks such as the ones used in the present study. Due to a combination of factors such as teacher and student absenteeism, delayed openings, early closings, and extended recess, primary schools in Mozambique offer only thirty days of actual instructional time per 183-day school year (DeStefano, 2012); more than 30 percent of children in Nepal are overage in first grade (UNESCO, 2015); fifteen countries in sub-Saharan Africa have primary school completion rates lower than 50 percent (UNESCO, 2015).

And yet as I described, researchers, practitioners, and policymakers are convinced that the Education for All movement needs to move away from access and toward quality. The belief in such a shift is so entrenched that advice is offered on how to inspire it: "To shift the focus of education improvement from access to achievement, it is critical to determine how serious and widespread low learning levels are among a country's students" (Wetterberg & Gove, 2011: 2). Brief synopses of the shift have become standard in the literature, such as, "Children in sub-Saharan Africa are attending school more than ever before in history—but once in school, they learn very little. In response, the development community has shifted away from a focus on school enrollment and towards the goal of improving learning outcomes," (Kerwin & Thornton, 2020: 1); "While education interventions have traditionally focused on getting children into school, researchers and decision makers are now focusing their attention on efforts to improve learning for all" (Snilsveit et al., 2015: ii); and "Global discourse has shifted from access to education for all towards focusing on the quality of education available to students" (Davidson & Hobbs, 2013: 283).

Low learning levels are unquestionably a critical concern, but to shift the field of international education away from access is an overly simplistic response to the problem. This shift overlooks the persistent challenges of access and the way in which they are related to the challenges of children's learning. Access, like quality, is a multidimensional concern and continues to define the average child's experience, not just particularly disadvantaged or marginalized children. Throughout the world, challenges related to age of entry into primary school, attendance, grade progression, and school dropout are the norm. Issues of access and quality are highly interconnected and quality should also be recognized as more than just test scores. Our understanding of the learning process depends upon understanding these concerns and any response to the Global Learning Crisis must address them.

Access and Quality: A Trade-Off?

Given the need to recognize the complexity and durability of access-related issues, in addition to low learning levels, the question is how to consider access and quality together. The Education for All discourse includes two implicit theories. The first is that access and quality are relatively independent concerns; you can change one without significantly affecting the other. The second is that access and quality are inversely related; gains in access cause decreases in quality. Together, these two theories represent the access vs. quality paradigm, in which access and quality are at best separate concerns competing for attention or, more commonly, in which gains in access have undermined quality. I define and illustrate these theories with quotes from research, policymakers, practitioners, and multilateral development institutions.

Literature that advocates for a shift in focus from access to learning often implies that access and quality are independent concerns. The first theory of the relationship between access and quality is accordingly that there is no relationship. For example, the assessment "Over the past fifteen years, major advances have been made in enrolling millions of children into school worldwide. However...learning levels remain unacceptably low" (UNESCO & Brookings, 2013: 9) suggests a disconnect between access and learning outcomes; progress in one does not necessarily transfer to the other.

Similarly, the statements "While many countries have made impressive gains in access to education over the past decade, improvements in quality have not always kept pace" (UNESCO, 2014: 190) and "Access is not sufficient. The quality of learning is also crucial" (UNESCO, 2013: 1) illustrate this same theory of independence. The Global Learning Crisis is, accordingly, a result of overlooking learning or falsely assuming that there is a link between access and learning. Diagnosing the crisis in this way might suggest a certain sequence: access can be addressed first and then attention can shift to quality. Or access might be an easier issue to address, and so progress might be faster on that front. With either of these interpretations, viewing access and quality as separate leads to either an exclusive focus on quality or a strong emphasis on quality with access presented as a separate, secondary concern.

The second theory of the relationship between access and quality is that the two constructs are inversely related. Specifically, this theory argues that increases in access cause decreases in quality. The Global Learning Crisis is, therefore, a direct result of the progress made on access; it is "a function of the near-unilateral focus, over decades, on educational quantity (access/enrollment data)" (Wagner, 2012: slide 4). For years the experiences of countries around the world have been interpreted in this framework, both to confirm it and to challenge it. I illustrate the ubiquity of this theory by providing examples from research, policymakers, practitioners, and multilateral development organizations. I begin with research.

Much of this discourse centers around a single question: "Is there a quantity-quality tradeoff as enrollments increase?" (Duraisamy et al., 1997: 1) Conclusions are both specific, such as this analysis of data from a study in Yemen: "the analyses point to a trade-off between improved access and quality of learning," (Yuki & Kameyama, 2013: 1) and general, such as this summary "during primary school expansion there was a quantity-quality trade-off" (Al-Samarrai, 2003: 109), thought to encapsulate the experience of countries around the world.

Several studies confirm the theory that increases in enrollment in various contexts were associated with declines in quality. Research on increasing enrollment in Tamil Nadu, India, finds that negative impacts on examination pass rates were the greatest in districts with greater enrollment rates (Duraisamy et al., 1997). Sifuna (2007: 687) documents how examination scores "stagnated at best or declined" in Kenya and Tanzania after increases in access. Similarly, Somerset (2011: 483) describes that in the wake of Kenya's Free Primary Education policies, the education system experienced "quality shocks" where sudden massive enrollment increases led to over-crowded classrooms, and shortages of physical facilities, qualified teachers, and learning materials. Research in Yemen found that school-level increases in total enrollment and also in gender parity across three years were nega-tively associated with current students' test scores (Yuki & Kameyama, 2013). The most extreme cases appear to be in sub-Saharan Africa: "in some African cases, the expansion of the primary system appears to have been accompa-nied by sharp declines in school quality, such that literacy and numeracy are no longer so readily delivered by the primary system" (Colclough, Kingdon, & Patrinos, 2009: 2).

The research in support of a trade-off between access to education and education quality, however, is far from definitive. The same countries are sometimes referenced to argue both for and against the existence of a trade-off. For instance, research on the Central Region in Ghana concludes that "reported improvements in access to education do not correspond to improvements in the provision of educational facilities to assure the delivery of quality education," (Amakyi & Ampah-Mensah, 2016: 61), while a World Bank report argues that "the experience of Ghana and India has shown that the tradeoff [between access and quality] is not inevitable" (World Bank, 2006: 38). There does not seem to be any irrefutable evidence either in support of or against the notion of a trade-off, though there is significantly more research literature in support. In most cases, the challenges to the idea of a trade-off come from policymakers and practitioners rather than from research.

Communities of policymakers and practitioners continually return to the question of a trade-off. Conversation among multilateral and bilateral donor agencies, NGOs, and ministry officials calls for a research agenda to respond to the unanswered question "Is the quantity/quality trade-off inevitable?" (Education for All: Fast-Track Initiative, 2007: 4) A World Bank Report poses a similar question, "Trade-off between improved access and student learning gains: Is it inevitable?" and answers, "Pursuing the popular expansion agenda can often be done in ways that undermine the learning improvement one (as when classrooms become overcrowded or trained teachers are not provided); effectively pursuing both at the same time is rare" (World Bank, 2006: 38).

The notion of a trade-off is so pervasive and entrenched, that it is often presented as a false truism that needs to be challenged. Countries that appear to have improved both access and quality are noted as exceptions that "call into question the widespread claim that increased enrolment across the region has been universally accompanied by a steep decline in quality, implying a tradeoff between learning levels and access" (UNESCO, 2011b: 86). The eleventh meeting of the Education for All Working Group concluded: "Improving the quality of education requires an integrated approach. There is no inevitable trade-off between access and quality" but "The knowledge base on the relationship between access, quality and equity needs to be elaborated" (UNESCO, 2011a: 1).

How, then, to elaborate? Existing literature presents some options. One way to rethink access vs. quality proposed by the Consortium for Research on Educational Access, Transitions and Equity (CREATE) research initiative is to include quality within the definition of access. This expanded view of access is described by arguing, "Full access is not secured unless enrolment is linked to high attendance rates and time on task, progression occurs with little or no repetition, indicators of learning outcomes confirm that basic skills are being mastered, and most if not all have opportunities to enter and complete lower secondary schooling" (Lewin, 2007: 21). The work of the CREATE initiative is invaluable. It produced both empirical and theoretical insight that has been indispensable for the field of international education. Certain questions remain, though, as conflating access and quality into a single construct does not describe or explain the association between access and quality.

Similarly, another approach combines access and quality into a single measure of educational performance per age-specific population cohort (Taylor & Spaull, 2015). Country average test scores reflect only the performance of those children attending school. As enrollment patterns change, the socioeconomic background of the children enrolled in school changes. Thus, "viewing country average test scores or enrolment rates in isolation is misleading" and a decline in country average test score does not necessarily reflect a deterioration in the education system (Taylor & Spaull, 2013: 9). With this approach, Taylor and Spaull (2013: 9) find that expanding access to primary education in the countries of the Southern and East African Consortium for Monitoring Educational Quality (SACMEQ) improved overall production of literacy and numeracy in many of those countries. Again, this is an important contribution to the discourse, and it challenges more simplistic views of either access or quality.

However, this argument does in some way circumvent the issue; the quality of education any single child received might have decreased while population-level literacy and numeracy increased. Additionally, Taylor and Spaull (2013: 26) note that experiences across different countries varied, in relation to both the way in which access was expanded and patterns of learning outcomes; in some cases, average learning levels declined overall, as in Mozambique. Other population-level measures also indicate that learning declined along with expanded access, as in the ASER assessments, which find that learning levels declined in the wake of the Right to Education Act (ASER, 2013). What this population approach does unquestionably illustrate is that learning cannot be assessed independently from access, just as much of recent literature has been arguing that access can no longer be assessed without attention to learning.

Recent work on Learning Adjusted Years of Schooling (LAYS) is a similar contribution (Filmer et al., 2020). This initiative combines data on years of schooling with data on learning performance into a single measure. While it is a valuable initiative to highlight the importance of both access and quality, as with the previous example, the combination masks important variation. For example, a country's LAYS might appear unchanged if more children are staying in school longer but those children have lower levels of learning or, alternatively, if learning levels go up but more children drop out.

To summarize, over the past several years, the field of international education has been defined by a shift away from access-oriented issues toward quality and learning outcomes. This orientation can be expected to continue: "A discernible shift in emphasis towards quality and learning is likely to become more central to the post-2015 global framework" (UNESCO, 2015: 189). Some of the ideas behind this shift are extremely important, most notably that many children are learning very little in their time in school. Some of the other underlying assumptions of this shift are problematic.

First, issues of access are far from being solved. Challenges related to delayed enrollment in school, infrequent attendance, repetition of grades, and early dropout define the average child's educational experience, and not just that of extremely disadvantaged children. Recognizing the importance of learning should incorporate issues of access and not leave them behind, and access, like quality, should be recognized as a complex, multidimensional, and culturally situated concern.

Second, if access and quality are to be investigated and addressed in tandem, their association must be better understood. Two theories exist in the discourse: that access and quality are independent concerns and that there is a negative linear relationship, a trade-off. Research on the subject has mixed results. Researchers and practitioners alike recognize the need for improved understanding of educational access, educational quality, and their interaction. A more dynamic, interdependent, and multidimensional understanding of access and quality is needed. To rethink this question, which is central to the Education for All movement and efforts to achieve Universal Primary Education, I turn to the study of systems and complexity.

3

Complexity as a Subject and Method in International Education

The first definition of "complexity" offered by the *Merriam-Webster Dictionary* is "the quality or state of not being simple." This definition might initially seem like an unhelpful tautology, but it does serve as an informative starting point, ironically, because of what it suggests about an endpoint. To call something complex can be just as uninsightful as calling something simple. My work to apply complexity theory to the Global Learning Crisis, and accordingly rethink the access vs. quality paradigm, will be remarkably unsuccessful if its sole conclusion is "It is complex."

At the heart of the difference between what is simple and what is complex is the idea of parts. Simple, building off of the root *sim-*, meaning *one*, is distinguished from complex, defined as "composed of many interconnected parts; compound; composite" and "characterized by a very complicated or involved arrangement of parts, units, etc." A second distinction, to use an education metaphor, is legibility. Complex implies hard to read: "so complicated or intricate as to be hard to understand or deal with." Simplicity connotes "easy to understand, deal with, use, etc" (Merriam-Webster, 2020). In this way, the concept of complexity is inherently tied to the idea of a system.

No single word might so accurately describe a national education system as the word "complex." Composed of many different stakeholders (from individual children to national policymakers), organized into many different setting levels (family, classroom, school, nation, etc.), and engaged in many hard-to-understand processes (what is learning/an effective teacher/a high quality classroom/a successful school?), education systems can appear to defy understanding.

The challenge of viewing an issue or subject as complex is that embracing complexity goes against the grain of traditional hypothesis-based, mechanistic scientific inquiry. Understanding large systems has traditionally been attempted by breaking them down into their component parts or isolating specific interactions and using lower-level insight to build up to higher levels of complexity. From the very beginnings of scientific inquiry, what still

Access, Quality, and the Global Learning Crisis: Insights from Ugandan Primary Education. Sarah Kabay, Oxford University Press.
© Sarah Kabay 2021. DOI: 10.1093/oso/9780192896865.003.0003

appears to be a natural approach to research is (as described by Descartes, 1637; Zittel et al., 2008) "to subdivide each on the problems I was about to examine: into as many parts as would be possible and necessary to resolve them better."

Reductionism remains the dominant and prevailing approach to science (Mitchell, 2009). First steps in analysis are often to isolate an issue, control for other variables, and consider very specific and bounded questions. Derived from the Greek word *analusis*, meaning "dissolving," our very understanding of *analysis* is based on the idea of breaking complexity apart. Definitions for analysis include "the separating of any material or abstract entity into its constituent elements" and "this process as a method of studying the nature of something or of determining its essential features and their relations." Even as notions of complexity have gained traction, it has been hard to break out of a reductionist mentality; as it was described in relation to the biological sciences, until very recently, complexity was seen as "a by-product of incomplete understanding, an illusion that would fall away once the parts were fully understood" (Dorit, 2011: para 11).

Research on various systems, however, has found that collective behavior or traits cannot always be understood as the aggregation of individual behavior or traits. While a single ant is "behaviorally one of the least sophisticated animals imaginable," five hundred thousand ants together operate as a "superorganism" with "collective intelligence," capable of building complex structures, communicating information, and adapting to changing circumstances (Franks, 1989: 138). Similarly, the brain functions as more than a collection of neurons. Weather systems and market economies are composed of and influenced by infinite and varying factors.

The need to consider a system as something more than a sum of parts was just one challenge to traditional scientific thought and process. Advances in the physical sciences in the late nineteenth to early twentieth centuries also began to contest an understanding of the world that was predictable, linear, and nonrandom. In 1887, mathematician Henri Poincaré predicted a whole field of thought when he described what has come to be known as sensitive dependence on initial conditions. In 1927, Werner Heisenberg's "uncertainty principle" argued that we cannot measure exact values of the position and momentum of a particle at the same time.

In 1948, in what has become a seminal text for complexity theory, Warren Weaver named and distinguished between *disorganized complexity* and *organized complexity*. A mechanistic understanding of the world, Weaver believed, had been able to address "problems of simplicity." In the twentieth century, an alternative approach to scientific inquiry became widespread.

Using statistical analysis, the motion of atoms or the behavior of a gas could be understood as a system comprised of very many variables interacting randomly. Systems in which many variables interacted randomly Weaver christened "disorganized complexity" (Ramalingam, 2013: 133–5).

What was left unaddressed was systems defined by organization. Attention had not been drawn to "problems which involve dealing simultaneously with a sizable number of factors that are interrelated into an organic whole" (Weaver, 1948: 541) and "interrelated in a complicated, but nevertheless, not helter-skelter fashion" (Weaver, 1948: 541). This, Weaver defined as "organized complexity" (Weaver, 1948: 541). Problems of this nature include "How can one explain the behavior pattern of an organized group of persons such as a labor union?" as well as "What is a gene, and how does the original genetic constitution of a living organization express itself in the developed characteristics of the adult?" (Weaver, 1948: 541).

Over several decades, these and other insights related to evolution, relativity, chaos, and networks have developed into numerous fields of research. They represent a significant and insightful departure from a more mechanistic understanding of the world. There is no single, unified complexity theory arising from several different theories and schools of thought. Instead, complex systems are seen as exhibiting similar principles. These principles offer a language and set of concepts which lend themselves to a new way of thinking and seeing and can be used as an explanatory framework (Mitleton-Kelly, 2003, 2008).

The field of international development has been engaging ideas of complexity and systems thinking in a variety of ways. Notably, Ben Ramalingam's (2013) book *Aid on the Edge of Chaos* and lectures and writings by Owen Barder (2012) of the Center for Global Development explicitly explore how the theory and principles of complex adaptive systems can inform work in international development and humanitarian settings. Several ideas from this work resonate with my work on the Global Learning Crisis, such as the need to recognize and work with the dynamism of systems, as opposed to fighting against it.

Systems, Complexity, and the Global Learning Crisis

My application of complexity theory to the Global Learning Crisis has two initial implications: first, that primary education should be recognized as a system defined by complexity, or a complex adaptive system, and second, that access to education and the quality of education are interconnected. These two inferences serve as the motivating premise and initial argument of this book.

In relation to the first, one approach to the study of complexity is described as the study of complex adaptive systems (CAS), organizations defined by interconnectivity that cannot be fully understood by understanding their individual parts (Chan, 2001). Examples of CAS include a biological cell, an immune system, an ecosystem, a city, and a climate system. CAS are often defined by self-organization, spontaneous order that arises from localized interactions rather than an external agent or top-down order. CAS can also be hierarchical, though, as in education, where there is self-organization and also top-down intervention and control. Viewing education as a CAS will emphasize the interrelationship, interaction, and interconnectivity of elements within education, and between education and the broader environment (Chan, 2001).

Complex Adaptive Systems exhibit many similar principles, such as the aforementioned self-organization, which offer a language and conceptual framework for the study of such systems. In my case study of Ugandan primary education, I highlight one principle of complex adaptive systems for each of the three issues I study. My analyses of grade repetition, privatization, and school fees are defined by the principles of nonlinearity, interdependence, and emergence, respectively. I will briefly describe each of these principles here.

Nonlinearity, typically understood in relation to fields such as mathematics, physics, and computer science, refers to a situation in which the output is not proportional to the input, which is also known as disproportionate cause and effect. A good example would be the comparison between throwing a tennis ball and throwing a paper airplane (Hardesty, 2010). While it is relatively easy to predict the speed and direction of the tennis ball, the same would not be true for the paper airplane. Linear dynamics (throwing a tennis ball) are relatively well understood; nonlinear dynamics (throwing a paper airplane) are not. The relationship between grade repetition and school dropout is often presented as a simple linear cause and effect, in that repetition is believed to lead to dropout. I argue that the association would be better described as nonlinear.

Interdependence is defined as mutual dependence, often used in the discussion of international relations and environmental science. A popular concept relating to the former is the interdependence of nations' economies, describing how states can be inextricably tied together, relying on a web of imports, exports, and trade regulations. In relation to the environment, interdependence is illustrated by the existence of ecosystems, in which different organisms live together, exchanging nutrients and resources. Remove any individual organism, and the entire ecosystem can change dramatically. In international education, research often presents the issue of privatization as a comparison between two discrete and independent sectors: private and public. In my work, I highlight the overlap, connections, and exchange between the sectors, illustrating that private and public primary schools are highly interdependent.

Emergence describes a phenomenon where a system has properties that its parts do not have. The stock market serves as one example, where trends and patterns are analyzed at a market level, and no individual or small cluster of stocks can explain the behavior of the market as a whole. Language can also be seen as exhibiting the principle of emergence, in that languages are governed by structure and rules that develop across multiple speakers, as speech is a social activity and thus requires interaction and exchange at a systems level. I argue that in my sample of Ugandan primary schools, the payment of school fees is affected by emergent, systems-level properties. Individual parents are influenced by community-level attitudes and awareness in relation to coordination and solidarity.

My study of access and quality in primary education recognizes primary education to be a Complex Adaptive System and accordingly begins with the principle of connectivity; it then highlights three additional principles: nonlinearity, interdependence, and emergence. Though I associate each principle with a particular topic, these designations are not exclusive. Nonlinearity applies to the study of school fees, just as emergence can relate to cultural perceptions of grade repetition, etc. I focus on one principle per topic, though, for clarity and concision. Taken together, these principles create a new view of primary education, one that moves beyond a simple input-output framework.

Complexity and Systems as Methodology

In addition to offering a set of principles and theoretical framework, the study of complexity and systems also has methodological implications. Though they might not explicitly reference specific theories or schools of thought, there are many different studies and research projects which have embraced an understanding of complexity. In their book *Complexity and*

Education, Davis and Sumara (2006) offer a few illustrations: "Deborah Gordon's multi-year observations of the life cycles of anthills, Friedrich Engel's studies of the emergence of social structures in the free-market world, Rachel Carson's examinations of the ecological implications of industrialized societies, Humberto Maturana's research into self-producing and self-maintaining biological unities" (Davis & Sumara, 2006: 19). Another frequently cited example of complexity is Jane Jacob's work on cities. In the *Life and Death of American Cities,* Jacobs even references Weaver's work, writing, "Cities happen to be problems in organized complexity" (Jacobs, 1961: 433).

These studies were each principally observational and descriptive in nature. Davis and Sumara (2006: 19–20) reason, "The theme that unites these diverse projects is the desire to generate rich accounts of specific phenomena, oriented by a suspicion that anthills, cities, biological unities, cultures, and so on must be studied at the level of their emergence, not in terms of their sub-components—and certainly not in terms of fundamental particles and universal laws."

Many of the most influential texts in international development have also employed such an approach. The work of Albert O. Hirschman, particularly *Development Projects Observed* and *Exit, Voice and Loyalty: Responses to Decline in Firms, Organizations, and States,* analyzed projects in detail, from multiple perspectives, incorporating complex principles such as emergence, feedback, and self-organization. James Scott's *Seeing like a State* is primarily a critique of a reductionist view of development, detailing government and development institutions' inability to recognize and appreciate complexity and concepts such as interconnectivity and coevolution. James Ferguson's *The Anti-Politics Machine* critiques a development intervention in Lesotho as overly one-dimensional and linear, importing simplistic ideas from other areas to a dramatically different context and failing to recognize irreversibility.

Complexity thus informs both how we view certain problems and the methodologies we use to investigate these problems. Back in the 1940s, Weaver was extraordinarily prescient, recommending a "mixed-team" approach to research. He references operations teams from World War II and notes:

It was found that in spite of the modern tendencies towards intense scientific specialization, that members of such diverse groups could work together and could form a unit which was much greater than the mere sum of its parts. It was shown that these groups could tackle certain problems of organized complexity, and get useful answers.   (Weaver, 1948: 542)

More current complexity research builds on these same ideas. Mitleton-Kelly and Puszczynski (2006) have detailed an integrated approach of working with organizations in collaborative, action research:

> The integrated methodology uses both qualitative and quantitative tools and methods, which provide rigor by triangulating the data and the findings and by testing against interpretation bias. They also provide different but complementary information about the organization and offer a very rich and deep understanding. The findings can then be used as an informed basis for co-creating an enabling infrastructure and an environment conducive to change and the emergence of new ways of organizing. The methodology however is not just a set of tools and methods—it is about facilitating connectivity, emergence, self-organization, etc. and about helping to co-create an environment which acknowledges organizations as complex social systems that co-evolve over time, both internally and with their broader social ecosystem.
>
> (Mitleton-Kelly and Puszczynski 2006: 2)

Following these examples, in this book I include descriptive statistics, multiple perspectives, and analysis of different levels of the education system (individual parents, children and teachers, classrooms, schools, national policy, and broader context). I combine quantitative and qualitative data and analysis collected over multiple years. My focus on a single sample and particular issues within that sample enables me to develop a "rich account of specific phenomena" (Davis & Sumara, 2006: 19).

This methodology allows for educational interventions and policy to be analyzed outside of a basic input-output framework. Emphasizing the interconnectedness of actors and influences in education systems moves the discussion beyond basic cause and effect and toward unintended effects. Focusing on a single case study allows for the possibility of multifinality (in which similar conditions can lead to multiple and varied outcomes) or equifinality (in which dissimilar conditions result in the same outcome), which is difficult in the analysis of multiple contexts.

Existing Approaches to Systems and Complexity in International Education

A number of new and exciting developments in the field of international education are drawing attention to the importance of systems and issues of complexity. The research initiative Research on Improving Systems of Education (RISE) might be the one most closely associated with complexity thinking. With over US$45 million in funding, it is also among the most prominent. In seeking to address the Global Learning Crisis, the RISE initiative exhibits many principles of complexity theory, supporting multidisciplinary research teams, engaging in local contexts, and focusing on systems. The initiative is one of the most inspiring and transformative research groups in the field of international education.

One of the key tenets of the RISE program is that in order to understand the world's low learning outcomes, research has to consider systems-level concerns. This has introduced new perspectives and discussion into the discourse on the Global Learning Crisis, highlighting, for example, the role of politics and political economy.

One rationale for this argument is that lower-level processes of education, such as basic teaching, are already understood. For example, RISE researchers argue that:

> At one level, we already know the answer. Unlike producing controlled nuclear fusion or a viable vaccine for Ebola, we already know how to teach children to read or do basic mathematics. Researchers have carefully calibrated the learning gains from specific interventions, like school feeding programs, computer assisted learning and remedial education.   (Beatty, 2015; Sandefur & Oye, 2015)

Accordingly, what is needed is "research that goes beyond the proximate causes of test score performance to understand the underlying ingredients of a well-functioning system" (Beatty, 2015; Sandefur & Oye, 2015).

It is extremely important to investigate the underlying ingredients of a well-functioning system, but the claim that "We know how to teach children to read or do basic mathematics" is problematic. Although the number of rigorously evaluated educational interventions conducted in low-income countries has increased, and multiple meta-analyses have compiled and assessed over 100 interventions (McEwan, 2015; Ganimian & Murnane, 2016; Glewwe & Muralidharan, 2016; Ladd & Loeb, 2013), to say "We know the answer" is misleading. For example, in one of these recent meta-analyses, McEwan (2015) illustrates that effect sizes of thirty-two different computer or technological interventions range from -0.6 to 0.4. With little information on the interventions and almost no information on how they were implemented, it is hard to draw any strong conclusions on technologically assisted learning interventions.

Additionally, "the review found zero or small learning effects of health interventions such as deworming and school meals" (McEwan, 2015: 380). And of the interventions that were reviewed on cost-effectiveness criteria, almost 50 percent of the interventions were more cost-effective than remedial education (McEwan, 2015). Of the three examples mentioned by the RISE researchers, accordingly, neither school feeding programs, nor computer-assisted learning, nor remedial education seem to suggest a clear way forward, across contexts, for how to teach children to read and do basic mathematics. Even the very theory of meta-analysis has come into question, as work to synthesize research in meta-analysis in education finds that the results of educational interventions are highly unpredictable (Masset et al., 2018).

Over the past ten years, there has been considerable progress in research on teaching and learning in low-income countries. Major large-scale initiatives such as the Tusome project and Pratham's Teaching at the Right Level initiative have demonstrated that pedagogical and teacher-training initiatives can improve children's basic reading and math performance (Piper et al., 2018; Banerjee et al., 2016). The field of international education has positive findings that are encouraging.

But many questions remain. Current reforms often focus on moving away from traditional rote learning and assess very basic outcomes such as letter recognition and very basic reading—do we know what it would take to get all children reading advanced text with comprehension? New initiatives such as the Teacher Instructional Practices and Processes System (TIPPS) (Seidman et al., 2018) are working to develop measures of classroom quality, but what do we know about high-quality classroom management and teacher-learner interactions in classrooms with over 100 children? What is the best approach to working with not just bilingual but multilingual populations, where tonal languages do not yet have an established orthography? What is the best way in which to engage illiterate parents in children's schooling? Even in high resourced settings such as the US, where there is significantly more research and investment, we are far away from knowing how to deliver high quality education for all children.

A focus on systems should not lose sight of lower-level processes. In education, there is still much to be learned about what happens at an individual, classroom, and school level, especially in diverse, global contexts. In arguing that issues of access should not be overlooked, the point is not that attention should not be drawn to issues of quality but instead that the two issues should be investigated together. In the same way, arguing that lower-level education processes are not fully understood is not meant to detract from the need to better understand larger systems, but that they should be investigated in tandem.

In applying complexity theory to the study of education, Davis and Sumara (2006: 107) define "level-jumping," a focus on multiple levels of a system, as an analytic strategy that will "simultaneously examine the phenomenon in its own right (for its particular coherence and its specific rules of behavior) and pay attention to the conditions of its emergence (e.g., the agents that come together, the contexts of their co-activity, etc.)" This appears to be a much more powerful strategy than simply moving from one level of analysis to another and my goal in choosing to focus on grade repetition, privatization, and school fees aiming to incorporate national policy-, school-, and individual-level perspectives.

In order to address the Global Learning Crisis, education systems must be recognized for their complexity. Learning itself must also be recognized as a complex phenomenon influenced by what occurs both in and outside of the classroom. Insight from complexity theory calls for interdisciplinary research and the integration of different methodologies. It also calls for a re-envisioning of the problem. The approach, as articulated by Mitleton-Kelly (2008), is to first "understand the problem space when addressing apparently intractable problems" (Slide 3), and then "create enabling environments" (Slide 3).

My work to understand low learning levels in Uganda begins by "understanding the problem space." I identify access and quality as two fundamental, underlying constructs of the movement to achieve Universal Primary Education. I argue that current theories of access and quality are overly simplistic and need to be rethought. The association between these two constructs needs to be seen as multidimensional, dynamic, and varying. Put more simply, it needs to be seen as complex.

I choose three independent but interrelated phenomena within Ugandan primary education that exemplify the complicated relationship between access and quality. My empirical analysis is accordingly focused on phenomena "at the level of their emergence" (Davis & Sumara, 2006: 20) For each of grade repetition, private primary schools, and school fees, I include observational data, using descriptive statistics to illustrate the limits of previous data collection and better define the three phenomena. For each topic, I conduct quantitative analysis to investigate the association between access and quality. I complement this analysis with qualitative research on different stakeholders' perspectives and beliefs surrounding these topics. And finally, I interpret my findings in relation to the access vs. quality paradigm.

This work can serve as an example of a complexity-inspired research approach. To borrow the description of the London School of Economics'

Complexity Group, a study that employs an "integrated methodology" (Mitleton-Kelly, 2003: 2), is one that "uses both qualitative and quantitative tools and methods, which provide rigor by triangulating the data and the findings and by testing against interpretation bias" (Mitleton-Kelly, 2003: 2) in order to develop "a very rich and deep understanding" (Mitleton-Kelly, 2003: 2). Honoring the complexity of education and the challenges of learning, my work ultimately aims to generate insight that will help "co-create an environment, which acknowledges organizations as complex social systems that co-evolve over time, both internally and with their broader social ecosystem" (Mitleton-Kelly, 2003: 2).

4
Ugandan Context and Description of Sample and Data

Primary education in many ways reflects the society in which it takes place. In this book, I have chosen to focus on a single country context, Uganda, and in particular, on a specific sample of children, schools, and communities. With this focus, I am able to contextualize the educational issues I study and integrate local news, politics, and culture into my empirical analysis. This focus also supports my objective to explore the connections between various actors, influences, issues, and levels of the education system. Throughout the book, I work to balance an interdisciplinary and inclusive approach with a case study's focus and specificity.

In any country-specific case study, how we perceive the country will frame how we perceive the subject of the case, as well as its broader relevance. Familiarity, or the lack thereof, with Uganda or sub-Saharan Africa will color how we view its primary education and the extent to which we believe in its significance. What about Uganda's primary education is unique, determined by site-specific factors? What, if anything, about Ugandan primary education is relevant for Kenya, Laos, or the United States? In this chapter, I provide some details to help frame the Ugandan context and inform any application to other contexts. I intend for this to serve as a brief sketch of the issues that define the population of children served by Uganda's primary education and the factors that influence and define that education. I also provide a basic description of the data and methods of analysis that I use in this work.

Uganda is located in East Africa (Figure 4.1). It borders Rwanda, Kenya, Tanzania, the Democratic Republic of Congo, and South Sudan. It covers 241,038 square kilometers, which makes it slightly smaller than the United Kingdom, slightly larger than Ghana, and roughly the size of the American state of Oregon (CIA, 2016). The country's southern border comprises the northern shore of Lake Victoria, the world's largest tropical lake and the source of the Nile River. The Equator cuts across the southernmost part of the country. The Rwenzori Mountain range in the east contains Ngaliema,

Figure 4.1 Location of Uganda

the African continent's third highest peak, which, at 5,109 meters, is permanently snow-capped.

Uganda's population is estimated to comprise around 44 million people (World Bank, 2020). Incorporating data on language, ethnicity, and religion, research into ethnic fractionalization has found Uganda to be the most diverse country in the world (Alesina et al., 2002). Currently, Uganda has fifty-six legally recognized ethnic groups. The Baganda, from whom the British derived the name Uganda, and the ethnic group with the largest share of the population, comprise 17 percent of the total population. They are followed by the Banyankore and Basoga with 10 percent and 8.9 percent of the population, respectively (UBOS, 2016). There are forty-three listed languages in Uganda, of which five are institutional (including English), twenty-seven are developing, seven are vigorous, two are in trouble, and two are dying (Simons & Fennig, 2017). Forty percent of Uganda's population identifies as

Catholic, 32 percent as Anglican, 14 percent as Muslim, and 11 percent as Pentecostal/Born Again/Evangelical (UBOS, 2016).

Uganda is the second youngest country in the world, a demographic trend highly relevant to education (UNDP, 2018). The United Nations estimates that nearly half (46 percent) of Uganda's population is under the age of 14 and 18 percent is under the age of 5 (United Nations Population Division, 2018). The fertility rate is 5.8 births per woman and life expectancy is fifty-nine years (UBOS, 2016; UNDP, 2016). The literacy rate is 77 percent (UBOS, 2016, UNDP, 2016). Eighty four percent of the population lives in rural areas (UBOS, 2016).

In 2013, 34.6 percent of Ugandans lived on $1.90 purchasing power parity (PPP) or less (World Bank, 2016). Though there has been considerable progress in reducing monetary poverty (in 2006, 53.2 percent lived on $1.90 PPP or less), much of this progress has been concentrated in the Central Region, where households generally have higher levels of human capital, more assets, and better access to services and infrastructure than in other regions. The proportion of poor households living in the Northern and Eastern regions, for example, increased from 68 percent to 84 percent from 2006 to 2013 (World Bank, 2016). Of the 185 countries included in the 2016 Human Development Index, Uganda was ranked at 165, as one of the countries with "low human development" (as compared to medium, high, and very high human development) (UNDP, 2016).

As in every country, Uganda's development is a mix of progress and enduring challenges. However, the strengths of low-income countries such as Uganda often receive less attention. Due to the recent outbreak and rapid spread of Ebola in West Africa, though, Uganda has recently been recognized for its history of successful disease management. Between 2000 and 2015, Uganda experienced six outbreaks of the Ebola viral hemorrhagic disease, along with outbreaks of Marburg virus disease and yellow fever. Each of these incidents was controlled, with limited spread beyond the initial locus of the outbreak (Mbonye et al., 2014).

Uganda's strong health surveillance system is longstanding. In 1947, scientists with the Uganda Virus Research Institute were monitoring a monkey as part of their yellow fever research. When the monkey developed a fever, they took a blood sample and isolated a previously unknown virus. They named it after the forest in which it was found, Zika (Green, 2016). Uganda has continued to monitor the Zika virus, even before its recent outbreak in the Americas made it international news.

Uganda is also known for the decline in its population's HIV/AIDS prevalence, which is often touted as "one of the earliest and most compelling national success stories in combatting the spread of HIV" (Green et al., 2006: 335). Uganda's national HIV prevalence for all adults is estimated to have declined from its peak in the early 1990s at around 15 percent to about 4 percent in 2003 (Green et al., 2006). While some have argued that both measurement bias and "natural die-off syndrome," where the rate of new infections is outweighed by the number of AIDS deaths, have played a significant role, it seems unlikely that they could completely account for the decline in Uganda's HIV prevalence (Green et al., 2006). Uganda's proactive and high-level political and multisectoral response to the epidemic, its mobilization of religious leaders, and its anonymous voluntary counselling and treatment center have all been cited as key elements in its work to combat the virus (Green et al., 2006).

At the same time, Uganda still struggles with many health concerns, particularly for women and young children. Three in ten children in Uganda tested positive for malaria, with prevalence rates ranging from 1 percent in the capital city of Kampala to 69 percent in the Karamoja region (UBOS & ICF, 2017). Nearly a third of all children under 5 are stunted, an indication of chronic undernutrition (UBOS & ICF, 2017). Both infant and under-5 child mortality rates have decreased, though. The infant mortality rate, for example, decreased by half between 2001 and 2016, from eighty-eight deaths per 1,000 live births to forty-three in 2016 (UBOS & ICF, 2017). Still, Uganda's rates for early childhood and maternal mortality are among the worst in the world. Of 225 countries, Uganda had the twentieth worst rate of infant mortality and thirty-sixth worst rate of maternal mortality (CIA, 2016).

Uganda also faces many challenges in critical infrastructure, such as access to electricity and improved sanitation, particularly in certain regions. Figure 4.2 provides an illustration of Uganda's regions. While 32.3 percent of households in the Central Region have access to electricity, only 3.7 percent, 5.8 percent, and 8.6 percent of households in the Northern, Eastern, and Western Regions, respectively, have access. Similarly, 29 percent of households in Northern Uganda do not use any type of toilet facility, compared to 8 percent in Eastern, 2 percent in Western, and 5 percent in Central Regions.

Uganda's population, infrastructure, and broader development both influence and are influenced by the country's education sector. Primary education is a critical concern. As previously mentioned, the vast majority of Ugandan children are struggling to learn basic skills of literacy and numeracy. Even within the context of East Africa, Uganda's learning outcomes are comparatively low, as students in both Kenya and Tanzania outperform those in Uganda on comparable exams (Jones & Schipper, 2015; Uwezo, 2015). This is especially concerning given the emphasis placed upon primary education in

Figure 4.2 Maps of Ugandan (a) regions and (b) ethnic groups
Global Hunger Index https://www.globalhungerindex.org/case-studies/2018-uganda.html

Uganda's education system and society at large. Issues related to primary education are often front-page news and the subject of campaign promises and debates. I will now briefly describe some background on Uganda's education system.

Uganda's Primary Education System

Indigenous education in Uganda was arranged around the homestead and integrated into regular economic, political, and social activity, as opposed to being set aside in schools and classrooms. Education's general purpose was to enable each member of society to be helpful to herself, her family, her society, and her state (Ssekamwa, 1997). Education included everything from

(b)

Figure 4.2 Continued

the history, laws, and customs of the tribe to agricultural practices and local geography. Certain skills and knowledge were differentiated by sex—for example, boys were taught to raise livestock and make cloth and clothing from skin and bark, while girls were taught the production of food crops and cooking. Education was not literate, but was dynamic and continually updated. Older members of families would teach younger members, experts and professional organizations would teach specialized knowledge such as healing or metallurgy (Kalibala, 1934; Tiberondwa, 1998), and people seeking particular knowledge were known to travel long distances to seek out known experts (Feierman, 1985).

In the mid-1800s, Arab and Swahili traders introduced Islam into Uganda and, along with it, exposure to literacy. Ugandans began learning to read, teaching others as well. Formal schools were first established in Uganda by

British missionaries in the late 1800s, but as early as the 1870s "village schools" were being built, run, and staffed by Ugandans, as many embraced literacy and Christianity (Hanson, 2010). Although some sources depict the instruction of Protestant and Catholic missionaries as a complete break from what came before, others argue that village schools in particular illustrated the ways in which indigenous patterns of education were combined with the new knowledge brought by missionaries (Hanson, 2010).

African Christians were interested in expansion, but the Protectorate Department of Education established by the British in 1925 withdrew funding from the majority of village schools in order to more directly fund a small sample of primary schools that could operate at a higher standard and ultimately lead to the establishment of a university. In this way, actors such as the Governor of Uganda Sir Philip Mitchell aimed to recreate a British model of elite education of which they themselves were a product. The idea was that educating an elite minority would lead to the benefit of the uneducated majority more effectively than attempting to educate the majority. Subsequent policies continued to reinforce the choice of "investment in quality education over mass education" (Hanson, 2010). Historians argue that the resulting inequality became the main source of "social conflict in Uganda generating the structural violence from which all subsequent political, military, and civilian violence would erupt" (Kasozi, 1994: 7).

Another enduring consequence of these early education policies was the perception of education as the work of trained professionals rather than the responsibility of local actors. Assessments of the Protectorate policy concluded that it "rooted out a great deal of effective African influence" (Ranger, 1965: 73). Many of the debates and issues from this period continued to be relevant for Ugandan education, such as determining the balance between basic and tertiary levels of education, the credentials of the teaching workforce, and the comprehensiveness of the curriculum.

The current Ugandan school system still resembles the British system with, for example, O and A level exams. The system begins with seven years of primary school intended for children ages 6–13 years of age, followed by four years of lower secondary school and two years of upper secondary school, with each section concluding with high-stakes exams: Primary Leaving Examinations (PLE), Uganda Certificate of Education (UCE–Ordinary Level) and Uganda Advanced Certificate of Exams (UACE–Advanced level). Primary education in Uganda also has policies and programs for technical and vocational education and tertiary education.

Pre-primary education is not currently included in public basic education, and the government plays only a regulatory role. Enrollment in pre-primary education in Uganda is very low. In 2011, the Net Enrollment Ratio (NER) in pre-primary education was 6.6 percent. Though this increased to 15.6 percent in 2016, enrolment rates are mostly driven by high enrollment in urban areas. However, informal and unregistered early education opportunities have also been increasing, and are not reflected in official rates; though still relatively low, actual enrolment in early childhood education can be expected to be higher.

Enrollment in secondary education is also relatively low, with a NER of 25 percent in 2011 and 24 percent in 2016 (MoES, 2017). The government does play a very active role in secondary education; in 2007, Uganda because the first country in sub-Saharan Africa to institute a policy for universal secondary education. In comparison, in 2011, the NER for primary education was 97.5 percent, which indicates that nearly all Ugandan children are at some point enrolling in primary school (MoES, 2017).

Primary education accordingly comprises a significant share of the government's education budget. Of the entire education budget, 38 percent was spent on primary education in 2011 (MoES, 2017). This is due in large part to Uganda's Universal Primary Education (UPE) policy. Implemented in 1997, UPE is still seen as the "most fundamental and far reaching program" of the country's education sector (National Planning Authority, 2015).

The seven grades of primary school are referred to as classes, for example, the Primary 1 or P1 class, and are divided into lower (P1–P3) and upper (P5–P7) primary, with P4 as a transition year. In 2016, the Ministry of Education and Sports' registry of schools included 19,718 primary schools, serving 8,655,924 pupils. Uganda's primary school population, accordingly, represents about 20 percent of the country's total population. About 20 percent of primary school pupils are enrolled in private schools (more information on the private sector is included in Chapter 6).

Uganda's experience with Universal Primary Education (UPE), as in other sub-Saharan African nations, is often interpreted in terms of access vs. quality, making it a clear example of the access vs. quality paradigm. The country's UPE policy, first implemented in 1997, abolished tuition payments all at once. This strategy has been christened the "big bang" approach and is interpreted as an access-oriented intervention aiming to get children into schools. As described by Bertoncino et al. (2002: 4), "the big bang approach can be a very powerful policy instrument for getting all the children into school and Uganda has managed to do this very well," but "the downside of the big bang approach is that there can be a dramatic decline in quality and the key is to anticipate the likely impact of big bang approaches on quality and prepare accordingly." In other words, increasing access, especially on such a large scale, can be expected to lower the quality of education provided. In the case of Uganda, researchers often make this conclusion very explicit: "Studies on the impact of the Universal Primary Education policy have highlighted how educational attainment increased whereas the quality of education declined" (Huylebroek & Titeca, 2008: 350).

Uganda's experience in this regard is not particularly unique. The country can be seen as a representative case of many issues in primary education. In reviewing the school fee abolition initiatives of Ethiopia, Ghana, Kenya, Malawi, and Mozambique, for instance, researchers concluded:

> All five case studies raise questions about the impact of fee abolition on the qual-
> ity of education, both because the revenues from fees typically provided for learn-
> ing materials and because resources must be shared among more pupils to cater
> to the enrollment surge. This results in crowded classrooms and increased pupil-
> teacher ratios (PTRs). Low quality was a serious concern before fee abolition and,
> without a funded strategy to address quality issues, the situation has often been
> more serious after the removal of fees. While the case studies differ in many
> aspects, the question of quality features in all of them.
>
> (World Bank & UNICEF, 2009: 12)

Fee abolition is a prominent issue, and one of the defining policy questions of the Education for All movement. I explore this issue in greater detail in Chapter 7, which is focused on the costs associated with attending school. As one of the first countries in sub-Saharan Africa to abolish school fees for primary education, Uganda set an important precedent and might have served as inspiration for other countries, particularly in East Africa. Uganda eliminated tuition payments in response to a presidential election campaign promise in 1996; in the following decades, thirteen other countries in sub-Saharan Africa did the same (Harding & Stasavage, 2016). Uganda's long history with the policy makes it an interesting case for analysis.

Many of the challenges facing Ugandan schools and the primary educa-tion system are widespread. Low-income countries around the world have to confront large class sizes, poorly trained and underfunded staff, and a lack of learning materials, as well as numerous issues outside of the classroom that affect children and their educational experience. Insight from Uganda's pri-mary education is accordingly relevant to a number of different countries facing similar challenges. As was previously illustrated by differences in access to electricity and sanitation across Uganda's regions, there is also great variation within Uganda.

Sample

For this book, I use data from schools in Uganda's Busoga Region, which is part of the Eastern Region. Busoga includes some of the extreme poverty that characterizes much of the Eastern Region, but also has some areas with more economic activity and affluence. The Basoga are the country's third largest ethnic group. Though 81 percent of this population is considered rural, the area is densely populated, with 543 people per square kilometer (UBOS, 2016). If this region were its own country, it would be the twenty-third most densely populated country in the world, while Uganda as a whole is the seventy-seventh.

The Basoga speak Lusoga, a Bantu Language like Luganda, the language spoken in the Central Region by the Baganda and the most established of Uganda's local languages. Though there are definite similarities between the regions and languages, this proximity and likeness can overshadow significant differences. To offer one indicator as an example, the Bible was first translated into Luganda in 1896 (Pawlikova-Vilhanova, 2006); the Lusoga translation of the Bible was only recently released, in 2015 (Walukamba, 2014).

Although in general the Busoga Region, and accordingly the sample of children I analyze, is primarily low-income and rural, it also includes significant variation. Among Busoga's ten districts are some that are well established, with town centers that can be categorized as urban, but also recently created districts that are not yet connected to an electrical grid, are run entirely from generators, and have communities that are many kilometers from the nearest tarmacked road. Similarly, students in my sample come from many different villages and towns. This includes struggling communities that are no longer able to rely on subsistence agriculture, having sold off their land to sugar cane plantations, as well as more affluent urban populations in the town municipalities.

Quantitative Data

In this book, I focus my empirical analysis on a single sample of schools and their associated students, pupils, and communities. The sample started as 136 government primary schools, representing all government-supported Universal Primary Education (UPE) schools in one district (ninety-six in total), as well as neighboring schools in three sub-counties of three adjacent districts (forty schools). The quantitative data I analyze were originally collected as part of a longitudinal randomized controlled trial (RCT) evaluating a school savings program. That program was implemented in grades 5–7 in a subset of seventy-eight of these 136 schools. I describe this savings program and the original study by Karlan and Linden (2017) in detail in Chapter 7, in which I conduct secondary analysis of this intervention.

As the Project Associate for the original RCT study, I assisted the principal investigators, Karlan and Linden, in all aspects of the project, from designing the intervention to the drafting of data collection instruments. I trained and managed the research teams and directed all of the fieldwork across the four years of the project. In relation to the savings intervention, I found and enlisted the Ugandan partner organizations and worked with them to design the intervention. I trained and managed the implementation team to conduct a year-long pilot of the intervention in eight schools, and then scaled up the team to implement the intervention to an additional 78 schools for the full study. The research and any possible ethical concerns associated with it were approved by Uganda's National Science and Technology Council as well as Yale University's Institutional Review Board.

We chose the Busoga Region for its location and because it was fairly average for Uganda in terms of poverty levels and educational performance, according to national statistics. Though relatively close to the capital, the Busoga Region is generally defined by rural poverty, like much of Uganda. Over the past two decades, the Busoga Region has experienced an economic decline mirrored in the region's educational performance. Schools in the Central and Western Regions significantly outperform those in Busoga (Uwezo, 2010, 2011, 2019). For the pilot of the savings intervention, we began working in a district where our Ugandan implementation partner had a branch location. For the RCT, we included all government primary schools in this district (excluding those from the pilot) and also added neighboring schools in the sub-counties of three adjacent districts in order to reach the sample size recommended by our power calculations.

Schools varied in size from sixty to over 1,400 pupils, with teaching staffs of four to thirty-nine teachers and an average P5 class size of eighty-eight students. Sixteen schools were located within and managed by the municipal government, which I classify as the urban sample. The remaining 120 schools were rural, and managed by the district governments. These 136 schools represent just less than 1 percent of all Ugandan government primary schools nationwide (MoES, 2013). To conduct this research, we coordinated with the relevant District Education Offices, School Inspectors, and a local NGO and financial institution. The baseline sample, as it includes every school within a radius of approximately 20 kilometers, accurately represents the population of children attending P4 and P5 in government schools in this area. All selected schools agreed to participate in the research. At baseline, all selected pupils also individually assented to participate. One of the schools which was randomly selected to receive the intervention declined to participate in program implementation, but, as in the original study, I use "intent to treat" analysis, and include this school with all other schools assigned to treatment.

My quantitative analysis uses the baseline, endline, and monitoring data collected as part of this RCT. In this chapter I will provide a brief description of this sample and the procedures used to collect the data. For both the baseline and endline, I hired and managed a team of approximately fifty Ugandan enumerators, auditors, and field managers. We extensively pretested all data collection instruments in order to ensure that language and content were appropriate for the sample. Special attention was paid to ensure that the sample included children who were frequently absent (as described in the previous chapter). During the baseline, if a child was not present on the day on which the survey team visited the school, an enumerator would track the child to his or her home or workplace to conduct the interview. Thirty-five pupils were randomly selected from each school, eighteen from the Primary 4 class and seventeen from the Primary 5 class. My quantitative data accordingly include 4,716 children.[1]

In October 2009, children in the sample were individually surveyed on basic demographics and educational experience. Almost all interviews were conducted in Lusoga, but a few students were more comfortable in Luganda, Ateso, and English, and those interviews were accordingly conducted in those languages. Surveyed children also took an aptitude exam. In order to design this exam, I obtained examples of Uganda's national curriculum and tests for both the P4 and P5 classes, and created two comparable exams, one for each grade. The goal was to create an exam that would reflect the content of children's schooling in a familiar format and assessment approach. These exams were reviewed by local primary school administrators and pretested in two area schools.

The aptitude exams included three sections: math, English grammar, and reading comprehension. The math section included addition, subtraction, multiplication, and division, along with fractions, decimals, and calculating the perimeter of a rectangle. The English grammar section included verb tenses, alphabetization, and sentence formation. The reading comprehension section included two prompts—an itemized shopping list and a paragraph story, each with several comprehension questions. The P4 and P5 exams

---

[1] Two schools were very small and did not have thirty-five total students in the P4 and P5 classes combined, which thus made the total number of students fewer than the 4,760 there would have been if all the schools had had thirty-five students.

were very similar, except that the P5 exam included a more advanced reading comprehension prompt which required children to both read a paragraph and make calculations.

Summary statistics from the baseline sample provide a rough sketch of the population of students in my sample. Fifty-three percent of the sample is female. This slight imbalance is most likely due to the dynamics of school dropout. While boys are much more likely to enroll in secondary school, in this region of Uganda, young boys tend to have many more economic opportunities than young girls and are thus slightly more likely to drop out in the upper grades of primary school.

Eighty-five percent of the children in the baseline sample were barefoot. Ten percent reported that they never ate lunch during the week. Forty-two percent reported that they worked to earn money. The distribution of children's ages is provided in Figure 4.3. It reflects the similarly wide heterogeneity of the nationally representative sample of children in third grade that I described in Chapter 3. The heterogeneity of Ugandan classrooms is caused by a number of factors: delayed entry into school, grade repetition, and breaks in schooling. Seven percent of this sample reported that they had at one point dropped out of school and then re-entered.

A follow-up survey was conducted two years after baseline, in September-November 2011. The research team tracked children to different schools if they had transferred and to homes and workplaces if children were absent or had dropped out of school. More details on the number and type of schools children transferred to are provided in Chapter 6. In addition to the original

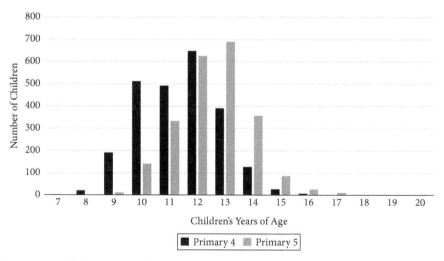

Figure 4.3 Children's years of age by grade at baseline

sample area, the team traveled to neighboring districts to track children who had moved. Of the original sample, 83 percent or 3,838 children were located, which illustrates a relatively low attrition rate for studies in low-income countries (Thomas et al., 2012). Each child was individually interviewed using the follow-up survey and given the follow-up exam—both of which were based upon and very similar to the baseline versions. I will refer to the first data collection as the baseline and the follow-up as the endline.

Qualitative Data

To complement these quantitative data, I conducted two qualitative data collection exercises. The first was conducted in October 2012. Three representatives from each of the original 136 schools in the quantitative sample were invited to attend one of three dissemination events. Transport allowances were provided, and participants were given lunch at the event. Basic descriptive findings from the quantitative research were presented, including the incidence of repetition and transferring. Across the three events, there were a total of 398 participants. All but two schools were represented. The majority of participants were class teachers from the Primary 5, 6, and 7 classes. We requested the presence of these individuals as they would be the teachers of the children from the quantitative sample and would best be able to comment on phenomena observed in that population.

Participants were divided into groups of approximately twelve people in order to conduct focus group discussions (FGDs). FGDs are particularly well-suited for "in-depth exploration of a topic about which little is known" (Stewart et al, 2007). The groups discussed three different topics: grade repetition, transferring, and the school savings program (the subject of the original RCT for which I conduct secondary analysis in Chapter 7). Quotes and discussion points from the participants were recorded. At the conclusion of each event, I conducted a debriefing session with the facilitators to discuss general impressions and feedback. I collected all notes from the events and transcribed them.

I conducted the second qualitative data collection in July 2014, when I was a graduate student. With a Ugandan colleague serving as a translator, I conducted semi-structured interviews in two communities. Using the quantitative data, I identified a rural community that had particularly high rates of repetition and transfer, but that otherwise represented the majority of communities in the sample in that it was rural and predominantly Basoga. In this community, I conducted eight individual interviews and two focus group discussions with parents and community members. I also conducted four individual interviews in a non-representative urban community, many of whose residents have moved from other regions in Uganda, and an interview with the main district's head School Inspector. All respondents who were approached agreed to be interviewed, but one preferred not to be recorded.

I developed a basic protocol to guide the interviews. I began with very general questions about education and schooling. The questions served as initial prompts and helped to ensure completeness across different respondents, but the interviews were semi-structured and pursued different subjects and themes as they emerged. In this way I hoped to take advantage of the strengths of qualitative research "to discover variation, portray shades of meaning, and examine complexity" (Rubin & Rubin, 2005).

I took notes during and after the interviews, highlighting trends and developing ideas, and also recorded and later transcribed the interviews. The protocol and questions evolved over the course of the interviews, inspired by emerging themes and following the guidelines of "responsive interviewing" (Rubin & Rubin, 2005). In later interviews, I shared theories and beliefs from previous interviews to check my interpretation and see how certain hypotheses resonated across different respondents. I recorded and transcribed all interviews, except for the individual who preferred not to be recorded, for whom I have the notes I took during the interview.

My analytic approach to these interview data followed the "hybrid model" proposed by Rubin and Rubin (2005). With this approach, I integrated ideas from the literature and continued with the responsive interviewing strategy, but also used insights from methods more related to grounded theory (Corbin & Strauss, 2008). Having already completed some analysis before conducting the interviews, I began with a few specific ideas that I wanted to investigate. At the same time, I wanted to allow the interview data to speak for themselves. Using grounded theory analytic methods enabled me to investigate ideas that emerge from the data, not necessarily in response to my own research questions or preconceived notions. "Open coding" according to Corbin and Strauss "requires a brainstorming approach to analysis because, in the beginning, analysts want to open up the data to all potentials and possibilities available to them. Only after considering all possible meanings and examining the context carefully is the researcher ready to put interpretive conceptual labels on the data" (Corbin & Strauss, 2008). By completing line by line analysis with this more grounded theory approach, I aimed to balance out the formal coding analysis I complete in relation to my research questions.

In each of Chapters 5–7, I combine analysis of quantitative and qualitative data to explore each of the three topics. For grade repetition, I use the quantitative data first to explore the incidence of grade repetition in the sample. I then use logistic regression to determine whether repeating a grade was associated with dropping out of school. I use the focus group discussions with teachers and administrators as well as the interviews with parents and community members to explore how grade repetition is perceived, and how various stakeholders make meaning of it and approach their decision making.

For my analysis of private schools, I use the quantitative data and logistic regression to determine what predicts transfer to private primary schools. I use the qualitative interviews and focus group discussions to investigate how parents and other community members view the private and public education sectors, independently and in comparison. And for the costs associated with attending school, I conduct secondary analysis of the savings intervention. Using the experimental design, I investigate whether the impact of the savings intervention was moderated by children's socioeconomic status. I then use instrumental variable analysis to test the hypothesized mediation pathway, that the program's positive impact on test scores was mediated by the purchasing of scholastic materials.

My data and analysis are not without their limitations. The key concern for this work is that the quantitative data only cover a two-year period in children's educational experience. As my sample began with children enrolled in P4 and P5, it misses a significant population of children who have dropped out of school before that point. It, of course, would have been preferable to track children from their initial enrollment through the point at which they either completed P7 or discontinued their education. However, my quantitative data do cover the transition year of P4 and the early years of upper primary school, an important period in primary education. Focusing on this particular time period could bring to light certain issues that might be obscured or overlooked when considering the entirety of primary education. One downside of the qualitative data is that interviews and focus group discussions included parents and children from the same schools and communities, but do not directly correspond to the specific students interviewed in the quantitative data. Had this work been conducted concurrently, this would have been a great opportunity for truly integrated analysis.

Another important limitation of the data concerns the individual measures. As previously mentioned, if access and quality are to be recognized as multidimensional and dynamic, measurement of these constructs must also be multidimensional and dynamic. While I am able to measure access and quality in a number of different ways and at two different time points, the picture of these two constructs that I present is still relatively constrained. For example, though I have data on teacher attendance, the presence of scholastic materials in the classroom, lunch programs, the frequency of tests, and test scores, a more complete picture of quality would include information on teachers' backgrounds, time on task, instructional styles, teacher-child interactions, and direct assessment of multiple skills and aptitudes rather than a self-administered standardized exam. Similarly, a more informed view of access would include much more information about children's background and household. As our data collection was focused on the school, I have very little information about households' poverty level, children's position in the household, or other factors which would influence their ability to attend and progress through school.

And finally, while certain variables were able to be observed directly (for example, whether a child was wearing a uniform), many of the questions from the quantitative survey instrument relied on children's self-report. It is possible that children are not accurate respondents –they could not know the information or feel pressure to respond a way that does not accurately represent their experience. The impression of our team, though, was that children seemed very forthright in what they did not know (for example, many children did not know their parents' education level), were more honest than other potential respondents (for example, when compared to teachers in reporting ghost pupils), and were very informed and aware of their educational experience. Generally, though, any form of self-reported data should be recognized for its limitations.

In spite of these concerns, the data analyzed in this study present a unique opportunity to rigorously analyze Ugandan primary education. My use of mixed methods and interdisciplinary analysis aligns with the methodology of complexity theory and offers a rich and detailed picture of primary education that is relatively rare in international development education. Chapters 5–7 use the data I have just described to investigate three issues in Ugandan primary education: grade repetition, private schools, and school fees. In each chapter, I review the existing literature on the subject, considering a wide variety of international contexts but focusing on low-income countries and sub-Saharan Africa. I then conduct empirical analysis to answer the particular research question that illustrates the issue's connection to the access vs. quality paradigm.

5

Grade Repetition and School Dropout

Grade repetition, also referred to as grade retention, is the practice of enrolling a child in the same grade for more than one year. It is typically contrasted with social promotion, also known as automatic promotion, in which children are routinely promoted from one grade to the next.

At times, grade repetition can be a high-profile issue. In discussing the country's education system in his 1998 State of the Union Address, for example, US President Bill Clinton admonished, "We must also demand greater accountability. When we promote a child from grade to grade who hasn't mastered the work, we don't do that child any favors. It is time to end social promotion in America's schools" (Clinton, 1998: 133). Similarly, in a parliamentary meeting in Uganda in December 2017, Members of Parliament contended, "Automatic promotion is not a good policy. The way Ugandans are implementing it is extremely poor and if we continue like that, it is going to erode and destroy education in this country" (Parliament of the Republic of Uganda, 2017: 19).

Whether it is used to usher in a wave of accountability reforms, as in the US, or to signal the decline of the education system, as in Uganda, grade repetition has a way of standing in for major educational debates. It serves as an unfortunate proxy for some of the more intractable challenges of the education sector. This is particularly true in international education. In place of thoughtful investigation into the practice of repetition, the issue is simply seen to represent "inefficiency and wastage of resources" (Brophy, 2006: 3), that is, spending multiple years' worth of resources for a child to complete a grade rather than just one year's.

Defining repetition in this way depends in large part on its commonly assumed association with later school dropout. This association is often taken for granted in the international literature where "Discussions of repetition are often subsumed in larger discussions of 'wastage'—the combination of repetition and dropout rates" (Gomes-Neto & Hanushek, 1994: 117). If repetition is aligned with dropout and defined as "wastage," its opposite might be considered efficiency; indeed, repeaters as a percentage of total enrollment is used to represent "the efficiency of student flow in the education system"

Access, Quality, and the Global Learning Crisis: Insights from Ugandan Primary Education. Sarah Kabay, Oxford University Press.
© Sarah Kabay 2021. DOI: 10.1093/oso/9780192896865.003.0005

(Mingat et al., 2002: 12). With a linear, positive, association cited between repetition and dropout and the use of both as indicators of a system's inefficiency, countries have been advised to decrease their rates of repetition (Mingat et al., 2002; Berete et al., 2005; Ndaruhutse, 2008).

The greatest extension of this argument is found in the claims that repetition, as an inefficient use of resources, is a drain on a country's economy. For example: "If resources spent on repeating a grade were instead spent on enrolling new entrants into school, annual GDP in countries like Burundi, Madagascar and Malawi could grow potentially by 1.3, 0.7, and 0.6% respectively" (UNESCO, 2012: 52). This line of reasoning relies upon extensive assumptions and extrapolation, aligning not just repetition and dropout, but entry into school, primary school completion, and later life outcomes. The idea that resources spent on repetition could be simply transferred to new entrants in such a way that GDP would increase seriously oversimplifies education and the challenges facing educators.

This framing of grade repetition can also be seen as a clear illustration of the access vs. quality paradigm. By definition, repetition halts a child's progression through school, limiting access to upper grades. Repetition's possible association with later school dropout suggests an even greater constraint upon access. Conversely, grade repetition is believed to reinforce performance standards, learning, and, accordingly, quality (Okurut, 2015; Roderick et al., 2002; King et al., 1999). In the same way, automatic promotion policies are seen to decrease the overall quality of an education system (Koppensteiner, 2014; Chohan & Qadir, 2011).

The issue of grade repetition can thus be seen as reinforcing the idea of a negative association or tension between efforts to improve access and efforts to improve quality. Repetition is an intervention intended to improve the quality of education by emphasizing standards and performance, but it has the potential to constrain access, as it prevents a child from progressing through school and is often associated with school dropout. An education system that demands that all children be at grade level might be seen as one that prioritizes quality over access. An education system that prohibits repetition might be seen to be accessible, but of poor quality. This conceptualization of repetition perfectly aligns with an understanding of access and quality as competing concerns.

The study of grade repetition could greatly benefit from an approach that acknowledges its complexity, both of the practice itself and of the systems and contexts in which it takes place. Though repetition is an issue faced by education policymakers and practitioners around the world, it is rarely the focus of research on education in low-income countries (Taniguchi, 2015).

Stylized Dynamics of Selected indicators of Student Flow, 2000–2015

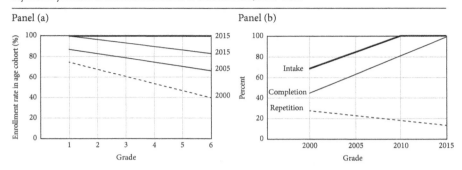

Figure 5.1 Example of grade repetition's representation in the literature (reproduced from Mingat, Rakotomalala & Tan, 2002, page 7)

In place of a detailed literature, grade repetition is treated as a stylized fact, particularly in relation to its possible association with school dropout, which, as illustrated by the reproduction of Mingat, Rakotomalala & Tan, 2002 in Figure 5.1, is often visualized as a direct, negative linear association.

In this chapter, my goal is to rethink the issue of grade repetition. I begin by surveying existing research on the subject. Given how little research has been conducted on grade repetition in low-income countries, I begin with the literature and discourse from the United States and Europe, identifying key concepts and insights that will apply to multiple contexts, and then focus on what research exists from low-income countries, and in particular, sub-Saharan Africa. This review helps to identify what we know about grade repetition, and also the limits of our understanding. In addition, it exposes the overly simplistic framework that currently defines so much of the international literature.

I then turn to my case study, and empirical analysis with data from my sample of Ugandan primary schools and pupils. I focus on the assumption at the heart of the issue: that grade repetition and school dropout are positively linked. My primary question for empirical analysis is: Did repeating a grade increase the likelihood that child would drop out of school? The empirical analysis of this chapter thus aligns with the theoretical question of whether emphasizing quality negatively impacts access. It also investigates the supposed linearity of the association between repetition and dropout.

In my literature review and empirical analysis, my approach to the subject of grade repetition is informed by systems thinking and the principles of complexity. If my primary critique of the discourse on repetition is that it is oversimplified and reductive, the challenge will be to assess the issue in a way that embraces its complexity. I first argue that grade repetition must be analyzed within the contexts and systems in which it takes place. For this reason, I include qualitative investigation into local perceptions of grade repetition. I analyze focus group discussions and semi-structured interviews with parents, teachers, and school administrators to explore the experiences of these key stakeholders and what they think of grade repetition.

I also incorporate principles of complexity theory in my quantitative analysis. While the literature presents a direct, linear association between repetition and dropout, I explore variation and change over time. I question the idea of a constant association between the two issues, and instead hypothesize that repetition might lead to dropout under certain conditions but not others, or maybe only for some children. I investigate not just whether repeating a grade is associated with dropping out of school, but also whether the repetition of specific grades or the frequency of repetition might be associated with dropping out of school, as complex systems exhibit high levels of nonlinearity.

Finally, I consider how my empirical analysis speaks to the access vs. quality paradigm. Does it support and provide evidence for the theorized trade-off between access and quality? Should grade repetition be seen as an improvement in quality that threatens access or, alternatively, that its absence might increase access but at the expense of quality? Or both? What other relationship might exist between access and quality when viewed through the lens of grade repetition?

Grade Repetition in the United States and Europe

Given how little rigorous research exists on grade repetition in low-income countries, I first review literature from the United States, and then Europe. Grade repetition is a contentious issue in the US educational discourse. One side of the debate argues that repetition is not a positive educational intervention. As Ernest House contended in 1989, "it would be difficult to find another educational practice on which the evidence is so unequivocally negative" (West, 2012: 3). Estimates for the annual national cost of grade repetition range from $12 billion to $18 billion, which draws attention to the fact that an additional year of school could be one of the most expensive educational interventions (West, 2012; Xia & Glennie, 2005). Additionally, the literature highlights the connection between grade retention and later school dropout, concluding that "early grade retention is one of the most powerful predictors of later school withdrawal" (Jimerson, Anderson, & Whipple, 2002: 452). Given the high cost, the limited benefit to academic achievement, and the strong positive association with negative consequences such as dropout, a large body of work contends that the practice of grade repetition should be significantly reduced.

However, research on grade repetition has long suffered from methodological limitations. As West (2012: 3) puts it:

> To the extent that much of the evidence available on a topic suffers from a common flaw, however, a consistency of findings should not increase confidence in their validity. In the case of grade repetition, the central challenge facing researchers is to distinguish the effect of being retained from the effects of those factors that triggered the retention decision in the first place.

In particular, this quotation speaks to the presumed connection between repeating a grade and dropping out of school. Those students at risk of repeating a grade are also likely to be the same students that are at risk of dropping out of school. It is, therefore, difficult to determine whether it is the experience of repeating a grade that might lead a student to drop out of school or whether those students might have dropped out regardless.

Nationally, there are no systematic attempts to monitor the number of students who repeat every year. In general, there are very few data that directly measure repetition; estimates are usually inferred from census or demographic data on students' age per grade (Alexander, Entwisle, & Dauber, 2003; Eide & Showalter, 2001). Noting the absence of even basic data on repetition, researchers have argued, "I doubt that governments currently make important policy decisions about any other social process with so little sound, basic, descriptive information" (Hauser, 2001: 155).

In what research exists on repetition, variation emerges as an important theme. The impact of repetition has been shown to vary across different settings and educational contexts, as well as for children of different ages and at different points in their education. The psychological consequences of repetition in California (Anderson, Jimerson, & Whipple, 2005), for example, seem to differ dramatically from those in Baltimore (Alexander, Entwisle, & Dauber, 2003). While sixth-grade students in a California study rated grade repetition as a potentially more stressful event than losing a parent or going blind, in Baltimore, where nearly 50 percent of students repeat a grade at some point (as in many other high-poverty school districts), the experience of repetition was much more normalized. Research in Chicago showed a short-term positive effect of grade repetition on third graders' test scores but not on sixth graders' scores; the researchers also found that repeating sixth grade did not affect high school completion, but repeating eighth grade increased the probability that struggling students would later drop out of school (Jacob & Lefgren, 2004, 2009). Impacts may also differ for white and black students, as one study found clearly negative effects of retention for white students, but inconclusive results for black students (Eide & Showalter, 2001).

While the American discourse focuses on determining a correct policy or approach for a single national setting (Xia & Glennie, 2005), Europe has a diverse array of approaches to and practices of grade repetition. Some countries, such as Iceland and Norway, have policies of automatic promotion, with less than one percent of students repeating (Eurydice, 2011). In other countries repetition is much more frequently practiced, with rates ranging from 12.2 percent in Spain to 22.4 percent in the Netherlands and Portugal.

One of the most interesting findings from research on grade repetition in Europe is the disconnect between policy and practice: "The comparison of statistical data (Eurostat 2008 and PISA 2009) indicates that there is no linear relationship between the provision of grade retention in legislation and its actual use in practice" (Eurydice network, 2011: 60). In Belgium, Spain, France, Luxembourg, the Netherlands, and Portugal, grade repetition is embraced as a pedagogical tool believed to be beneficial for students' learning. This view is supported by parents, teachers, and education professionals. Simply changing policies and regulations may not affect prevailing assumptions or attitudes, which seem to be more influential (Eurydice network, 2011). Similarly, in the US context, teachers, parents, and the public at large support repetition and believe in its importance, in spite of a large research literature that condemns the practice (Xia & Glennie, 2005).

The experiences of the United States and Europe offer three key points relevant to the study of grade repetition in sub-Saharan Africa. First, the phenomenon of grade repetition is complicated, and it is difficult to determine its impact, particularly across diverse contexts that vary not only in relation to which students are selected to be retained and why, but also at what point and in what kind of education system and cultural context repetition occurs. Second, the question of whether or not to practice grade repetition is not a binary yes/no. There are many different approaches to the implementation of repetition, which accordingly might result in many possible outcomes. And finally, the practice of grade repetition includes multiple actors such as parents, teachers, and policymakers and is highly influenced by prevailing attitudes and the culture of the education community. Any intervention or policy on repetition would need to address these various actors and their perspectives. Each of these three points highlights the complexity of grade repetition and the need to consider the practice within the systems and contexts in which it takes place. These ideas inform my approach to studying grade repetition in sub-Saharan Africa, both in how I assess existing literature and in how I conduct my own research.

Grade Repetition in Sub-Saharan Africa

There is very little research on grade repetition in sub-Saharan Africa (Taniguchi, 2015), but the general consensus of extant literature is that the practice is negative and should be discouraged (Brophy, 2006; Ndaruhutse, 2008). Another key conclusion of the literature is that grade repetition is practiced more frequently in Francophone (French-speaking) and Lusophone (Portuguese-speaking) Africa than in Anglophone (English-speaking) Africa (Bernard et al., 2005; Michaelowa, 2003; Ndaruhutse, 2008; UNESCO, 2012). This difference has been interpreted from a historical perspective. Colonial education systems reflected various European approaches to grade repetition; their lasting influence led Francophone and Lusophone countries to embrace repetition as a pedagogical practice, while Anglophone countries tend to have policies of automatic promotion (Bernard et al., 2005; Eisemon, 1997).

Comparisons between more than forty different African countries find average national rates of repetition in Francophone countries to be consistently higher (18–19.9 per year across primary) than average rates of repetition in Anglophone countries (8.5–10.3 percent) (Bernard et al., 2005; Michaelowa, 2003). Accordingly, the discussion of repetition in Africa tends to focus on Francophone countries, arguing that they should decrease their rates of repetition (Brophy, 2006; Ndaruhutse, 2008). Anglophone countries, with their lower official rates, are presented as the alternative approach to repetition (Bernard et al., 2005; Michaelowa, 2003).

Aside from the Anglophone-Francophone comparison, the primary conclusion of research on repetition in sub-Saharan Africa is that it is related to school dropout. Multi-country studies of grade repetition find a direct, linear, and positive association between grade repetition and dropout. Using 2002 UNESCO data from forty-four African countries, Bernard, Simon, and Vianou (2005) find that an additional 1 percent of repeaters in a country's repetition rate was associated with a 1.3 percent increase in dropouts. They argue that a country with a repetition rate of 20 percent and a primary school completion rate of 60 percent could increase completion rates by 13 percent if the repetition rate were lowered by 10 percent (Bernard, Simon, & Vianou, 2005; Ndaruhutse, 2008). Directly linking repetition to dropout is prevalent in the international literature on repetition. It extends back to at least 1971, when a study of forty-two low-income countries found that "a one percent increase in the average repetition rate is associated with an almost one per cent increase in the cumulative dropout rate," concluding that "high repetition rates clearly discourage school continuation" (Levy, 1971: 58).

The most extensive application of this argument is found in the World Bank's Africa Country education status reports. Across fifty African countries, the World Bank estimates that, on average, a one percent increase in grade repetition is associated with a 0.7 percent increase in the student dropout rate (Berete et al., 2005). Therefore, if the repetition rate is lowered by 10 percent, a "typical African country" can anticipate an increase in the primary school completion rate of around 7.7 percent (Berete et al., 2005: 90). Costs have been estimated as well—with one report stating that in 1998 in Francophone Africa, nearly 40 percent of total education resources were "wasted" due to high repetition and dropout rates, while only 25 percent of resources were wasted in Anglophone countries (Amoussouga, Cuenin, & Rakotomalala, 2002; Ndaruhutse, 2008: 6).

These studies of African education systems align repetition and dropout and characterize both as the "wastage" of educational resources. The idea of repetition as a simple precursor to dropout is the prevailing representation of grade repetition in international development education discourse, and it is used to argue that countries, particularly those in Francophone Africa, should decrease their rates of repetition. It also presents the dynamics of primary education as strictly linear.

This line of research has four critical flaws. First and foremost, it makes little mention of learning. It either assumes that repeating a grade has no effect on a child's academic achievement, positive or negative, and that its removal would have no effect, or it presents learning as a secondary and separate issue (Amoussouga et al., 2002; Berete et al., 2005; Mingat, 2002). At the very least, grade repetition alters the composition of a classroom, with implications for both peer-to-peer learning and teachers' instruction. Recommending that a country decrease its repetition rate by 50 percent would likely have consequences other than simply making an education system more "efficient."

Second, this literature does not adequately address issues of endogeneity. Existing country and multi-country data sets do not have any features that allow for causal inference. It is not possible to determine whether repeating leads to dropping out or whether the same underlying factors that influence repetition also influence dropout. In the discussion of grade repetition in sub-Saharan Africa, Glick and Sahn's (2010) work in Senegal is an exception.

Using panel data, the authors were able to exploit variation in schools' repetition policies to determine a causal estimate of the impact of repetition on both academic achievement and later school dropout. They found that repeating the second grade increased the likelihood that a child would drop out of school by 11 percent. Students who repeated the second grade also appeared to have a small reduction in third-grade test scores, but this finding was not statistically significant, and the study only analyzed repetition in second grade. The authors note that "there appear to be no similar studies in other African contexts that plausibly attempt to control for repetition endogeneity" (Glick and Sahn, 2010: 115).

The third flaw is that this literature assumes the practice of repetition, except for its frequency, does not vary across different African countries. In one of the only qualitative study to focus on grade repetition in sub-Saharan Africa, N'tchougan-Sonou (2001) compares teachers' practices of repetition in Togo and Ghana. Togo practices large-scale repetition. Whether or not a pupil repeats is determined by her performance on national exams, which limits many students' progression through school. In contrast, Ghana's education system has a policy of automatic promotion, severely limiting repetition. Ghanaian teachers reported that they held back only the very competent and academically able students who might be behind due to extended absence, illness, or immaturity, whereas they promoted students with very poor academic abilities through the education system in the hope that they might acquire vocational, technical, or other skills (N'tchougan-Sonou, 2001).

Repetition practices in Ghana and Togo represent two dramatically different phenomena that vary not only in their historical and policy contexts, but likely in their consequences as well. Ghana's reported rate of repetition of 3.6 percent suggests a distinctly different phenomenon from Togo's reported rate of repetition of 28.4 percent (N'tchougan-Sonou, 2001). Given the significant difference in rates of repetition, it seems likely that the practice of repetition affects not only the students who have undergone it directly, but also their peers and the larger dynamics of the education system as well. Grade repetition cannot be isolated from the settings and complex systems in which it takes place.

Other countries' differing practices of repetition have also been noted, such as those in Kenya, where repetition is common in the later grades of primary school, when students are working to improve their performance on standardized exams (Zuze, 2008). Even within the same context, the impact of repetition may vary for a number of reasons. Repeating the first grade due to age or immaturity might have different consequences than repeating the seventh grade in order to perform better on the entrance exams to secondary school. The examples of Ghana, Togo, and Kenya offer three important sources of variation in the practice of repetition: the selection criteria used to determine which children repeat, the overall percentage of children repeating, and the developmental or educational point at which a child repeats; each might be expected to influence a child's experience of repetition and the system at large. Analysis which combines data on repetition across multiple countries potentially conflates dramatically different phenomena.

A final flaw in existing studies is data quality. The calculations that link grade repetition with school dropout and completion rates across different countries often rely on national-level data and official statistics (Bernard et al., 2005; Mingat, 2002). There are significant concerns about the accuracy of these data. Official statistics often underreport grade repetition for a variety of reasons (Brophy, 2006; Eisemon, 1997; UNESCO, 2012). Teachers, for example, might be reluctant to draw attention to the practice if it is discouraged by national policy. Malawi serves as a good illustration, where the repetition rate reported by administrators in the school census is 15.5 percent, or just under half the average repetition rates found in two household surveys (25.8 and 28.4 percent) (Nellemann et al., 2004).

In summary, most of the existing literature on grade repetition in sub-Saharan Africa is narrow in scope, has significant methodological flaws, and does not account for variation in either the experiences or consequences of the practice. Perhaps the literature's most significant limitation is that in so closely aligning repetition with dropout, it fails to focus on repetition itself, rarely looking into why the practice of repetition exists in the first place. In the absence of a focused literature on the subject, grade repetition is viewed through the lens of the access vs. quality paradigm. In Uganda, the issue is explicitly understood in these terms; the headline of a Ugandan national newspaper, for example, asked "Automatic Promotion: Quality or Numbers?" (Businge, 2007).

Repetition in Uganda

Like many other countries in Anglophone Africa, Uganda has long promoted a policy of automatic promotion. First proposed in 1998, the policy was intended to address a number of problems (high dropout, low primary school completion rates) and potentially save the Ministry of Education an "estimated Shs 58bn" (approximately 51 million USD) (Talemwa, 2014). Due to imperfect implementation of the policy, significant numbers of pupils still repeat; starting in the year 2000, Uganda's Ministry of Education has reported annual rates of repetition of between 10 and 15 percent (MoES, 2015). In 2009, the president of Uganda appointed a Judicial Commission of Inquiry to investigate the mismanagement of funds under the country's Universal Primary and Secondary Education. The commission calculated that the Ministry of Education's failure to enforce the policy of automatic promotion from 1998 to 2010 resulted in "a loss to Government of UGX 53,803,884,000/= [approximately 57 million USD] in funds wasted on children who clog the system" and recommended that the ministry better enforce the policy "to minimize wastage in the education system" (Commission of Inquiry, 2012: 58).

Ugandan newspaper articles and editorials, like the Judicial Commission, often reflect the rationale of the international development discourse, that repetition is a waste of resources, leads to school dropout, and should be minimized. An editorial in the national newspaper the *Daily Monitor* argued, "Grade repetition undermines the internal efficiency of education as the unit costs of provision get inflated. School completion and retention rates plummet as a result" (Okurut, 2016: para 1). Similarly, an article titled "Government Defends Automatic Promotion of UPE Pupils" reported that the Education Minister Namirembe Bitamazire was a lead advocate of the policy, frequently arguing that repeating classes is a waste of money (Ssenkabirwa & Miti, 2010).

On the other hand, Ugandan media has also chronicled significant resistance to automatic promotion policy. Individual schools and districts have challenged it. A head teacher, preferring anonymity in order to "keep her job" explained, "We are no longer implementing that policy. We let children repeat, and once they improve we promote them to another class" (Nangonzi, 2017: para 23). The District Chairman of Iganga, in response to students' poor test scores, banned the policy, stating "I am ready to face any charge for that" (Kirunda, 2015: para 5). In a 2017 report, a parliamentary committee on education reported, "The committee is concerned that the 'no repeat' policy has compromised the quality of [learners] emerging from the schools" (Nangonzi, 2017: para 16).

Very little research or data exist on either the promotion policy or the country's practice of grade repetition; accordingly, there is little evidence to support any argument in relation to repetition, either in favor or against. Information on repetition in Uganda is limited to officially reported rates of repetition from the MoES (2015) and data from one or two other surveys, such as the Southern and Eastern Africa Consortium for Monitoring Education Quality (Hungi, 2011). The little research that exists suggests that official rates are significantly underreporting the practice. One study collected five different reports of first-grade repetition: the official rate, teacher records, teacher interviews, and parent interviews. Teacher and parent interviews ranged from 4 to 14 times higher than the official repeater rate (Weatherholt et al., 2017). A second research paper to address grade repetition in Uganda is by Okurut (2015) and investigates the country's automatic promotion policy by comparing government and private schools. As with most of the research on repetition in sub-Saharan Africa, research in Uganda faces significant methodological limitations, enabling few conclusions.

Stakeholders in Uganda are accordingly caught between competing objectives. In response to critiques, the government has pulled back from its hardline stance, offering poor performance and low attendance as potential reasons why pupils might repeat. In discussing the issue, "Dr. Rose Nassali, director, Education Standards Agency (ESA) said the Ministry's aim is to ensure all the children go through the school system while minimizing wastage and ensuring quality" (Eremu, 2003: para 11). Similarly, assistant commissioner Dr. Tonny Mukasa-Lusamu recently stated, "One of the challenges stakeholders point at as the cause of poor performance of UPE is automatic promotion. It is imperative that we revisit the policy by providing some adjustments to ensure that more learners access school as well as improve the quality of education" (Nangonzi, 2017: 28).

I organize my own research on repetition into three parts: basic descriptive statistics, which I use to get a sense of the phenomenon and complement the limited administrative data on the topic, analysis of the association between repetition and dropout, and qualitative research. I start with my descriptive analysis.

Empirical Analysis: Incidence of Grade Repetition and Dropout

Given that the phenomenon of repetition is believed to be significantly underreported in official reports (Weatherholt et al., 2017, 2019), I begin my quantitative analysis with descriptive statistics on the incidence of both repetition and dropout. As described in Chapter 4, my quantitative data include an original sample of 4,117 primary school pupils initially distributed across 136 Ugandan government primary schools and tracked for a period of two years. I accordingly have data from two time points. At each point, children were asked how many times they had repeated a grade. In the endline, children were also asked which grade(s) they repeated. I summarize these descriptive results in Table 5.1.

Table 5.1 Survey responses: How many times have you repeated a grade? Which grades did you repeat?

	Repeated once	Repeated 3 or more times	Repeated Primary 1	Repeated Primary 2	Repeated Primary 3	Repeated Primary 4	Repeated Primary 5
Baseline	73%	8%					
Endline	88%	11%	8.42%	8.99%	24.13%	40.91%	34.45%

The incidence of grade repetition was extremely high, with 88 percent of the endline sample reporting that they had repeated a grade and more than 11 percent reporting that they had repeated three or more times (see Table 5.1). Additionally, because of the high rates of repetition, in order to get a more complete picture of primary schooling, this sample would have to be tracked for at least three more years to see all children either graduate or discontinue their primary school education. I therefore expect that a total estimate of repetition for all of primary school would be even higher.

In the endline survey, 259 children reported that they dropped out of school during the two-year period between the baseline and the endline, comprising 6.7 percent of the endline sample. We asked each child who reported dropping out of school their primary reason for dropping out. Of these children, 38.19 percent reported that they dropped out due to a lack of money for fees or scholastic materials, 14.17 percent because of their poor performance, and 12.20 percent due to pregnancy. Other responses such as sickness or "not interested" each represented less than 10 percent of the dropout sample.

Empirical Analysis: Repetition and Dropout

My central research question for this chapter is whether repeating a grade increases the likelihood that a child will drop out of school. In my quantitative analysis, I address this question in a number of different ways, corresponding to the different measures of repetition I just reported in my descriptive analysis. I analyze whether ever repeating a grade is associated with dropping out of school, whether the number of times a child has repeated is associated with dropping out of school, and whether the repetition of specific grades is associated with dropping out of school. The results tables for this analysis are included in the Technical Appendix.

One important concern is the timing of the study. When the baseline survey was administered, all children were at the end of either fourth or fifth grade. The endline survey was completed two years later. Without repetition, children would be at the end of sixth and seventh grade when the endline survey was conducted. Repeating fifth or sixth grade occurred during the study period. Repetition of these grades, accordingly, does not serve as a valid predictor of dropout, as the two phenomena would have to be concurrent. I accordingly do not investigate or report findings related to those grades.

Generally, I do not find that grade repetition was associated with dropping out of school. Children who repeated a grade were not more likely to drop out of school than children who did not repeat. The number of times a child repeated a grade was also not associated with dropout. Two of the factors that were associated with dropout were if a child worked and test scores. Children who reported at the baseline that they worked to earn money were more likely to drop out than children who did not, and children with lower test scores were more likely to drop out than children who performed better on the baseline exam.

The strongest predictor of dropout was a child's age. An additional year in age made a child two times as likely to drop out of school. This foreshadows one of the themes of the qualitative research, as teachers suspected that over-age children struggle with access to school and are at risk of dropping out. Teachers believed that overage children should not be made to repeat a class. As one teacher said, "Better let children who are aging go to the next class."

Across all of my analysis, a child's age appears to be the strongest, most consistent, and statistically most significant predictor of dropout. I hypothesize that age could be an important confounder in understanding the relationship between repeating and dropping out, as it predicts dropout and is also highly associated with repetition. A child cannot repeat a grade without getting older. As previously mentioned, age is an important issue in the qualitative data, to be described in the next section. I investigate whether excluding age as a covariate in my analysis changes the relationship between repetition and dropout, and it does.

When age is not included in the analysis, there does appear to be a statistically significant association between repeating a grade and dropping out of school. If research does not account for age, it could be mistakenly aligning repeating a grade with dropping out of school. A child's age might be an important confounding variable in the analysis of repetition.

Absence from school also appears to be a strong predictor of school dropout. In the baseline survey, children were asked "How often do you miss school per term?" I coded responses on a zero to three scale from one to two times per term (0) to more than ten times (3). The association between earlier school absence and dropout indicates that dropping out of school should not be seen as a discrete event, but one that is foreshadowed by frequent absence. A child who reports being absent from school three to five times per semester was 1.5 times more likely to drop out of school than a child who reported she was absent only one or two times per semester. A child who was absent more than ten times in a semester was 4.5 times more likely to drop out than a child who was absent only once or twice.

Though I do not find that repetition overall is associated with school dropout, I also investigate the repetition of specific grades. Repetition of the first two grades of school, P1 and P2, was not associated with dropout. Repetition of third grade, though, did have a positive association with dropping out of school. Children who repeated P3 had a higher likelihood of dropping out. This suggests that repeating third grade (P3) might differ in some ways from repeating first or second grade (P1 or P2) and potentially later grades as well.

As I mentioned in Chapter 4, during the endline we were able to locate, resurvey, and retest 83 percent of the baseline sample. Especially in relation to repetition and dropout, attrition is likely not a random process. To address this concern, I use additional information to conduct a robustness check. During the endline data collection, if a child from the sample could not be located, an enumerator met with family members, neighbors, and friends in order to determine how best to locate the child. Many of these people were able to provide information on the lives of children in the sample.

We collected information on the schooling of 453 of the 878 children we were unable to locate. Reports included stories such as "Her father said that she went to Kampala to work as a maid" or, conversely, "She is staying with her aunt in K——, and she goes to school there, but the uncle doesn't know the school." Reponses were coded as either "in school" or "dropped out." Including this information increased the endline sample to 91.1 percent of the original sample. After rerunning some of my analysis using this additional information, there were no substantial changes in relation to the main findings on repetition and dropout.

To complement these quantitative findings, I turn to my qualitative research on repetition. With semi-structured interviews and focus group discussions I am able to explore the perspectives and opinions of key stakeholders. How do parents, teachers, and school administrators perceive and make sense of grade repetition? This qualitative work also serves to contextualize the issue, grounding my study of grade repetition in the lived realities of the Ugandan primary education system and the students it serves.

Empirical Analysis: Perceptions of Repetition

First, I analyze my semi-structured interviews and focus group discussions with parents and community members. These were extended, in-depth conversations with individuals or small groups of people. I explored respondents' thought process and decision-making, trying to uncover the meaning behind their words and actions. Second, I analyze data from focus group discussions with teachers and school administrators. These focus groups were conducted across three different events and included almost 400 participants. As these data consist of short quotations from participants, my goal is to define how teachers and administrators understand, frame, and make sense of repetition in their own words.

In my research with parents and community members, I began by talking about education generally. In some instances, respondents brought up the issue of grade repetition themselves. For example, one father used repetition to describe the difference between public schools and private schools, in that private schools do not have to follow automatic promotion policy and thus repeat children more freely. He saw this as positive. This father described repetition as "a form of accountability" for parents, ensuring that children are not just wantonly moved through the education system.

If respondents did not bring up the issue of grade repetition themselves, I would ask whether any of their children had ever repeated a grade and, if so, could they talk about it. About half of the respondents had children who had repeated, but even those who did not have direct experience still had clear opinions. In one focus group discussion, for example, though their children had not repeated, one parent stated, "We would make them repeat if they had to, [so that our children would] understand."

The parents I interviewed believed grade repetition was an effective pedagogical tool. In all the interviews, they described repetition as an opportunity for children to improve, noting that their children performed better on exams after repeating a grade. Parents did not appear to attach any stigma to the practice, believing, as one father said, that it was "no problem."

These parents saw low test scores as justification for repetition, thinking low scores represented a child's failure to grasp the material and necessary competencies. One mother admitted that "It's hurting to see a child repeat once, twice, same class," but she wanted her child "to understand." Though parents did not reference any specific curriculum, skills, or standards in discussing repetition, they always referenced reports or exams. As one father explained, "If their performance is bad, they don't deserve to go to the next class." Though he admitted that it might be costly, "they deserve to work better and move to the next level."

This is not to say that parents and community members viewed repetition as a wholly positive experience. Parents referenced various negative concerns to explain why it happened (poor teaching, children's capacity) as well as its impact (toll on household finances, halts children's progression through school). As one mother described, she "felt bad" because she was spending money when her daughter repeated, but her daughter's performance on exams had improved. This mother disagreed with parents who did not let their children repeat. She explained, "That child actually needed to repeat and understand better."

The issue of cost is important. Repeating a grade means parents have to pay for an additional year of school. This is a primary reason why parents are key decision makers when it comes to repetition, as they are seen to bear the cost. Almost all the parents I interviewed self-identified as primary decision makers. Teachers might suggest that a child should repeat, but ultimately parents believed that it was their decision.

The mother who "felt bad" because she was spending money on repetition quoted a radio show where she heard a doctor say, "I told my child that I've put your bank in your brain...through education, so that you don't have to come back to me." This mother explained what she meant by saying, "If you invest in a child, like the children here, they grow up, maybe find a job and start working, they get independent...and go with their own life without coming back to give you a burden." Parents felt that repetition, like education in general, is an investment. Ensuring that children are learning what they are supposed to will enable them to ultimately become independent.

In the focus group discussions with class teachers and school administrators, most discussion participants were not surprised by the high incidence of repetition in their schools. Like the parents, teachers recognized many potential benefits of repetition: "Children should repeat so as to master the content for that class." "It is good to repeat because the child may get [faculties] he didn't get before." "Learners should not be promoted to another class unless he/she knows how to read and write." Multiple participants described repeating as "normal," and one teacher explained that "Repeating is inevitable and professional." Others said that "Repeating helps a child to attain the minimum standards."

These comments illustrate teachers' and administrators' emphasis on learning outcomes and the quality of education. This relates to both the development of an individual child—as in "the child may get [faculties] he didn't get before"—and the maintenance of standards, as in "Learners should not be promoted to another class unless he/she knows how to read and write." Like parents, teachers viewed repetition as a pedagogical tool working to serve the interests of individual children, as well as the education system as a whole. The comment from a teacher that "Repeating is inevitable and professional" suggests that repetition can be seen as a natural part of a functioning school system. From the perspective of key stakeholders, grade repetition is intended to improve the quality of education.

Though the discussion of repetition was mostly positive, teachers and administrators also voiced some negative impressions. Two participants mentioned "loss of time and resources" and said that repetition can be costly to parents. Only a few of the nearly 400 teachers and administrators referenced Uganda's automatic promotion policy, which made the policy more notable for its absence than for its discussion. The few references were almost neutral, simply stating that "It is government policy to promote every learner." It seems the policy was not a pressing concern for teachers and barely factored into their consideration of the issue. Technically, though, given Uganda's automatic promotion policy at this time, teachers' decision to repeat students was against the law.

Teachers and administrators also mentioned age and suggested that repetition might not be appropriate for all children. They argued, "Better let children who have repeated many times go to the next class," and "Better let children who are aging go to the next class." As one participant explained, repeating is "healthy to those who go to school when they are young, but can also lead to school dropout for those who are grown."

School officials accordingly believe that for some children, their presence in school is not to be taken for granted, and rather than emphasize learning outcomes, which might threaten access, these children should at least be able to progress through the system. These quotations also illustrate that teachers recognize the varying needs of different students and that key factors outside of the classroom influence children's education. Teachers consider more than a child's academic performance when deciding to repeat a child and understand the influence of a child's environment. In short, they recognize repetition to be a complex concern.

These findings align with my quantitative analysis in two key ways: that it might not be repetition so much as age that makes children more likely to drop out of school and that the impact of repetition might vary for different grades. It also illustrates a point at which parents' and teachers/school administrators' perspectives diverge. Parents appear singularly focused on test scores and children's performance, while teachers and school administrators take a more holistic approach. Similarly, while parents typically mentioned poor teaching practices to explain why children repeat, the teachers and school administrators presented a much broader perspective. While some teachers and school administrators mentioned poor teaching practices and related concerns, they ultimately focused on broader societal issues. A good illustration of this perspective is the statement that repetition "is normal due to prevailing problems."

Teachers' and school administrator's holistic approach to grade repetition contextualizes the practice within Uganda's education system and also in relation to Ugandan society more broadly, aligning with complexity theory's emphasis on the interaction between a system and its environment. School administrators and teachers provided a wide range of answers to the question "Why do children repeat?," most of which could be described as "prevailing problems." Of the various themes, approximately half concerned issues within the classroom: "high teacher pupil ratio," "negative attitudes toward the curriculum by some teachers," "misinterpretation of government policies," "transferring between schools," "poor motivation of teachers," "poor assessment of learners."

Though these scholastic concerns prompted some discussion, the most frequently cited cause of repetition came from outside the classroom. In response to the question "Why do children repeat?," some educators simply answered, "Poverty" or "Child labor." Others more fully explained "Most children absent themselves and go to work." Throughout all the discussions, the most frequently mentioned theme was parents' and communities' lack of support for education. School officials explained this issue by describing a "lack of support from home," "parents [who] are not concerned," a "negative attitude toward education by parents," a "lack of role models," and "parents [who] don't follow up with the children's academic progress." This theme speaks to a pressing challenge of Uganda's primary education: the figurative distance between the school and the community.

The division of roles and responsibility among parents, communities, and the government is still being negotiated. In answering the question "Why do children repeat?," teachers and administrators gave the same exact responses as when asked the question "What are the greatest challenges facing primary education?" Teachers' and administrators' alignment of grade repetition with primary education as a whole reveals their belief that grade repetition is just one indicator of an entire system that is struggling. As a practice that takes place within the complex system of primary education, repetition is influenced by a range of interconnected issues, both inside and outside of the classroom. Simply reducing grade repetition would not actually address the issues grade repetition represents, such as low learning levels and high levels of absenteeism.

Parents', teachers', and school administrators' perspectives offer a stark contrast to framing repetition as "wastage" and the assertion that educational inefficiency can be defined as the ratio between actual resources consumed and the quantity of resources that would be "strictly necessary" to produce primary school graduates in the absence of grade repetition and dropout (Mingat, 2002: 2).

Beyond Wastage: Grade Repetition in a Complex Education System

Grade repetition can seem like a simple problem with a simple solution. The problem: Repetition is a drain upon limited resources; it prevents children from progressing through school, and it might even increase the likelihood that they dropout. The solution: Education systems should limit grade repetition, if not eliminate it altogether.

But what happens when a child fails? Or if a school system is full of children failing to grasp its basic standards? Ugandan parents seem to take a clear stance: Children "deserve the best, not to just promote them... they deserve to work better and [then] move to the next level." Parents believe repeating a grade gives a child an opportunity to improve, to "understand." They recognize the inanity of a school system that just moves children along regardless of how they perform.

With little longitudinal research on grade repetition in low-income country contexts, however, it is hard to know whether grade repetition actually improves learning. Are Ugandan parents choosing grade repetition only because of the lack of better options? In the absence of nuanced, focused research on the subject, the discourse on grade repetition is vastly oversimplified. Grade repetition and dropout are viewed as indicators of inefficiency or school "wastage," which suggests that the primary goal of education is to move the greatest number of children through school as fast as possible. There is little to no mention of learning. If learning is recognized, its role is interpreted in terms of the paradigm, not from detailed evidence. Does repeating a grade actually increase the likelihood that a child will drop out of school? Or has a common association between repetition and dropout been assumed to be causal? Does an emphasis on standards and quality always constrict access?

In this chapter I approach my study of repetition from a standpoint of complexity. This approach opened up several possibilities. Might the impact of grade repetition vary by the grade repeated? Could different students experience repetition in different ways? Might grade repetition vary across different settings and contexts? Rather than use the access vs. quality paradigm to interpret the issue of grade repetition, I analyzed the dynamics of grade repetition itself to see what this focus might highlight and bring to the fore.

In my qualitative data, a number of teachers argued that repetition might not be good for overage children or for those who have already repeated multiple times. It could further increase the risk that these children might drop out of school. The importance of age was also reflected in the quantitative data, where a child's age was the largest statistically significant predictor of dropout, even when controlling for repetition. This introduces age of entry as an important concern.

Over 50 percent of Ugandan children are overage when they begin school (Education Policy and Data Center, 2012). Research shows that Ugandan children begin school far behind their peers in Kenya and Tanzania in terms of basic skills, which suggests that pre-primary education and early childhood experiences should be addressed (Jones & Schipper, 2015). It seems that children's later educational experiences are strongly defined by how and when they enter school.

The strong associations between children's age and later educational experiences in my data suggest that improving children's entry into primary school might have the potential to reduce later dropout rates, increase test scores, and otherwise improve their educational experience. A growing field of research is drawing attention to the importance of children's early education and the long-term impact of these experiences (Knudsen et al., 2006; Shonkoff & Phillips, 2000). Ensuring that children enter school at the appropriate age can be considered an access-oriented intervention, but an access-oriented intervention that also improves quality.

A second finding in my results concerns the specific grade repeated. I find that the association between repeating and school dropout is different for third grade than for either first or second grade. Third grade represents an important transition in Ugandan primary school. In P1 through P3, local languages are used as the medium of instruction; in P4, English becomes the medium of instruction. This is a dramatic transition. In P3, local languages are used in the classroom 76.8 percent of the time; in P4 local language use is reduced to 13.2 percent (Piper, 2010).

In my sample, I find that P4 had the highest rates of repetition, which possibly signals the need to adjust to the increased use of English in the classroom. Repeating P3 may represent teachers' concern that children have not fully mastered English and are not able to continue their education. English might accordingly serve as a gate-keeping skill, a constraint upon access.

Research has suggested that instead of an abrupt transition between languages of instruction, a more gradual transition that includes supports for struggling children would be preferable (Piper, 2010). This could be conceived of as a quality intervention: an improved language policy. In light of the current high rates of repetition around the years of the transition and the association between repetition in these years and dropout, it could be hypothesized that improving this language transition could lead to lower rates of repetition and less school dropout. Improving quality could improve access.

My analysis of grade repetition thus highlights two important challenges within Uganda's education system: age of entry into school and the transition between languages of instruction. Both of these issues suggest interventions that operate outside of the access vs. quality paradigm. Improving age of entry into school addresses an access-related issue, but also has the potential to improve quality at the same time. Improving the transition between languages of instruction is a quality intervention that could positively impact access. These dynamics suggest ways in in which efforts to improve educational access and efforts to improve educational quality could be mutually reinforcing.

I come to these conclusions by approaching the study of grade repetition with principles of complexity theory. Much of existing research presents a direct, linear, and unchanging association between repetition and dropout, along the lines of the access vs. quality paradigm. My results suggest that the issue is far more complicated and, in particular, that the issue of grade repetition is better understood through complexity theory's principle of nonlinearity. The practice of grade repetition must be contextualized within the contexts and settings in which it takes place. Analyzing grade repetition in isolation and across multiple countries overlooks the interconnectedness and interdependence of different issues within primary education. In my analysis of Uganda, early childhood education and language policy appear to be highly relevant to grade repetition and dropout. The teachers and school administrators of my qualitative analysis viewed grade repetition as one indicator of a complex system, recognizing that a single policy on grade repetition will not address these underlying concerns. Simply eliminating repetition and moving students through the education system are unlikely to achieve the desired outcomes. Additionally, grade repetition might not always, for all children, increase the likelihood of school dropout.

In general, I do not find that ever repeating a grade is associated with dropping out of school. Grade repetition's emphasis on quality, therefore, does not necessarily have a negative impact on access. My analysis does not rule out this possibility, and at the very least, some children might experience grade repetition in this way. But there is also space for a different dynamic in which there could be a positive association between educational quality and educational access. To further investigate this relationship, I turn to my next empirical study of the access vs. quality paradigm and focus on the low-fee private primary education sector in Uganda.

6

Private Primary Schools

Low-fee private primary schools are a powerful illustration of how quickly an educational issue can move from relative obscurity to prominence. As late as 2004, private schools were considered to be of little consequence to the Education for All movement (Srivastava, 2013). In the past decade, their recognition as an issue of significance has become indisputable. Discussion of basic education and efforts to achieve Universal Primary Education now invariably include reference to the private sector and analysis of the phenomenon has grown from a handful of technical reports to a burgeoning field of research (UNESCO, 2015).

Several different developments can explain this attention: growing recognition that private schools can and do serve poor students, concerns that states alone might not be able to meet education goals, reservations over the relationship between privatization and the right to education, and a contentious debate in policy and practice about the current and future role of private schools in the movement to achieve Education For All (Day Ashley et al., 2014; Srivastava, 2013). An important ideological debate also exists about the role of the state and its responsibilities to its citizens. At the same time, practitioners and researchers around the world are struggling to determine what is actually happening in an education landscape that is rapidly changing.

From one perspective, the crux of the issue of privatization can be described in terms of access and quality. The promise of the private sector is that it could provide a higher quality alternative to public education, and one that might be more cost effective (Pritchett & Viarengo, 2008; Tooley et al., 2010). The threat of the private sector is that it might deepen educational inequality, providing access to quality education for only some children and potentially making education worse for others (Srivastava, 2013; Härmä, 2015). In sum, privatization might improve quality, but at the expense of access, a clear illustration of the access vs. quality paradigm.

We are limited in our ability to determine whether private schools actually offer higher-quality education and whether access to these schools is in fact inequitable. One of the primary challenges for research is that the private

Access, Quality, and the Global Learning Crisis: Insights from Ugandan Primary Education. Sarah Kabay, Oxford University Press.
© Sarah Kabay 2021. DOI: 10.1093/oso/9780192896865.003.0006

sector is often comprised of unregistered and informal schools for which data are unavailable. Official administrative data are unable to capture the full extent of the sector, especially when certain schools deliberately avoid such attention (Srivastava, 2013; Phillipson, 2008). The shortcomings of current data collection result in inaccurate enrollment estimates and, in particular, routinely underestimate enrollment in the non-state sector. This is one reason why low-fee private primary schools have historically been so overlooked.

In this chapter I investigate my sample of Ugandan primary school children's engagement with the private sector. As a longitudinal sample from a low-income country, my data present a unique opportunity. At baseline, all children were enrolled in either fourth or fifth grade in a regionally representative sample of Ugandan government primary schools; two years later, 10 percent or 389 children had transferred to private primary schools. Children were interviewed at baseline and endline, i.e. before and after they transferred, which presented the opportunity to both predict transfer and collect data on the schools they had transferred to.

My research questions focus on the two key premises of the private sector, and, accordingly, access and quality. I ask what aspects of a child's socioeconomic status, school, or test scores predict transfer to private school/ And do children's later test scores and educational experience vary by whether they are enrolled in a private or government school? If a child's socioeconomic status strongly predicts transfer to private school, this might suggest that access is a concern, that only certain children are able to access these schools. If issues such as teacher absence and extra lessons differ significantly between private schools and public schools, this might suggest that there is a difference in quality between the two sectors.

As in Chapter 5 on grade repetition, if I am to critique the way in which the issue of private primary schools in global primary education is framed, I believe it is important to seek an alternative. Understanding how key stakeholders perceive the issue is a necessary first step. In my research on the private sector, I accordingly conduct and analyze semi-structured interviews and focus group discussions with parents, children, and community members. I explore the issue of school choice, and in parallel with my quantitative analysis, focus on the perceived differences between private and public schools.

Together, my quantitative and qualitative analyses highlight a key principle of complexity theory: interdependence. While current research on the private sector tends to focus on its distinctions from the public sector, my research reveals more of the overlap and connections. Considering private and public as part of the same complex adaptive system offers a different framework to view the issue of privatization.

First, I review the existing literature on private schools in low-income countries, focusing on the challenges inherent in research on such schools, some of which I aim to address in this chapter. Much of the literature relates to my two research questions and the themes of access and quality, so I organize my review in relation to those two research questions. As there is very little research on transfer, I focus more generally on what defines enrollment in private primary schools (access) and then investigate the evidence as to whether private primary schools offer a higher-quality education than public schools.

Research on Private Schools in Low-Income Countries

Research on private primary schools is still relatively new, but growing rapidly, and in low-income countries, researching these schools and the populations they serve presents many challenges. First among these challenges is definition. Traditionally, private schools were seen to be primarily elite-serving institutions that charged high fees and generally served only a very small percentage of the total population of potential students. Over the past decade, a growing field of research has drawn attention to a different type of private school and the dramatic increases in enrollment in such schools around the world (Srivastava, 2013). Referred to as low-cost or low-fee private primary schools, these schools are typically characterized as being "independently funded through comparatively lower tuition fees (relative to elite or higher-fee private schools), [and] financially sustained through direct payments from poorer or relatively disadvantaged households (though not necessarily the poorest or most disadvantaged)" (Srivastava, 2013: 11–12). However, what might constitute "comparatively lower" and "poorer or relatively disadvantaged" is not well defined. Nor is whether these schools are primarily characterized by their funding source or the population they serve.

No standard or universal definition exists for low-fee or low-cost private primary schools (Day Ashley et al., 2014; Srivastava, 2013). Attempts to define the landscape of the private sector are better able to convey the diversity of the sector rather than a clear characterization of school type. One approach is to argue that "Defining precisely what we mean by a 'low-cost private school' is easier to do in terms of what it is not rather than what it is" (Philipson, 2008: 1), that a low-cost private school is *not* a school that serves the children of elites. Even the terms of this negative definition have been controversial, as certain distinctions are still unclear and many points can be debated, such as whether to include schools run by NGOs or schools that receive funding from the government but are independently run (Walford, 2011).

In this chapter, I rely on terms used colloquially in Uganda and by the country's Ministry of Education. A "government primary school" is a school that is under the jurisdiction of the Ministry of Education and receives funding from the government as part of its Universal Primary Education (UPE) policy. A "private primary school" is a school that is independently run and does not receive funding from the government's UPE policy. In this way, Uganda's definition aligns with the definition used in a review of research on private schools in low-income countries: private schools are "dependent on user fees to cover all or part of their operational and development costs" and are "managed largely independently of the state and are owned and/or founded independently of the state" (Day et al., 2014: 4). These definitions do not address the issue of "low cost," though, and accordingly include schools at all levels of costs or fees.

A second, related challenge for research on low-cost private primary schools is the issue of ideology. Privatization is a contentious issue, strongly influenced by certain beliefs and principles, such as support for a market-based approach or education as a public good. From a research standpoint, the topic of private primary schools seems particularly difficult to approach neutrally. There is concern that ideology influences how schools are identified and analyzed. Controversial accounts and misinterpretation or misrepresentation of previous research are fairly common (Walford, 2013; Tooley & Longfield, 2015). On one hand, the belief that "'public' was better and more equitable than 'private'" is described as "a hegemonic idea that dominated (and to a large extent still dominates) the major global institutions in the development field and most of the academic work that was commissioned" (Barber, 2015: 7). On the other hand, some argue that the research reviews that support private education selectively filter evidence (Srivastava, 2015; Härmä, 2015).

Definition and ideology both depend upon distinguishing between public and private schools. Definition can be seen as the work to identify what differentiates private schools from public schools, dividing primary schools into two separate and discrete sectors. The ideological debate suggests that there is a choice between these two distinct options and that governments, policymakers, parents, and educators choose between them. Indeed, as research has become increasingly focused on private primary schools, much of this work concerns comparison, implying both difference and choice. Two illustrative titles of research studies are "Are Private Schools Really Performing Better than Government Schools?" (Wadhwa, 2009) and

"How Do Government and Private Schools Differ? Findings from Two Large Indian States" (Goyal & Pandey, 2012).

The issues of difference and choice directly correspond to the themes of access and quality, and, accordingly, my two research questions. I review the literature on these two issues, beginning with access and the question of choice and then continuing with quality and the question of difference.

Factors Associated with Private Primary School Enrollment (Access)

Examining correlates of private school enrollment is a central research topic in the literature on private primary schools, as in many ways the significance and potential of these schools are determined by the type of children they serve. One of the primary critiques of the privatization movement is that it might be aggravating educational and social inequality (Srivastava, 2013). Although there is a growing body of evidence to illustrate that children of poor and sometimes very poor families attend private primary schools (Muralidharan & Kremr, 2007; Tooley et al, 2008), there is also evidence that children from very poor or otherwise disadvantaged families are excluded from these schools (Pal 2010; Singh & Sarkar, 2012). A review of research from 2014 concludes that the evidence is weak and does not support any definitive conclusions as to whether private primary schools are affordable for the poor (Day Ashley, 2014), but there is a growing number of studies that find that the private schools are not reaching the poorest children.

Across many different contexts, a host of different demographic characteristics have been shown to relate to enrollment in private primary schools; generally, results suggest that the most disadvantaged groups have limited access to private primary schools. Several studies in multiple low-income countries find that schools are not equally accessed by boys and girls, as girls are less likely to enroll in private primary schools, both as compared to boys and also compared to the gender differentials in public schools (Härmä, 2011; Aslam, 2009; Nishimura & Yamano, 2013; Datta & Kingdon, 2019). Caste, family size, and religion have also been shown to influence enrollment in private primary schools, but context is always an important factor. For example, Muslim children were shown to be less likely to attend private primary schools in one region in India (Härmä, 2011) and more likely to attend in another (Sarangapani & Winch, 2010). Research in Lagos found that, throughout the state, private primary schools appeared to include an equal number of boys and girls, but in the poorest and most marginalized area, girls comprised only 41.9 percent of private primary school enrollment (Härmä & Adefisayo, 2013). Qualitative data indicated that extreme poverty was related to girls' underrepresentation (Härmä & Adefisayo, 2013). Research in a rural state in Nigeria found that only 13 percent of children in rural areas are enrolled in private primary schools, including only 3.3 percent of children in the poorest 40 percent of the population (Härmä, 2016). Affordability is a key concern. Even if at one point children enroll, research in Ghana found that the financial strain of private education led to later absence and dropout (Akaguri, 2013), and research in Kenya found that the fees of private schools were a heavy burden on poor families (Zuilkowski et al, 2018).

The issue of later absence and dropout suggests that access is not a static concern and change over time is an important dimension of the study of privatization. A related issue, and the focus of my own study, is students' transfer between schools. There are only two existing studies on students' transfer in low-income countries, both from Kenya. The first finds that in informal settlements in Nairobi, children were more like to transfer to schools that had a feeding program, upper grades, and male headmasters; children were less likely to transfer to schools with electricity, piped water, and more teachers (Oketch et al., 2010). These findings seemed to be determined primarily by which schools had vacancies. The second study finds that wealthier and male children were more likely to transfer to private schools (Nishimura & Yamano, 2013).

Differences between Private and Public Schools (Quality)

The hypothesis that private schools offer a higher-quality education than public schools is perhaps the most pressing question in the field, and, accordingly, the largest body of evidence for research on low-cost private primary schools concerns whether children in private schools achieve higher learning outcomes than children in public schools (Day Ashley, 2014). This issue is intimately linked to the previous theme of enrollment, as differences between the sectors are often determined by the sorting of children between schools. A number of studies in South Asia find that children in private schools have higher learning outcomes than children in public schools (Desai et al., 2008; French & Kingdon, 2010; Goyal, 2009; Javaid et al., 2012), though there is significant variation in relation to the scale of difference, which subjects it applies to, and whether it represents standard schooling or the additional tutoring or extra lessons often offered in private schools.

Additionally, some research in India has found that differences between private and public schools are larger in rural rather than urban areas (Singh, 2013; Chugdar & Quin, 2012).

Research in sub-Saharan Africa is more mixed, such as the work of Akaguri (2011) in rural Ghana, which finds that systematic differences in performance between children in public and private schools do not persist after controlling for children's characteristics and previous test scores. While there is moderate evidence that children in private schools have better performance outcomes, most studies are unable to effectively control for selection bias. It is difficult to determine whether better outcomes should be attributed to the services offered by private schools or children's underlying characteristics (Day Ashley, 2014). An informal review of research from 2015 on highlights that the effects of private schools drop sharply when controlling for such selection effects (Akmal, Crawfurd, & Hares, 2020).

Recent studies from East Africa have found outcomes to be higher for children in private primary schools, but still conclude that the chances of the poorest children learning in private schools are still very low (Baum & Riley, 2017; Alcott & Rose, 2016). A study from Kenya used longitudinal data to analyze gains over time and improvement in children's learning, controlling for initial level of achievement. The researchers find that children in low-cost private primary schools did not experience significantly higher growth than their peers in public schools (Zuilkowski, Piper, & Ong-ele, 2020).

Aside from learning outcomes, there are a number of other factors used to compare the quality of education in private as compared to public schools. Teachers' absence is a common indicator. Aside from one study in India which found that teacher attendance and activity were similar between private and government schools (Goyal & Pandey, 2009), most studies find that teachers' absenteeism is worse in public schools than in private schools. Research in India, Pakistan, and Nigeria finds that rates of teacher absence are significantly higher in public rather than private schools (Kingdon & Banerji, 2009; Andrabi et al., 2008; Tooley et al., 2011).

Research has also addressed pupil-teacher ratios, approaches to teaching, general teacher activity, and teachers' background and training. As with all research on the private sector, these findings are significantly constrained by the limits of available data and the likelihood that a significant proportion of schools and typically the unregistered/unaided schools are missing from analysis (Day Ashley, 2014).

A final and critically important point is that the relative quality of education could almost be seen as a distraction, given how low learning levels are for children across all schools (Day Ashley, 2014). If children in primary school are generally unable to read, write, and perform basic calculations, it might not be particularly useful that outcomes are marginally better in some schools, particularly given the methodological concerns about controlling for selection bias.

It is possible that pitting private against public is not the right question. In focusing my research on students' transfer between public and private schools, my work illustrates that there are connections between sectors, not just distinctions. It is also important to note that schools themselves transfer between sectors by changing their status. In Uganda, this transition typically comes in the form of community-run schools being incorporated into the government schools. Between 1997 and 1999, for example, the Ministry of Education was able to establish nearly 2,000 more primary schools mainly by assuming ownership of community schools (Kisira, 2008; MoES, 2001). Though this happens much less frequently now than in the early nineties, schools continue to change in status—in the sample of schools for this study, for example, we dropped and replaced one school that was technically still a community school in the process of becoming a government school.

In the region in which my study takes place, as many as 40 percent of all students are enrolled in private schools (author's calculations, Uwezo, 2011 data). It might not be feasible to choose one sector over the other in Ugandan primary education. In my sample of government schools, single classrooms frequently include more than 100 pupils and there are limited textbooks, desks, and other supplies. Given such resource constraints, these classrooms could never absorb an additional 40 percent of children from the private sector.

Connectivity is perhaps the most fundamental principle of complexity, and approaching the study of privatization from a standpoint of complexity could alter the way in which the issue is understood. Viewing private and public sectors as interdependent schools within the same system could inspire different interventions and approaches. I shall return to this idea and explore what might be the most important question to ask of the issue of privatization, but first I analyze the two defining themes of access and quality as they are present in my sample and data. I investigate what predicts transfer to private primary schools and then what differences exist between the schools in the private and public sectors.

Quantitative Measures of Quality and Access

Details for my analysis and results are provided in the technical appendix, but I provide some key information here. To predict transfer to private school, I use data from the baseline survey, focusing on variables that might influence a child's access to private school. *Urban* is an indicator variable to represent whether or not a child was originally enrolled in a school in the one urban municipality included in the sample (the rest of the children were located in rural sub-counties). *Child assets* refers to an index of three items: whether or not a child was wearing a uniform and the condition of the uniform, whether the child was wearing shoes or was barefoot, and whether the child reported sleeping on a mattress, shared a mattress, or slept on the floor. These three items were considered by the local research team to best reflect the variation in children's economic status. *Mother's* and *father's education* are dichotomous variables to indicate whether or not the child's mother or father completed primary school.

Previous research in Uganda has shown that the ability or willingness to invest in primary education is strongly influenced by children's socioeconomic background (Deininger, 2003; Nishimura et al., 2008). These three basic assets, a uniform, shoes, and a mattress represent a household's investment in an individual child that is easily observed (uniform, shoes) or easily reported by the child (mattress). Although it is not a perfect measure, this index was able to reflect both between school and within school variation and was strongly and significantly correlated to other factors such as parents' education level and urban setting, though not so correlated as to be redundant.

The achievement exam administered at baseline was based on Uganda's national curriculum and included three different sections: basic math, grammar, and reading comprehension. The variables included in the regression are normalized scores of each of these individual sections, as well as a total mean score. The *class 4* variable is an indicator variable for initial enrollment in class 4, to control for the child's grade, as at baseline all children were in either grade 4 or 5. Children were also asked the education level of their mother and father. I have recoded these data into a binary indicator to signal whether the parent had completed primary school. The sample size decreases significantly for these variables, as many children did not know their parents' education level. This issue will be more fully discussed in the results section. *Class size* reports the size of the fifth-grade classroom in the child's original school, measured by enumerators in a classroom survey, and inspired by the findings of Nishimura and Yamano (2013) in Kenya, where children in classes with higher pupil-teacher ratios were more likely to transfer to private schools.

For the second research question, To compare children's experiences in government and private schools, I use quantitative data from the endline. As with the baseline, children were individually interviewed on a range of topics. Many questions focused on children's experience in school, including how often teachers were absent, how many tests they had taken, and whether they eat lunch.

I describe the questions in my analysis in the results section. Together these variables represent something of the quality of education that children receive.

Private School Enrollment: Descriptive Findings

Descriptive findings illustrate a high volume of movement of children across many different schools, both government and private. In two years, 24 percent of children in my sample transferred to a different school. During the follow-up survey, children who had transferred were asked the name of the school they were currently attending. The majority (75.8 percent) of these children were interviewed in their new school compound, which made it easy for enumerators to record the name. Two lead enumerators with years of experience working in these schools later identified which of these schools were private and which were government. When necessary, they consulted other education stakeholders to confirm the sector of particular schools.

In the follow-up survey, 389 children were attending private schools, which indicated that 10 percent of the total follow-up sample and a little less than half of the children who had transferred between schools had transferred to private schools. These children reported that they were attending 204 different schools. Accordingly, the majority of children were the only child in the sample to have transferred to their private school. Seventy-nine schools were mentioned by more than one child, and the majority of these schools were named by only two or three children. The most popular private school in my sample was attended by ten children. In addition to the original 136 government schools, children had also transferred into 97 other government schools. The follow-up survey population was accordingly spread out over 233 government and 204 private primary schools.

Analysis of Transfer

In my analysis I find that neither gender, children's assets, class size, nor presence in an urban municipality appear to predict transfer to private school. In general, the data I have are able to explain little of the variation between children who transferred to private schools and those who remained in government schools. It is possible my data did not focus on the most relevant issues, that they are not an accurate measure, or that there are not many observable differences between these two groups of children. Nonetheless, a child's age, mean test score, and fathers' education level appear to predict private school enrollment. Older children and children with a higher mean test score were less likely to have transferred to a private school. The strongest predictor of transfer to private school was father's education level. A child with a father who had completed primary school was 1.5 to 2 times more likely to transfer to a private school than a child whose father had not completed primary school.

Comparison of Children's Responses in Private and Government Schools

In the endline survey, children were asked a number of different questions about their experience in the school they were attending at that time. I am, accordingly, able to compare responses from the 389 children attending private schools with those from the 3,190 children attending government schools.

School Fees

I begin with school fees. Uganda's UPE policy is a cost-sharing policy in which the government covers certain costs of schooling, but parents and community members are also expected to cover some costs. These costs are routinely negotiated by a school's School Management Committee, administration, and Parent Teacher Association, and are at times a contentious issue. I more fully explore this issue in Chapter 7. For now, I focus just on the comparison between fees in private and government schools.

In the endline survey, children were asked "What kinds of fees or payments does your school have?," "How much do they cost?," and "How much have you paid for them?" This line of questioning recognizes that many schools accept partial payment or payment in installments. Children were able to list up to four different fees, such as a general and inclusive school fee, and/or itemize a lunch fee, examination fee, ream of paper, etc. I added the costs of each fee together by student to create a variable for total fees cost and total fees paid. The question was focused on the concurrent school term, the third trimester of 2011. I report all responses in 2011 Ugandan shillings and USD.[1]

---

[1] During this time, the exchange rate between a dollar and the Ugandan shilling was 2,845 UGX per USD (Oanda currency converter https://www.oanda.com/currency/converter/, accessed February 18, 2021).

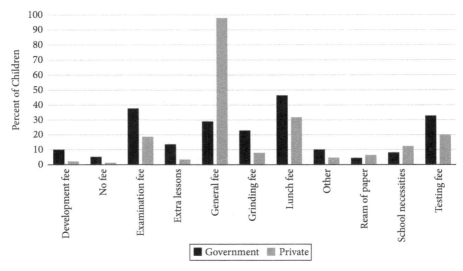

Figure 6.1 Children's reports of fees by school type

Nearly every child enrolled in a private school reported that their school had a general fee (98 percent) (Figure 6.1). In comparison, only 29 percent of children enrolled in government schools reported that their school had a general fee. Given that private schools rely upon school fees in order to operate, it makes sense that the vast majority of them would require a general fee, whereas government schools, which receive basic funding from the government, often only require fees for supplemental services such as a feeding program or practice tests.

The distinction between a general fee and fees for supplemental services is important, as it could relate to children's ability to attend school. In order to put pressure on parents and guardians to pay fees, children are sometimes excluded from the classroom, or "sent to look for fees" as one of the parents I interviewed reported. For supplemental services, children might still be able to attend, but do not participate in that service, such as lunch or taking a practice exam. These practices vary, however. Sometimes children without a uniform, for example, will be excluded from the classroom.

In the endline survey, children were asked "Have you ever been asked to move out of the classroom this year? If so, why?" 62 percent of children reported that they had never been asked. The responses of the other 38 percent of students were coded into different categories. Aside from poor behavior and sickness, all responses related to the payment of fees or supplies. They included "Sent to look for fees," "No materials," and "No uniform." I combine these three responses into a binary variable to indicate whether or not a child had been asked to leave the classroom due to not having made a payment toward fees, materials, or a uniform. A total of 31 percent of children in government schools had been asked to leave the classroom, while 50 percent of children in private schools had been asked to leave the classroom (a statistically significant difference, $t = -7.89$, $p < 0.00$).

On average, children attending private schools reported that their schools had higher fees. Mean values for the total fees charged by the primary school for the most recent trimester were 13,469 UGX (4.73 USD) for children in government schools and 52,524 UGX (18.46 USD) for children in private schools (a statistically significant difference, $t = -21.16$, $p = 0.00$).[2]

Children's reports of the fees they actually paid are lower for both government and private schools. The mean values of total fees paid as reported by children were 5,555 UGX (1.95 USD) for government schools and 23,097 UGX (8.12 USD) for private schools. This difference is also statistically significant, ($t = -12.20$, $p = 0.000$). It is noteworthy that, as a percentage, the fees paid in both government and private schools represent just over 40 percent of the total cost of fees reported by the pupils (41 and 44 percent, respectively).

More children reported paying no fees in government schools than in private schools, 49 percent as compared to 36 percent. In general, children's reports of the fees paid in government schools are highly skewed toward zero, while fees paid in private schools are less skewed. In Figure 6.2 I plot

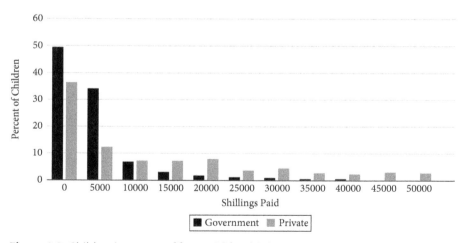

Figure 6.2 Children's reports of fees paid for third term in government and private schools

---

[2] The Ugandan scholastic calendar is divided into three trimesters. The survey was conducted at the beginning of the third trimester.

the percentage of children in government and private schools reporting that they paid a certain amount in fees, from 0 to 50,000 shillings ($17.57). This range represents 98 percent of the children in government schools and 90 percent of the children in private schools. The remaining children reported paying more than 50,000 shillings in fees.

In Table 6.1 I disaggregate the reports of fees paid by whether the child was originally enrolled in an urban or rural school, as this is a key factor in primary education generally, and specifically in relation to privatization. As in many parts of the world, children in urban areas in Uganda consistently outperform children in rural areas; 21 percent more children can read and understand a story and 10 percent more children can do division in urban areas as compared to rural areas (Uwezo, 2016). Private primary schools tend to cluster in urban areas, and there is accordingly far less research on rural private primary schools than on urban ones (Day Ashley, 2014). There is some research in India that finds that the difference between academic performance in private and public schools is greater in rural than in urban areas (Singh, 2013; Chudgar & Quin, 2012).

I do not find that children in the urban municipality of my sample were more likely to transfer into a private school than children in the rural sub-counties. Though I do not have the specific locations of all of the schools that children transferred to, I use the initial enrollment of a child as a rough proxy for their location in either the sample's one urban municipality or in one of the rural sub-counties. I report the mean values and standard deviations of the total fees paid by school status and whether the child was originally located in a school in the urban municipality.

All differences between these mean values are statistically significant except between urban public schools and rural private schools. With mean values of 18,231 and 18,284 Ugandan shillings (6.41 USD and 6.43 USD), children report paying nearly the same amount in urban public schools and rural private schools. An independent samples t test of these two means finds no statistically significant difference between them, $t = -0.02, p = 0.51$.

Table 6.1 Mean fees paid by school type and location

School type	Number of children	Mean fees paid	Standard deviation
Urban government	346	18,231 UGX ($6.41)	35,167 UGX ($12.36)
Urban private	34	73,349 UGX ($25.78)	125,714 UGX ($44.19)
Rural government	2,844	4,013 UGX ($1.41)	19,830 UGX ($6.97)
Rural private	355	18,284 UGX ($6.43)	31,153 UGX ($10.95)

Lunch

The most common fee required by government schools was a lunch fee. It was also the second most common fee reported for private schools. Sometimes schools accept in-kind payments, such as kilograms of maize, and then charge a grinding fee or a fee to pay someone to prepare the food (typically a maize meal porridge). School lunch was a particularly contentious issue in Uganda, as the country's president had repeatedly stated that it is not the government's responsibility to feed children, and, accordingly, children should bring food from home. Many schools, however, believe feeding programs are the most efficient and practical solution and still run them.

Across all schools, 8 percent of children reported that they never ate lunch. Twelve percent of children ate between one and four meals at school a week, and 80 percent ate lunch every day. In private and government schools, of the five days of the school week, children ate on average 4.3 and 4.4 meals, respectively (not a statistically significant difference, $t = -0.22$, $p = 0.59$).

Tests

Charges for tests or examinations are another common school fee. Given the resource-poor environment of both government and private schools, schools often charge fees in order for children to take tests. The funds are typically used for photocopying the test. Some schools simply require a ream of paper. Schools do sometimes charge fees in order to run national standardized exams, but private schools typically are not included in official examinations or have their students sit for exams at nearby government schools, so for a better comparison I focus on tests or "practice exams."

Children were asked, "How many times have you taken a practice test that was marked by your teacher in the first two terms of this year?" The mean number of tests taken for children in government schools was 3.9, and for children in private schools, 5.2, which suggests that, for these two trimesters, children in private schools took one more test than children in government schools on average. This difference is statistically significant, $t = -6.7$, $p = 0.000$.

Of the children enrolled in private schools, 6 percent reported that they had not taken a test in the past two trimesters. Of the children enrolled in government schools, 14 percent reported that they had not taken a test in the past two trimesters (not a statistically significant difference). It is important to note that this question conflates a few different issues: how often a school

Table 6.2 Number of tests taken in first two terms of the year

School type	Number of children	Mean	Standard deviation
Urban government	341	6.1	4.8
Urban private	31	6.3	4.6
Rural government	2,830	3.6	3.3
Rural private	349	5.2	4.4

offers exams, children's payment of fees, and children's attendance. A school could offer many exams, but children could be absent so frequently as to not take the exams or might not have paid the fee. Alternatively, another school might simply not offer many tests.

I again disaggregate responses by children's original location, either urban or rural. Children originally located in the urban municipality and enrolled in a government school at the second time point reported taking 6 tests on average. Children originally located in a rural sub-county and enrolled in a private school at the second time point reported taking 5 tests on average. This difference is statistically significant, ($t = -2.8$, $p = 0.002$). Children originally located in the urban municipality and enrolled in a government school at the second time point reported taking 6 tests on average. Children originally located in a rural sub-county and enrolled in a public school took 3.7 tests on average. I summarize these responses in Table 6.2.

Teacher Absenteeism

Children were asked two questions about their teacher's attendance. "Of the five days of last week, how many was your class teacher absent?" and "Of a normal week last term, how many days was your class teacher usually absent?" Responses were fairly similar across the two questions, but with higher rates of absence for the first question. This might be due to the fact that the survey was conducted in the third trimester of the year, when there are end of the year exams and other events that might lead to higher rates of absence, or issues with respondents' recall and memory.

Children attending private schools reported slightly lower rates of teacher absence than children attending government schools. Referencing the last week, children in private schools reported that their teacher was absent 1.4 days on average; in comparison, children in government schools reported that their teacher was absent 1.7 days on average. This difference is statistically significant, ($t = 3.57$, $p = 0.00$).

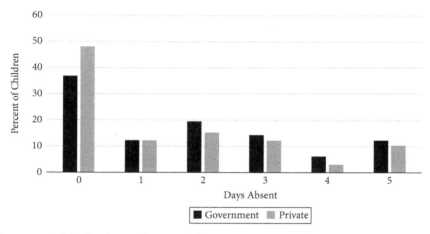

Figure 6.3 Of the five days of last week, how many was your class teacher absent?

The differences between reports from children in private and government schools are driven by the percentage of children who reported that their class teacher was never absent. Referencing the previous week, 48 percent of children in private schools reported that their teacher was never absent as compared to 37 percent in government schools. Similarly, in reference to the previous term, 68 percent of children in private schools reported that their class teacher was never absent, as compared to 59 percent in government schools. For one or more days of absence, rates are pretty evenly distributed, though, as illustrated in Figure 6.3. Teacher absence is clearly an issue in both government and private schools. In both schools, at least 10 percent of pupils reported that their teacher was absent for every day of the previous week.

Test Scores

As previously mentioned, as part of the original RCT, children in the study were given an exam based upon the national curriculum. It included three sections: basic math, grammar, and reading comprehension. Children who were originally enrolled in fourth grade were given an exam tailored to a fourth-grade level at both baseline and endline and children in fifth grade were given an exam tailored to the fifth-grade level at both baseline and endline. I compare test scores by section and as a mean normalized score across all sections. In Table 6.3 I report the endline mean normalized test score by school type and original location.

Differences between urban and rural schools are statistically significant, both within and across sectors. For example, the difference between the test

Table 6.3 Mean normalized test score by school type and location

School type	Number of children	Mean test score	Standard deviation
Urban government	338	1.22	0.83
Urban private	30	1.17	0.78
Rural government	2,812	−0.068	0.92
Rural private	340	−0.012	0.91

scores of children in the urban municipality in government schools and the test scores of children in the rural sub-countries in private schools is statistically significant, ($t = 18.38$, $p = 0.00$). Differences between the test scores of children across private and government schools *within* either urban or rural contexts are not statistically significant.

In a standard linear regression, the strongest predictor of endline test scores was a child's baseline test score, followed by location in an urban municipality. For example, children who were originally located in the urban municipality score almost half a standard deviation higher on the grammar section than those located in the rural sub-counties. Across all sections and as a mean score, enrollment in a private school had a statistically significant and positive association with test scores. (These results are included in the Technical Appendix.)

Qualitative Results

In the endline survey, children who had transferred between schools were asked why they had transferred. If a child had transferred more than once, he or she was able to report a reason for each transfer. The coded responses are reported in Figure 6.4. Children reported multiple reasons for transfer, and also simply that it was their parents' decision. As this survey instrument was designed for quantitative data collection, these responses offer only surface-level insight into the underlying meaning and significance of transfer to private schools. Additionally, it also suggests the limitations of children's perspectives, as one in four children simply reported that it was their parents' decision, which motivates work to understand parents' perspectives.

I use my qualitative data to more deeply investigate parent's perspectives. My goal was not to specifically explain the behavior of the exact individuals in my quantitative sample, but to develop theory that might lead to better understanding of attitudes, perspectives, and behavior more generally. Semi-structured interviews and focus group discussions provided the space and time for respondents to think deeply about the questions, use

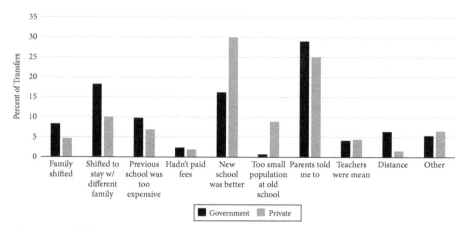

Figure 6.4 Children's responses to the question "Why did you transfer?"

their own terms, and explicate their perspectives and decision-making (Rubin & Rubin, 2005).

Though there are innumerable factors which influence the lives of parents, their children, and, accordingly, their approach to schooling, three important and unifying trends were revealed in the qualitative data: for these families, considering multiple schools is the norm; choosing a school is a dynamic process that continues throughout a child's time in primary school; and schooling choices are contextualized within extended family networks. I analyze each of these in detail below.

Every parent mentioned multiple schools when asked about the primary education of their children, and the selection of schools was described as an active process. Any individual child was not expected to attend a particular school, and certain communities or families did not default to a nearby or otherwise accessible school. Many parents described that their children were attending different schools. One mother of seven explained, "Three go to K—-, one goes to E—-, some others stay in another sub-county and they stay with a relative." Similarly, a father of three reported that each of his children attended a different school so that he could "see the difference between them." Both of these families had children attending both public and private schools.

Even parents who appeared uninvolved or disconnected from their children's education, answering "Don't know" to many questions and appearing uninterested in the subject, knew of and considered many schools. One mother stated, "There are schools that are nearby," but because of her "financial situation" she "chose the one that was far away," as it was the least expensive. This region of Uganda is densely populated and there are many schools. In a focus group discussion with primary school children, discussants easily listed eight nearby schools. School choice is not simply private or public, but includes many schools, and parents consider multiple and varied criteria.

Second, school choice was not a single decision for these families; almost all described continuously addressing the issue throughout their children's primary school careers. One reason is that children's experience is an important criterion by which to assess a school, and it can only be assessed by trying various schools. Another reason is that as family situations change or younger children enter school, family finances become constrained or available. These factors influence school choice for both younger and older children. A 9-year-old boy explained (through a translator) that, in his old school, "They used to punish them a lot, so [his parents] transferred him to another school, they didn't have money and he was taken to []." A mother stated, "Since the school was not getting any better, [she and his father] transferred him."

And finally, children's schooling is a decision to be made not simply on behalf of an individual child but as part of an extended family network. Particularly in relation to finances, parents have to consider all of their children when making school choices. They also take into account different relatives who might be able to assist with childcare or school expenses. Children often stay with different family members, as was explained by the mother who did not know the specific schools of all her children as "some others stay in another sub-county and they stay with a relative."

One father explained the benefits of having children attend different schools as, "if a child is attending one school and they send them home for fees, it [being sent home for fees] can't happen on the same day, so they [teachers or school administrators] will send the other one and then this one shall be in school so you don't have all of them sitting at home because of fees." This idea was echoed by a mother's statement, "It's not good to pile all the children in one school."

These findings relate to the quantitative data in two important ways. First, in the quantitative data, the high volume of student transfer between schools illustrates that the private and public primary education sectors in Uganda are not two distinct, separate spheres of education, but very interconnected, especially in relation to the populations of students who attend them. Similarly, the qualitative data reveal that many parents engage with both the private and public education sectors, considering a number of schools in relation to many different factors, not just whether they are private or public. Relatedly, the qualitative data show that change over time is a relevant concern in understanding parents' decision-making and their children's educational experience. It is important to consider the dynamism of enrollment in primary education.

Differences between Private and Government Schools

As illustrated by the quantitative data, in both government and private primary schools there are many costs associated with attending school. To encourage families to pay, teachers in both types of schools often send children home who have not paid their fees or do not have supplies. Private school proprietors also mentioned this issue, relating it to the students who transfer and describing them by saying "Some of them they are fee defaulters; they can't meet the minimum requirements of the school." And as a private school, "Actually that's the biggest problem."

Financial concerns were a key driver of school choice for many families. It was universally recognized that private schools cost more than government schools. During the time period of the study, Uganda had an average fertility rate of 6.1 (World Bank, 2011), Ugandan families often have to consider many children when making educational decisions. In light of the vast number of schools, large families, and multiple issues to be considered for each child, school choice is a dynamic, complex process.

Parents generally believed that children attending private schools had better outcomes than children in public schools. They mentioned a number of different indicators: that children in private schools have better English and standardized exam scores, better uniforms and appearance, and that children are allowed to repeat in private schools. In one of the focus group discussions a man said, "A child in P3 will speak better English than that the one in P7 if in a private school."

Exceptions were noted, though. For example, one father explained that "People are gifted differently" in relation to one particularly popular and charismatic headmaster who he believed was gifted with leadership skills. This headmaster's leadership was positive enough to make his public school better than the area private schools. The father noted, "People are now transferring to that school because of that individual, so it depends on the individuals there."

For parents, the defining difference between government and private schools was teaching. In private schools, one parent explained, "Teachers, they teach while paying attention to the children, whereas this government, they just teach anyhow." Some parents saw teachers as the key issue with government schools, such as the father who suggested, "The government should get rid of all the teachers because they are not serious." All other parents who discussed this issue identified the low salary of government teachers as the main concern.

Though one parent expressed uncertainty, saying, "We don't understand whether it's true up there, teachers are not being paid, we're just confused," the vast majority of parents and community members recognized that government teachers face serious challenges, described as "Government is failing to deliver on the side of teachers' payments and salaries. They are either delayed or they don't come on time so somehow they lose their morale and motivation to continue with their work." Another parent explained:

> It's because they are determined, you know in private schools the payment, they pay in time, they don't delay to pay and the government, it can even take two years, one year and people's teachers will strike, children are there they are not studying. But in private school I've never seen a school where they strike because they pay teachers and teachers are encouraged.

During the time of this study, there were multiple nationwide teachers' strikes in Uganda organized by the teachers' union to put pressure on the government to fulfill a promise to increase teachers' salaries. In addition, salary payments are often delayed, as is generally the case with lots of education funding, not just teachers' salaries. At this time, teachers earned 260,000 shillings per month (about 100 USD), which made them among the lowest paid of all civil servants, and payments were frequently delayed as much as six months (Bekunda & Walubiri, 2011, Biryabarema, 2013). When I interviewed the head School Inspector, he explained, "We have had a problem of delayed salaries for the teachers." Our interview was in July; he noted, "We have teachers who have not received their April salary. The fact is that the money is little, and if it doesn't come, how will the teachers survive?" He also recognized that "The privately owned schools, of course, they both have advantages and disadvantages. The advantage of the privately owned schools is that the parents pay the money; the money is readily there in the schools."

While many parents stated, "The government should come in and adjust the salaries of the teachers to give them something deserving," a few felt that the more direct connection between payment and services in private schools was preferable, as in, "In the private school a teacher will teach, knowing they are getting the money from the parents and eating that. However, in the public schools, a teacher is teaching like my money shall come either way; whether I teach or not my money will come."

Private and Public: Distinction or Interdependence?

My quantitative analysis focused on answering two questions, "What of a child's socioeconomic status or educational experience predicts transfer to private school?" and "Do children's test scores and educational experiences vary by whether they are enrolled in a private or government school?" These questions reflect the themes of access and quality, respectively, investigating the premise that privatization might improve educational quality but makes access to education more inequitable.

First, I address the issue of access, which I approximate by studying transfer to private primary schools. The most straightforward assumption would be that children from households of higher socioeconomic status would be more likely to transfer to a private primary school. In my sample, this would best be approximated by the variables *assets* and *urban*, which were not associated with transfer to private school, and also *father's education*, which was associated with transfer. Several factors that in other research were found to be associated with enrollment in private primary school were not associated with transfer in my data (gender, child's assets, urban). The three strongest predictors of transfer to private primary schools were lower mean test score, younger child age, and father's completion of primary school. Each of these variables could reflect socioeconomic status in various ways.

One possible interpretation is that a child's age and fathers' education level are indicators of parent engagement. My finding on age—that older children are less likely to transfer—could relate to children's age of entry into primary school, echoing my findings from Chapter 4, which also highlight the importance of age of entry into schooling. Fifty percent of Ugandan children start primary school late. It is possible that parents who are more affluent or more engaged and focused on education are more likely to enroll their child on time. Older children, and especially very overage children, might have less engaged parents. Less engaged parents might be less likely to transfer their child to private school.

Similarly, parents who themselves have had little experience with education might be less engaged in their children's education. Fathers who have finished primary school might be more likely to seek out options for their children or to generally perceive more choice in various aspects of life. Fathers' education might also relate to children's age of entry. Indeed, I find that both mothers' and fathers' completion of primary school are negatively correlated with children's age; the child of a mother who completed primary school is 0.38 years younger than a child of a mother who did not; the child of a father who completed primary school is 0.22 years younger than a child of a father who did not (both of these differences are statistically significant, $t = 6.92$, $p = 0.00$, $t = 3.35$ $p = 0.00$). Parents with more education appear more likely to enroll their children in school on time.

To summarize, my results do not indicate that there are clear, dramatic differences between the children who transferred to private schools and the children who stayed in government schools, but some distinctions reveal an important source of inequality: parents. More engaged, more experienced parents might be better able to support their children's education. This might be critical for the children who are struggling, as children with lower test scores were more likely to transfer than children with higher test scores. Perhaps more engaged parents are more aware of their children's struggles or poor performance and more likely to seek out alternatives.

To turn to quality, comparing the experiences of children in private schools with the experiences of children in government schools reveals a number of differences. According to children's reports, private schools charged higher fees. Children in private schools, on average, paid 290 percent more in school fees than children in government schools. Fifty percent of children in private schools had been asked to leave the classroom for not having paid fees or purchased basic scholastic materials, compared with 31 percent of children in public schools. Children in private schools took more tests and reported that their teachers were absent less frequently than children in government schools.

However, both government and private schools face similar issues; the differences between them are a question of degree. Both government and private schools charge fees and send children home who have not paid. Both government and private schools run school feeding programs, and children eat lunch, on average, four times a week. Both private and government schools have teachers who are frequently absent. Across almost all of these indicators, children report that private schools have slightly better performance, but the differences between the two school types are marginal.

Many of these differences were eclipsed by the comparison between urban and rural locations. Uganda is still primarily rural, with 85 percent of the population living in rural areas. In the original sample, sixteen of the 136 schools were located in the district town center, known as an urban municipality with a population of about 70,000 (Uganda Bureau of Statistics, 2016). When I disaggregate children by their original location, the urban-rural comparison is far greater than the private-government comparison. This is especially true for children's test scores. Children originally located in urban areas, whether they were in private or public schools, scored a full standard deviation higher than children in rural areas. Similarly, in the regression predicting test scores, the coefficient on the urban indicator was two to three times larger than the coefficient on enrollment in a private school.

It is notable, though, that enrollment in a private school was associated with higher endline test scores, even after controlling for children's previous test scores and basic demographics. This is especially interesting, given that low test scores were a predictor of transfer to private schools and that the period of enrollment in private school is unknown. Children could have transferred the day of the endline survey or have been enrolled in a private school for the full two years.

One possible explanation is that children in private school might receive more individualized attention. In the baseline sample, the average class size was eighty students and extremely heterogeneous. Anecdotal reports suggest that private schools have smaller class sizes, possibly enabling struggling students to be more directly engaged. This theory resonates with the qualitative data from parents and their focus on teachers. Parents believe the distinguishing factor between government and private schools is the attention and "determination" of teachers in private schools. However, with few extant data on private schools in Uganda, it is not possible to know whether class sizes are smaller or anything about the interaction between children and teachers.

Another possibility is that transfer to private school signals something about a child and her household. As illustrated by the association between fathers' education, a child's age, and transfer to private school, transfer is not random. It might be the case that the children who transfer would have had higher test scores even if they had not transferred due to the underlying differences between them and the children who did not transfer. I am limited in my analysis to the observable characteristics measured in the baseline data. Although on the basis of these, children who transferred did not appear to be categorically different from those who did not (aside from younger age, fathers' education, and lower test scores). Of course, this does not rule out further differences that were not observed.

Just as there did not seem to be large dramatic differences between the children who transferred to private schools and those who stayed in government schools, parents did not see private and public schools as two dramatically different options. Though they noted differences between the sectors, they also noted exceptions to those characterizations, for example, the mother who stated, "There are schools, yes, private schools that do teach well. Then there are those that, however much they are private schools, they also don't teach well." It seemed as though many parents were a little at a loss as to how to navigate their different options, given the limits of their resources and their information. Parents focused on issues such as cost and distance that affect all schools. For many families, it appeared to be the norm to have children enrolled in multiple schools, across both sectors.

My results, accordingly, offer some evidence to suggest that equity is a concern with the private primary education sector in Uganda in relation to both access and quality: Children with parents of a higher education level are more likely to transfer to private schools, which are generally more expensive than public schools. Similarly, I also find evidence that private schools outperform public schools on a number of different indicators, such as teacher attendance and test frequency. These results support the hypothesis that the private sector is defined by unequal access, offering a higher-quality education only to more advantaged children.

At the same time, my results also seem to suggest that this does not have to be the case. In the same way that parents do not categorically differentiate between private and public schools, it might be more constructive to view Ugandan private and public primary schools together, as one complex adaptive system rather than as separate, parallel systems. In this area of Uganda, private schools comprise as much as 40 percent of total primary school enrollment (Uwezo, 2011). It is simply not possible to consider primary education without the private sector, especially given the standard overcrowding of schools.

Additionally, with schools changing status, as in community schools becoming government-supported and children transferring between sectors, interconnectivity and dynamism might better characterize the issue than separateness and difference. Especially in relation to transfer, the public and private sectors are informed by each other; they are defined by interdependence. My analysis suggests that the most defining difference in educational indicators is between urban and rural, not private and public. Rather than simplify the issue of privatization to a dichotomy and an either/or choice, the question is how to consider them together, how might private and public schools complement each other.

Can the Private and Public Sectors Work Together to Improve both Access and Quality?

Just as Ugandan parents consider both private and government schools, policymakers and practitioners must also recognize that Ugandan primary education is defined by both types of schools, as well as the interaction between the two. The challenge is to determine how the two sectors can coexist in a way that improves both access and quality overall.

One possibility is present in the association between low test scores and transfer to the private sector. The private sector and school choice could offer an opportunity for remedial education. Research suggests that, especially for children who are struggling with basic literacy and numeracy, it is important to teach to their ability level rather than their age or grade (Banerjee et al., 2016). With multiple schooling options, it might be possible to group children by ability level, providing an alternative for children who cannot cope with large classes or are otherwise struggling with the content. Grouping by ability and providing targeted instruction (JPAL, 2018) are a clear example of an intervention in which access and quality are both addressed and positive change in the two dimensions is mutually reinforcing. This idea also offers the opportunity to build on a dynamic that already exists.

As with grade repetition, where age of entry was identified as a key predictor of children's later educational experience, age is also a relevant issue for the private sector. Older children are less likely to transfer to private schools. It is possible that less engaged parents might be more likely to enroll their children in school late, which means that that older children have less engaged parents, receive less support, and encouragement, and, as my data found, have lower test scores, are more likely to drop out, and are less likely to transfer to the private sector. As the qualitative data on grade repetition found, where teachers said, "Better let children who are aging go to the next class," parents and teachers of overage children might simply want to push them through the education system rather than focus on learning outcomes and transfer to private school.

This research suggests that it is critical for children to enroll in school on time. Public awareness, media, and other campaigns could be used as interventions to increase age-appropriate entry into school and take-up of early childhood education. Reaching out to parents and communities could also address the current imbalance whereby children with more educated fathers are more likely to transfer to private schools than their peers. Ideally, only those children who most need additional support would transfer, and school choice will be determined by children's pedagogical needs rather than by the interest level of the parents. Effectively engaging parents will be vital.

A key challenge in addressing equity will be addressing the issue of costs. School fees were a primary factor in determining parents' choice of school for their children. Just as it will be difficult to ensure that enrollment in school is determined by a child's best interest rather than the parents' level of engagement, it will also be difficult to define school choice by the educational needs of a child as opposed to a parent's ability to pay. An important starting point, though, is that all schools collect fees. The current difference between private and public schools is, accordingly, one only of degree.

Improving the payment systems for public school teachers will be a critical intervention. As was identified by parents in the qualitative data, the late and low pay of teachers in public schools is a primary source of dysfunction in the public sector and a key distinguishing feature between the public and private sectors. Improving it is likely to improve the quality of the public schools and lessen the difference between private and public, potentially improving both access and quality.

Viewing private schools within the same system as public schools might also help improve overall quality and reduce existing inequality. Inequity between the private and public sectors is a concern, but also within the private sector. Currently, the Ugandan Ministry of Education has a very hands-off role with the private sector. Without proper regulation, the quality of private schools varies dramatically. Improving registration and regulation of the private sector and encouraging the establishment of standards across all schools could help with both equity and quality concerns. Viewing all schools as one system could consider developing quality improvement initiatives that include both sectors. And with ability grouping, teaching to the right level, improved age of entry into schooling, and better teacher payment systems, the interaction and exchange between private and public schools could be used to create dynamics where access and quality are mutually reinforcing, rather than competing.

My results offer two primary conclusions: First, there is significant overlap, similarity, and exchange between private and government primary schools. Second, transfer from government to private primary schools is best predicted by a child's young age, the father having completed primary school, and low test scores. I used these two conclusions to argue that private and government primary schools in Uganda should be considered together as part of one complex adaptive system and that existing trends can be addressed or capitalized on in such a way as to improve access and quality overall. A key challenge to address, however, is the issue of costs. School fees are one of the most important issues in Ugandan primary education, and the focus of Chapter 7.

7
Understanding School Fees in Relation to both Access and Quality

Uganda first implemented its Universal Primary Education (UPE) policy in 1997, which made it the third country in sub-Saharan Africa to abolish school fees (Malawi and Ethiopia both initiated national school fee abolition policies in 1994). Uganda's policy eliminated tuition payments for up to four children per family and stipulated that two of those children had to be girls. The government committed to pay 5,000–8,100 Ugandan shillings per child, per year (approximately 4–7 USD), as well as to provide basic inputs such as teachers, textbooks, and materials for school construction (MoES, 1998).

Between 1996 and 1997, an additional 2.3 million children enrolled in school, representing an approximately 67 percent increase in Uganda's total primary school enrollment (illustrated in Figure 7.1). The policy was later extended to include all primary school-aged children, regardless of family size.

In the wake of this dramatic increase in enrollment, pupil-teacher ratios, pupil-classroom ratios, pupil-textbook ratios, and other similar indicators all significantly increased. Throughout the literature, these changes have been described as a decrease in the quality of Ugandan primary education; for example, "The introduction of UPE in 1997 was associated with a sudden drop in education quality indicators" (Bategeka & Okurut, 2006: 3).

Uganda is not alone in this experience of abolishing fees, or in its prevailing interpretation as a quantity-quality trade-off. Between 1990 and 2007, sixteen different countries in sub-Saharan Africa used national education policy to formally abolish school fees (Harding & Stasavage, 2014). A review of school fee abolition in Kenya, Lesotho, Malawi, and Uganda concluded, "In all four countries the sudden large influx of pupils led to 'access shock': overcrowded classrooms...acute shortages of teachers, textbooks, and materials." This report accordingly identified "quality issues" as the first of the "unintended and unforeseen negative consequences" of fee abolition (Avenstrup, 2004: 15) A review of school fee abolition in Ethiopia, Ghana, Kenya, Malawi, and Mozambique concluded: "The single most frequently

Access, Quality, and the Global Learning Crisis: Insights from Ugandan Primary Education. Sarah Kabay, Oxford University Press.
© Sarah Kabay 2021. DOI: 10.1093/oso/9780192896865.003.0007

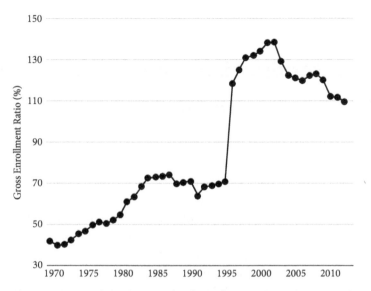

Figure 7.1 Ugandan primary school enrollment 1970–2013

expressed concern in the case studies is the need to avoid quality deterioration caused by the elimination of fee income at the school level" (World Bank, 2009: 25).

Nothing so clearly demonstrates the access vs. quality paradigm as the issue of school fees and, in particular, national school fee abolition policy. Fees are seen as restricting access. It is argued, that "The indirect and direct cost of education to families is the single most important factor excluding children from school. And the single most important policy measure to address this is to abolish school fees" (Institute for Domestic and International Affairs, 2006: 8). Dramatic increases in enrollment in the wake of school fee abolition have been interpreted as confirmation that school fees are among the primary barriers to access to education (Bategeka & Okurut, 2006, Bertoncino, Murphy & Wang, 2002).

On the other hand, school fees can also be viewed as a necessary supplement to limited government funding, or as a way to encourage parents' participation and sense of ownership over primary education (İşcan, Rosenblum, and Tinker, 2015)—all of which are seen as being a way to preserve the quality of education and standards. Engaging parents is an important concern, as research has shown that fee abolition policies can lead more affluent students to exit the public school system and enroll in private schools (Bold et al., 2010; Deininger, 2003). In sum, school fees are believed to constrain access but support quality, and the removal of fees is believed to increase access but decrease quality.

As described in Chapter 6, the issue of school fees should not be viewed as a discrete, dichotomous choice between whether or not to have fees. As Uganda's UPE policy is a cost-sharing policy, there are still many costs associated with attending school. Fees relate to multiple items (uniform, pen, paper), services (practice exams, extra lessons, feeding programs), and forms of payment (cash, kilograms of maize).

In 1913, Uganda's Board of Education stated, "Schools have to be built with money from school fees or from gifts from chiefs . . . funds will not be drawn upon for the purpose of building schools and running them" (Ssekamwa, 1997: 44). Teachers, however, were provided by the Board. In 2015, on the campaign trail, Uganda's President Yoweri Museveni explained: "When we started [Universal Primary Education], we wanted to share jobs where your parents would provide uniforms, exercise books, packed lunch, so that the government would pay teachers, build teachers' houses and school facilities." Museveni then proposed a new arrangement: "In order to support our children, we are going to buy them exercise books, text books, mathematical sets, pens and pencils. The parents will remain with the job of buying uniforms and providing lunch" (New Vision, 2015).

As these quotations illustrate, Ugandans have been discussing school fees and other education payments for more than one hundred years. The debate concerns not whether or not to have school fees, but specific expenses such as tuition, school lunches, or uniforms, as well as whose responsibility it is to provide them. Given the distance between policy and practice, there is also a significant difference between intent and the reality on the ground. In response to Museveni's aforementioned 2015 campaign promise, for example, a recent newspaper article ran with the headline "Pupils Wait for Museveni's Books, Pens Two Years Later" (Mufumba, 2018). At the same time, the Minister of Education criticized parents for "abandoning their responsibilities and putting every burden on the government and Museveni," as one journalist summarized (Rumanzi, 2016: para 4).

It is clear that school fees are an enduring issue of importance for Ugandan primary education, but what conclusions does the research literature offer to inform the debate? Is it simply that fees will reduce access, but improve quality? If we were to move beyond the assumptions of the access vs. quality paradigm, how might school fees be viewed?

As an alternative to the linear cause-and-effect framework of the access vs. quality paradigm, I interpret the issue of school fees using complexity theory.

First, school fees must be analyzed not just in relation to access, but also quality. Education systems are defined by connectivity and interdependence. An issue such as school fees can be expected to affect access to education, the quality of education, and potentially the interaction between the two. Second, the association between fees and either access or quality might not be a consistent, linear, or direct association. School fees might have varying effects for different individuals or under different conditions. While the literature on school fees presents the issue as a zero-sum trade-off, it is possible that school fees could represent a different association between access and quality, as I have found in my research on grade repetition and private schools.

The principles of complexity theory inspire questions such as whether school fees are *always* a constraint upon access and whether school fees could be used to improve the quality of education without threatening access to education. To date, no research has experimented with user fees within a public education system, either to increase or otherwise support them. The politically charged and legal nature of school fees often obviates this direction for research, making it difficult to determine the effects of certain initial conditions or differences in the implementation of fees.

The experimental evaluation of a primary school savings program in Uganda offers a unique opportunity to consider user fees in a new light. Between 2009 and 2011, the research organization Innovations for Poverty Action partnered with Ugandan organizations the Private Education Development Network and FINCA, Uganda in order to implement and evaluate a primary school savings program. The program created school savings accounts for children in the P5, P6, and P7 classes, and provided training and encouragement to both children and their families to save money for and invest in education. In this way, the program first acknowledged the existence of fees and other educational expenses, and then encouraged and supported families in their efforts to pay them. Children and schools did not receive any grants or any financial support. The program simply provided the infrastructure and training to enable children to save at school and encouragement to use those savings to contribute to fees and educational expenses. As the Project Associate for this initiative, I supported Principal Investigators Dean Karlan and Leigh Linden in all aspects of the project.

A research design that compared different treatment variations enabled Karlan and Linden (2017) to explore which version of the program might be most effective. The basic elements of the program were the same across all treatments: Bank accounts were opened for each school, and children were able to individually deposit money at their school. In the "cash" treatment schools, at the beginning of every trimester, children were given back in cash the exact amount they had saved during the previous trimester. In the

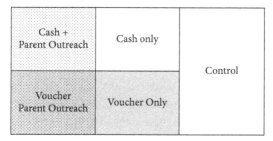

Figure 7.2 Research design

"voucher" treatment schools, children were given back the exact amount they had saved during the previous trimester in the form of a voucher, which they could use to make any education-related purchase—uniforms, school meals, etc. In a cross-cutting design, half of the treatment schools also received a parent outreach program, aiming to raise awareness of roles and responsibilities under UPE policy. This resulted in four different treatment variations: cash, cash+parent, voucher, and voucher+parent, in addition to a control group that received no intervention (Figure 7.2).

The study's authors found that only the combination of the cash savings and parent outreach interventions had significant impacts on targeted outcomes—specifically, increases in the number of children in the classroom with basic scholastic materials and improved test scores (0.11 standard deviation increase; Karlan & Linden, 2017). They hypothesized that the savings program enabled children and families to purchase basic scholastic materials, which led to the improvement in test scores.

The results of this study demonstrate that encouraging the use of fees to improve the quality of primary education does not necessarily have to negatively impact access. It is possible that improving school fee payment systems could be a potential strategy to improve the quality of primary education in low-resourced settings such as Uganda. Using savings or other financial tools to make the costs associated with attending school more affordable could be an avenue for future research and intervention. Additionally, in relation to the parent outreach program, improving the communication of fee policies and the division of roles and responsibilities between parents, schools, and the government could be another direction for future work and a way in which to improve both access and quality.

One concern, though, is that this impact evaluation did not investigate whether the savings program and its emphasis on fees in some way disadvantaged poorer children, or whether the benefits of the program were only experienced by more well off-children. This issue is important, given that "The principal argument against primary school fees is that they amount to regressive taxation, and that they have a disproportionately larger negative impact on the educational attainment of children from poor families" (İşcan, Rosenblum, and Tinker, 2015: 562). Research in Uganda has shown that, following the 1997 abolishment of tuition payments, increases in enrollment were experienced primarily by children from poor and rural families (Deininger, 2003; Nishimura et al., 2008; Lincove, 2012). The positive average treatment effect of the cash+parent intervention might have been driven by heterogeneous impacts or there might have been negative impacts on other outcomes.

This presents an opportunity for secondary analysis and to investigate possible moderation and mediation. Exploring moderation will determine whether the positive impacts of the program were universally experienced by all children or whether the improvements in test scores were driven by a subgroup of children. Exploring the mechanisms of impact and possible mediation pathways will also shed light on how user fees might lead to changes in educational outcomes, and for which children. Investigating a different outcome, dropout, will explore the possible tension between access and quality, that is, whether efforts to use fees to improve quality might have unintended consequences for access.

This chapter, accordingly, focuses on three research questions for empirical analysis: First, was the school savings program's positive impact on test scores moderated by children's socioeconomic status? That is, did poorer and more affluent children experience the benefits of the program equally? Second, was the proposed mediation pathway (that improvements in test scores were a result of the increase in scholastic materials) experienced in the same way by childred of different socioeconomic status? And third, did the program's objective to improve educational quality come at the expense of educational access? Specifically, did any of the treatment variations impact school dropout and would this impact have been moderated by children's socio-conomic status? The work to answer these questions will help explore both the potential and the drawbacks of emphasizing user fees in primary education.

Existing Literature on User Fees

In education systems around the world, there are many different costs associated with attending publicly provided primary school. Opportunity costs, such as the cost of a child's not working, are often a significant obstacle and should not be overlooked. In this chapter, though, I focus on "user fees," a term I will use to cover any direct payments made by a private household in order for an individual from that household to attend a particular school

(Kattan & Burnett, 2004). These fees can include anything from tuition fees to uniforms to PTA dues (Kattan & Burnett, 2004).

Research on user fees in primary education can be categorized by two different approaches: analysis of national school fee policies and randomized evaluations to experiment with the provision of educational resources at a more local level. Generally, the former literature tends to focus on tuition payments, covering teachers' salaries and school buildings, while the latter tends to address inputs such as uniforms, textbooks, and other supplies.

In one respect, these two research approaches have come to a single con-clusion: Costs decrease access to and the use of products and services. Reviewing the randomized evaluation literature, Kremer and Holla (2009: 4) draw from interventions in both health and education to conclude that "Imposing even small costs consistently leads to dramatic reductions in take-up." Whether it is for mosquito nets or school uniforms, "a range of studies on price and take-up of health and education services…find remark-ably similar results in very different contexts" (Kremer & Holla, 2009: 4).

Conversely, analysis of school fee abolition policies finds that, across multiple African countries, implementing a national school fee abolition policy tends to increase primary school enrollment (İşcan, Rosenblum, and Tinker, 2015; Kattan & Burnett, 2004; World Bank, 2009). One study estimates that in the year following fee abolition, primary school enrollment increased by 12 percent in Mozambique, 14 percent in Ghana, 18 percent in Kenya, 23 percent in Ethiopia, and 51 percent in Malawi (World Bank, 2009).

At this point, it seems to be something of a foregone conclusion that removing costs increases access to education. Governments and multina-tional organizations have worked to address this issue, possibly more than any other educational concern. The World Bank and UNICEF joined together to create the School Fee Abolition Initiative (World Bank, 2009); the Millennium Development Goals supported school fee abolition as an inter-vention that "works" for achieving universal primary education (UN, 2010: 34); and sixteen countries in sub-Saharan Africa abolished school fees between 1990 and 2007 (Harding & Stasavage, 2014).

Focusing exclusively on a direct link between costs and access, however, overlooks quality. This reflects the earlier trend in international education, in which "governments and aid agencies have given priority to improving access rather than improving retention and learning outcomes" (World Bank, 2009: 12). Though much more attention is now being paid to the quality of education, as illustrated by Goal 4 of the new United Nations Sustainable Development Goals (SDG), the shorthand for which could be simply "Quality Education" this attention has not yet been applied to the issue of school fees.

Understanding the connection between costs and access is important in relation to understanding the demand for education and the barriers that children face. However, given the backdrop of severely underfunded education systems and the fact that so many children are failing to achieve basic literacy and numeracy, it might be useful to also approach the issue of fees from another perspective.

The United Nations SDG Education Steering Committee estimates that there is an annual funding gap of US $39 billion to achieve basic education (UN, 2016). At the same time, it is estimated that around the world, 200 million young people leave school without having learned to read, write, or count well (UNESCO, 2013). In light of these two realities, what is important to understand about fees is not simply their one-dimensional association with access, but their "relative merits," i.e. do fees have the potential to improve the quality of primary education and is there always a trade-off between access and quality?

School fees are not just linked to other issues, but defined by them. The question of "relative merits" exemplifies complexity theory's principles of connectivity and interdependence. Investigation into the issue of school fees must consider issues of access to education as well as concerns for the quality of education. In this respect, the research on user fees in primary education is far more limited. As noted by İşcan, Rosenblum, and Tinker (2015: 560), in the literature on fees in primary education, "there is surprisingly little systematic empirical evidence regarding their relative merits."

İşcan, Rosenblum, and Tinker (2015) advance this literature by investigating the impact of reintroducing school fees as national policy, a strategy employed by many African countries in the 1970s and 1980s. In the 1960s, several African countries abolished school fees as part of liberation and independence movements, but facing economic challenges in the 1970s and 1980s, these same countries often reinstated them. Estimating across seven countries in sub-Saharan Africa, İşcan, Rosenblum, and Tinker (2015: 583) conclude that primary school fees were intended to improve the quality of basic education in sub-Saharan Africa, but in practice, they decreased enrolment without "achieving significant improvements in the quality of education delivered."

There are limited data available for this time period, and the authors recognize that the measures they use (teacher-pupil ratio and primary completion rate) are imperfect indicators of quality, but these indicators might be too directly related to access to be very insightful. For example, the study's key finding is that the reinstatement of primary school fees was associated with a 17 percent drop in primary school enrollment rates (negative access), but that primary school fees were also associated with an improvement in the pupil-teacher ratios of about seven pupils per teacher (positive quality). Many countries in sub-Saharan Africa aim to have a pupil teacher ratio of forty to one. A reduction of about seven pupils per teacher represents approximately 17 percent less crowded classrooms. It does not seem surprising that if enrollment decreases by 17 percent, classrooms are less crowded by 17 percent.

Another key point is that in this time period, many governments also reduced the amount of government spending on education after reinstating fees. There is an important distinction between asking whether *supplementing* government funding with user fees would improve primary education and whether *replacing* decreased government funding with user fees would improve primary education. And finally, İşcan, Rosenblum, and Tinker (2015) focus exclusively on the national policy side of user fees, recognizing that though the government might abolish school fees, in almost all contexts there are still many costs associated with attending primary school. Again, there is an important distinction between the question of whether school fees improve the quality of primary education and whether a specific type of school fee improves the quality of primary education. And finally, the reinstating of school fees during the 1970s and 1980s took place in a very different period than the current context of primary education and society more generally in sub-Saharan African countries.

Although several studies have investigated the issue of fees in primary education in sub-Saharan Africa (Caucutt and Kumar, 2007; Kattan and Burnett, 2004; World Bank, 2009), focused research on the connection of fees to quality is limited. It is generally hypothesized that "fees often ensure the quality of inputs, such as books, for those who do enroll" (World Bank, 2004: 2). Possibly because of the emphasis on fee abolition and the perceived negative impact of fees on enrollment, research has not investigated whether user fees have the potential to improve quality.

In sum, existing literature on school fees exemplifies the access vs. quality paradigm. At first, fees were understood only in relation to access, and the issue of quality was neglected altogether. Quality has since been incorporated into the discussion, but in a very narrow and limited way. Access and quality are presented as if on a single unidimensional scale: at one end, high fees result in high quality but limited access and, at the other, fees are limited, access is high, and quality is low. In relation to school fees, there seems to be a clear zero-sum trade-off between access and quality. To move beyond this framework, I investigate the issue of school fees in a single setting and in the context of an experiment, testing different treatment variations of a savings program that encourages the payment of school fees.

Ugandan Context and Savings Interventions

Uganda's policy of Universal Primary Education is a "cost-sharing" policy. It prohibits formal tuition payments (fees that would be used to exclude children from the classroom) but allows for schools to raise all types of "voluntary" funds from pupils, and their families and communities. Scholastic materials, from books and pencils to uniforms, are parents' responsibility to provide. These requirements are negotiated at a school level.

The communication of this policy, though, has been imperfect. Uganda's President Museveni, for example, has repeatedly made it clear that the government will not pay for school lunches, but that schools should also not be allowed to collect money for feeding programs (Sebano, 2015). Some local politicians further confuse this issue when they tell parents not to send lunch with their children, but then criticize the national government for not providing school lunches (Avenstrup et al., 2004). Even more concerning, local politicians often campaign on a platform of "free primary education," which is a clear misrepresentation of Uganda's policy.

In practice, user fees vary significantly between different Ugandan primary schools. As detailed in Chapter 6, children reported paying anywhere from nothing to 40,000 Ugandan shillings per term (16 USD), and 29 percent of children in the endline survey reported that they at some point had been asked to leave the classroom because they were not wearing a uniform, did not have scholastic materials, or were sent to "look for fees." Alternatively, children might remain in school, but not be able to participate in certain activities. For example, some schools in the present study charged "exam fees" to enable children to take a practice exam to prepare for the end of year standardized tests; children who had paid for the exam would take the exam, while children who had not would simply sit and wait for the exam to finish.

In Uganda's 2006 National Household Survey, the most frequently cited reason given why children had dropped out of school was that it was too expensive (Uganda Bureau of Statistics, 2018). At that time, the survey reported average annual educational expenses across all government primary schools in Uganda to be approximately $10 USD, including books, supplies, uniforms, school fees, and other expenses (Uganda Bureau of Statistics, 2008). Many Ugandan families struggle to raise this money. This was true for my sample as well: About 40 percent of children who had dropped out of school explained that a lack of money for fees or scholastic materials was the reason why they had dropped out, by far the most frequent explanation. The connection between household finances and education served as the motivation for the savings program. Could a savings program help families better afford educational expenses? And, accordingly, could a savings program improve educational outcomes?

There is some research to suggest that basic inputs can lead to improved educational outcomes. The distribution of free uniforms, for example, has been shown to improve both attendance and test scores (Evans, Kremer, & Ngatia, 2009). If the practice of saving enables the purchasing of supplies such as uniforms, the savings program could affect educational outcomes in the same way. An established body of research has also shown that school feeding programs can improve school attendance and educational achievement (Bundy et. al., 2009). Alternatively, research has also shown that scholastic materials can have heterogeneous impacts. For instance, providing schools with more textbooks affected only higher-performing students, authors hypothesize, because the level of the textbooks was too advanced for average and underperforming students (Glewwe, Kremer, & Moulin, 2009).

Certain families might simply not be able to afford any user fees. In 2016, 41.3 percent of Ugandans lived on less than 1.90 USD a day (World Bank, 2016). For this reason, conditional and unconditional cash transfers have been a popular intervention in many middle- and low-income countries (Baird, McIntosh, & Ozler, 2011; Behrman et al., 2011). The savings program might be ineffective because some families do not have any disposable income to save or to even afford to have children attend school, which might keep them from household or income-generating activities. It is also possible that the savings program might work for some children and families and not for those who experience more severe poverty or disadvantage.

Given that school fees "have a disproportionately larger negative impact on the educational attainment of children from poor families" (İşcan, Rosenblum, and Tinker, 2015: 562), investigating whether children of different socioeconomic status experienced the savings program in the same way is an important concern. Research in Uganda has found that the positive impact of school fee abolition on enrollment was experienced primarily by poorer children (Deininger, 2003; Nihimura et al., 2008; Lincove, 2012).

Analysis of mediation and/or moderation of the current savings program's impact can illuminate a number of these issues. Investigating whether the savings program's impact was moderated by children's socioeconomic status will help determine whether the program was experienced in the same way by children of different socioeconomic status or whether the effects of the program were only experienced by children of higher socioeconomic status. Testing the mediation pathway will also help answer this question by exploring whether the savings program's impact on test scores was indeed a result of the purchasing of scholastic materials and, if so, whether this pathway was experienced by children of both higher and lower socioeconomic status.

And finally, it is important to recognize that household finances affect not just a child's school supplies, but whether or not a child attends school in the first place. The literature on school fees has shown that the costs associated with attending school can act as a barrier excluding children from school. If abolishing tuition fees in Ugandan primary education led to an increase in enrollment, it is possible that the savings program, in emphasizing and encouraging fees, might lead to an increase in school dropout.

Though school savings programs are a relatively novel intervention and research on them is limited, existing research has highlighted the concern that encouraging children to save or think about money more generally might lead them to prioritize income-generating activities over schooling (Varcoe et al., 2005). An evaluation of a school savings program in Ghana found that financial education without any accompanying social education (information on children's rights and responsibilities) led to an increase in child labor (Berry, Karlan, & Pradhan, 2016). Although the savings intervention in the present study did not lead to an increase in child labor, it is possible that children who were already working might have experienced the program differently. In this sample, whether or not a child was working had strong negative associations with educational outcomes and can also be seen as an important indicator of children's socioeconomic status.

My three research questions are inspired by this possible tension between access and quality: First, was the program's positive impact on test scores moderated by children's socioeconomic status? I explore moderation in relation to two different indicators of socioeconomic status: an index of a child's assets and whether or not a child reported working. Second, was the proposed mediation pathway (that improvements in test scores were a result of the increase in scholastic materials) experienced in the same way by children of different socioeconomic status? As before, I investigate two possible moderators: an index of a child's assets and whether or not a child reported working. And third, did the program's emphasis on saving and school fees have any unintended consequences—specifically, did any of the treatment variations impact school dropout?

The Savings Intervention and Research Design

In the RCT design all treatment schools received the same basic intervention. A group savings account was designed specifically for this program and an account was opened for each school. Schools were given safety lockboxes to store savings in the time between collections by the bank, and children in the three upper grades of primary school (fifth, sixth, and seventh grades) were encouraged to save money. Children's savings came from multiple sources: Some children were given money by their parents, others performed simple chores for neighbors, and others had more formal work activities. As will be described later, 42 percent of the baseline sample reported that they completed some activities to earn money. Though savings were collectively stored, children were given passbooks in which to keep track of their individual savings, which were also recorded by teachers in a grade-level record. A program officer visited each school on a weekly basis to assist with saving and record-keeping. Children were able to save throughout the trimester, and then, at the beginning of each new trimester, the bank would return the savings to each school and individual savings would be paid out to each student. Neither children nor schools ever received any grants or any additional money.

In all treatment schools, children received the exact amount that they had saved, and on the day of the savings payout, educational supplies were made available for children to purchase as part of a savings day fair. In this way, children could easily buy supplies such as pens, uniforms, and exercise books, as well as make payments toward exam fees, extra lessons, or any fees present at a school. Treatment schools were randomly assigned to two variations: cash and voucher. In half of the treatment schools, children received their money as cash. In the other half of the treatment schools, children received their savings in the form of a voucher which had to be used to make education-related purchases or resaved. The terms of the voucher were inclusive, allowing children to spend their money on anything related to school, for example, uniforms, pens, pencils, exam fees, meals.

The savings program thus officially recognized the costs associated with schooling and worked to enable and encourage children and their families to pay them. This emphasis on fees resulted in some confusion amongst parents and the community—which costs are a parents' responsibility and which are the schools? As was discussed in the previous section, the cost-sharing nature of Uganda's policy has not always been clearly communicated. A complementary parent outreach program was implemented in the second year of the savings program to address some of the confusion previously mentioned about the role of fees in Uganda's Universal Primary Education policy. In particular, the program clarified that, under UPE policy, it was parents' responsibility to provide basic scholastic materials, not the governments' or schools'.

In a two-by-two evaluation design (Figure 7.2) half of the treatment schools, equally split between cash and voucher schools, were randomly selected to receive an additional parent and community meeting. Food was provided to encourage attendance, and a discussion was led by a program officer from the savings program in which the roles and responsibilities of various stakeholders was discussed. The program officer explained that while the government provided school buildings, teachers, curriculum, and other inputs, basic scholastic materials had to be provided by parents. This program was the same in both cash and voucher schools, except that, in the explanation of the program, the officer would describe either the cash or vouchers.

This intervention served to counter many parents' preexisting beliefs that, in implementing Universal Primary Education, the government assumed responsibility over all aspects of primary education. In an interview with a school inspector from this region, he explained to me that

> The major reason which is leading to poor academic performance in [this region] is poor attitude towards education, and this attitude is all round. The parents have a poor attitude towards education that they fail even to buy the basic needs of the children. Children come to school and they are not fed; they start school hungry. All through children are not given the scholastic materials, the books, the pens, mathematical sets, and so on.

The parent outreach program, in beginning with an explanation of the roles of different stakeholders in Uganda's UPE policy, sought to address this mentality.

The savings program was then introduced as a tool to help parents raise the money to cover these expenses. The treatment variation which combined the cash and parent interventions was the only variation that resulted in impacts on test scores or scholastic supplies (Karlan & Linden, 2017).

In their paper, Karlan and Linden (2017) focus on the cash-voucher comparison, relating their findings to a broader literature on conditional savings. The voucher program, a form a conditionality, was seen as being too restrictive; feedback from schools indicated that children wanted their savings in cash and disliked the voucher. For this reason, neither of the voucher treatment variations had any impact; it seems the program simply was not popular enough, and children did not save enough money for it to matter. Karlan and Linden (2017) find that cash schools saved significantly more than voucher schools. When combined with the parent outreach program, the cash schools increased the number and percentage of children in the classroom with basic scholastic materials and improved test scores by 0.11 standard deviations (Karlan & Linden, 2017).

In order to explain this finding, Karlan and Linden (2017: 11) turn to possible mechanisms of impact. The parent program did not appear to have any impact on the volume or frequency of savings in the cash treatment. They hypothesize that "while the cash treatment arm led to higher savings, the parent outreach component shifted *how* the funds were spent." This theory is supported by evidence from routine classroom surveys that found a statistically significant increase in the presence of scholastic materials only after the parent outreach program had been implemented. The interaction of the two treatments is accordingly explained in the following way: the cash savings program encouraged children to save money at school, and the parent outreach ensured that the money was actually spent on school supplies (Karlan & Linden, 2017).

Results of Secondary Analysis

For my secondary analysis of the savings intervention, I have three research questions: (1) Was the cash+parent treatment impact on test scores moderated by children's socioeconomic status? (2) Was the proposed mediation pathway (the impact on test scores was mediated by an increase in scholastic materials) experienced by children of high and low socioeconomic status? And (3) Did any variation of the savings program impact children's dropout from school, and, if so, did that impact vary by socioeconomic status? Details of my analysis and results can be found in the Technical Appendix.

In relation to the first research question, I did not find any evidence to suggest that the cash+parent treatment intervention was moderated by children's socioeconomic status. Children who were working and children who were not working seemed equally likely to benefit from the intervention, just as children with more and fewer assets were equally likely to benefit. The success of the cash+parent treatment intervention does not seem to have depended upon the success of more affluent children.

I did find evidence to support the mediation pathway. It appears as though the cash+parent treatment's impact on test scores did come as a result of children using their savings for scholastic materials and school fees, but again, I do not find that the cash+parent treatment intervention worked better for more advantaged children than for other children.

For my third research question, I evaluated all treatment variations, not just the cash+parent variation, and I found that a different treatment variation, the cash intervention without the accompanying parent intervention increased dropout, as compared with the control group. Children in schools that received the cash program without the parent intervention were 1.47 times more likely to drop out of school than children in control schools. No other treatment variation affected dropout.

The Potential and the Threat of School Fees

If school fees were to be personified, it might be said that they have been significantly maligned in the press. Over the past couple decades, serious charges have been made against school fees. This discourse is not just casting aspersions, as the negative portrayal of school fees is supported by a significant body of evidence. Multiple strands of research across many different contexts all find that user fees limit access to education.

But does this singular narrative on fees accurately represent the issue or do justice to the underlying concerns? In applying principles of complexity theory to my investigation of school fees, I expand the issue beyond a singular, linear cause-and-effect relationship between fees and access to education. My analysis of a primary school savings program and its potential to encourage the use school fees to improve the quality of primary education in Uganda illustrates both the potential of school fees and the threat they pose. My first two research questions focus on issues of moderation and mediation, testing whether the impact of a school savings program was moderated by children's socioeconomic status, that is, did poorer and more affluent children experience the benefits of the program equally? And was the program's proposed mediation pathway experienced in the same way by children of different socioeconomic status?

I do not find evidence to suggest that the positive impact of the program was moderated by children's socioeconomic status. This is a promising finding. It suggests that the savings program or other similar interventions could be a way to improve the educational experience of children without privileging the least disadvantaged. It is important to keep in mind that, on average, children were saving and spending very small amounts of money. In the baseline survey, children reported that families paid an average of 5,790 UGX (2.30 USD) to send a child to school for a trimester, which represents 0.5 percent of Uganda's per capita income in 2010 (Republic of Uganda Ministry of Finance, Planning and Economic Development, 2010). On average, children were saving 1,000 to 2,000 UGX (0.40–0.80 USD) per trimester, depending on the treatment variation. Basic scholastic materials cost from 200 UGX (0.08 USD) for a notebook to 6,000 UGX (2.40 USD) for a uniform or shoes. My analysis confirmed that the impact on test scores was mediated by the use of savings to purchase these basic supplies. My two measures of socioeconomic status did not predict whether or not children saved, or how much.

The fact that the positive impact of the program on test scores did not appear to be moderated by children's socioeconomic status, whether directly or through the mediation, indicates that savings and parent outreach programs have the potential to improve the quality of primary education by increasing educational resources and improving test scores. It also suggests that user fees might not always exclude children from school, as the program appeared to work equally well for children of high and low socioeconomic status. School fees do not necessarily result in a negative impact on access, and there does not have to be a trade-off between access and quality.

Current cost-sharing education policies could be improved by better communication and including financial tools such as savings to make the costs associated with attending school more affordable. The focus of research, practice, and policy can also shift away from an exclusive focus on abolishing school fees to instead recognizing that the current status quo in many countries includes some form of user fees and that improving user fee payment systems could be one way in which to improve the quality of education. School fees do not necessarily have to act as a limit on access.

In investigating dropout, however, I find that a different treatment variation increased student dropout as compared with the control group. Children in schools that received the cash intervention but not the complementary parent outreach program were 1.47 times more likely to drop out of school than children in control schools. My interpretation of this finding is that, without sufficient attention to community outreach and communication with parents, the cash savings program discouraged some children from staying in school.

To explore the impact of the cash only treatment on dropout, I refer to qualitative and anecdotal feedback from the program's implementation. It was widely recognized that the voucher program was relatively unpopular. As discussed in Karlan and Linden (2017), children preferred to receive their savings in cash, and the voucher program was discouraging. Schools with the voucher program saved less than schools with the cash program and generally did not have as much enthusiasm and energy surrounding the intervention. Perhaps because of this attitude, the voucher program did not have any impact on test scores, scholastic materials, or dropout. The voucher treatment variation resulted in no changes, positive or negative.

In cash schools, the program was more favorably received, and schools saved more. This success, though, appears related to negative consequences. Children who were unable to save or otherwise participate might have felt excluded and discouraged, which might have led them to drop out of school. Alternatively, children who participated in the program, possibly becoming more economically active, might have lost interest in formal schooling and sought more work or other opportunities outside the classroom, which also might have led them to drop out. Although all of the results of my moderation analyses were constrained by limited statistical power, for the dropout outcome, results were not as definitively null as the results for the moderation of test scores. A larger and less statistically insignificant coefficient on the work interaction term suggests that children who were working to earn money might have been more likely to drop out of school as a result of the program.

The potential connection between children's work and the savings program was often mentioned by teachers. When the program was first introduced, many teachers voiced the concern that saving and focusing on money might distract children from their academics and turn their attention to making money as opposed to staying in school. Research on a school savings program in primary schools in Ghana echoes this concern, as researchers found that when implemented on its own, a school savings program increased child labor (Berry, Karlan, & Pradhan, 2016).

Schools with the cash program that also received the parent outreach might have been able to mitigate these concerns or offset them with increased community engagement. The parent outreach program was originally implemented in order to address some of the confusion surrounding user fees and whose responsibility it was to pay them. The program's efforts to demystify and normalize user fees, as well as encourage parents to pay them, might also have been important in keeping children in school. Again, this issue is reflected in the research in Ghana, where researchers found that when the savings program was accompanied by a social program, child labor did not increase (Berry, Karlan, & Pradhan, 2016).

In my sample, whether or not a child reported that she worked to earn money during the baseline was a key predictor of later school dropout. Though I am not able to make any definitive conclusions in my moderation analysis due to limited statistical power, my results do suggest that rates of dropout were highest in the cash only treatment group among children who worked. There is also a possible connection between the intervention and how a child used their savings. Without the parent outreach program, the savings program might have encouraged children to use their savings to support their economic activity outside of the classroom, for example, by buying an animal to raise.

Primary education is situated within the broader context of Ugandan society, in which child labor, both formal and informal, is prevalent. Children's economic activities can coexist with primary education, taking place before or after school or on the weekends, or these activities can detract from children's educational experience. Similarly, the savings program could have encouraged children's financial activity, but still oriented them toward school, or it could have focused children outside of the classroom, turning their attention more toward work. Across all treatment groups, 56 percent of children reported in the endline that they worked for the money that they saved. It seems savings, money, and school fees can have either positive or negative properties.

The principle of emergence argues that systems can exhibit certain properties at the systems level that do not exist in relation to individual parts of the system. One way in which to explain the importance of the parent outreach program is that it changed something about the broader environment of the school. It is possible that school fees operate very differently in an area where parents are well informed and aware of their responsibilities as compared with an area where parents are skeptical of fees and less aware of their own responsibilities. A critical emergent property of Ugandan primary schools and communities could be attitudes toward fees.

Future research in Uganda should investigate children's work activities, the significance of this labor as an indicator of a child's welfare, and whether children's work supplements or detracts from experiences in the classroom. Research should also investigate which measures can be most useful in identifying at-risk or disadvantaged children. For example, whether or not a child is barefoot is often used as an indicator of socioeconomic status, but in this study, more than 80 percent of the sample and entire schools were barefoot, which limited its use as a single explanatory variable.

Interventions which address school fees must carefully consider the contexts in which they take place and, in particular, issues related to educational access. Emphasizing fees without enough parent and community outreach runs the risk of increasing school dropout or other possible negative outcomes, as these issues are all connected and interdependent. It is also important to note that the cash intervention without the parent program did not affect students' test scores. This treatment variation negatively affected access *and* had no impact upon the quality of education. Future interventions, programs, and policy should proceed slowly and explore avenues such as community outreach for how to alleviate negative consequences of fees.

The impact of the cash+parent treatment intervention, however, demonstrates that supporting a school fees system can have positive impacts. Anecdotal evidence from these and other primary schools in Uganda also suggests that school fees can be used to create a dynamic in which access and quality can be mutually beneficial. Though not present in every school, it is not an uncommon practice for Ugandan schools to accept school fees from some children and families and to use these resources to cover services for all children. School feeding programs are the most prevalent example of this dynamic, where schools collect kilograms of maize and donations to pay for a cook or grinding. The resulting porridge is then used to feed all students. Those who are able to contribute do, and then resources are spread as far as possible. Another local practice is for successful businessmen or other local leaders to donate land, labor, or other resources to schools. And a third practice is when schools "sponsor" children who are particularly disadvantaged, often orphans. Schools enroll a few children with an understanding that they will never pay fees.

Abolishing school fees and unilaterally discouraging their practice discourage these local support systems. The single, negative, top-down narrative of fees prevents these dynamics from coming to light. In addition, in speaking to Ugandan parents, many embrace their role in providing for their children's education. The single most popular response, and in some cases the only response to the question "What do you see to be your role in your children's education?" is to say paying for school fees. Parents in these communities described their role as "to provide scholastic materials like books pens and remind this child to go school and in case there are any other requirements at school that's where he comes in"; "My role as a parent, I have to make sure that I pay school fees"; "The role of the parent is to see that they pay for their children to go to school"; "Pay fees, buy books, uniforms."

While I do not intend to discourage the very real need for governments and multinational organizations to leverage more money for primary education, research, policy, and interventions need to investigate the issue of fees beyond a singular impact on access. The single, negative narrative on school fees is insufficient, if for no other reason than that school fees define the reality of Ugandan children's education and that of millions of other children around the world.

Fees can be used to improve the quality of education, to increase the presence of scholastic materials in the classroom, and to improve test scores. Fees can give parents a clear and concrete way in which to support their children. When supported by community dynamics, fees can also improve access to education for children who might otherwise be excluded. The direction for future work on school fees should be to determine how to advance both access and quality for all children.

8

Conclusion

We imbue education with great potential, as an end in and of itself, and for its relationship to other things. The latter is especially true in low-income countries, where education is seen as a key stimulus for many aspects of development. As the World Bank states, "Education is a human right, a powerful driver of development and one of the strongest instruments for reducing poverty and improving health, gender equality, peace, and stability" (World Bank, 2017: para 1).

Development, however, is not always a universally positive experience. To briefly explore this counternarrative—education can serve as protection *from* development. In one of the focus groups I conducted for this book, when asked about the purpose of education, participants replied that if you are not educated, "You can go to the courts of law, they write for you documents, you deliver to other offices without you knowing what you are carrying in your hands." Alternatively, "They don't take advantage of [educated people]; they can't cheat [educated people]." In places like Uganda, where there are accounts of people being forcibly evicted from their land to make way for World Bank-funded development projects (Oxfam, 2011), university expansion (Odongo, 2017), and the Ugandan National Roads Authority (Mbogo, Ssenkabirwa, & Kutamba, 2019), education can be crucial.

Every potential of education is threatened when children are not learning. Without the acquisition of basic skills, simply attending school might not lead to broader development outcomes. Research shows, for example, that economic growth and the distribution of income can be more powerfully related to a population's cognitive skills rather than schooling attainment (Hanushek & Woessmann, 2007). Similarly, we might expect one's number of years in school to be less relevant for defending one's rights in a court of law than the actual ability to read. The very concept of education is often inextricably tied to reading. In several Ugandan languages, such as Luganda, the words to "teach" (*somesa*), "teacher" (*omusomesa*), "student" (*omusomi*), and "school" (*essomero*) are all based upon the verb "to read" (*soma*).

Access, Quality, and the Global Learning Crisis: Insights from Ugandan Primary Education. Sarah Kabay, Oxford University Press.
© Sarah Kabay 2021. DOI: 10.1093/oso/9780192896865.003.0008

Yet the connection between attending school and basic literacy is not to be taken for granted. While this issue is typically understood in relation to low-income countries, it is present in many different contexts around the world.

On September 13, 2016, in the United States, a public interest law firm filed a class action lawsuit against the governor of Michigan on behalf of seven students from the City of Detroit's public schools. The suit argued that the state had denied these students a meaningful education: "Michigan's compulsory attendance laws require Plaintiffs to attend these schools, but they are schools in name only, characterized by slum-like conditions and lacking the most basic educational opportunities" (United States District Court Eastern District of Michigan Southern Division, 2016: 1). On June 29, 2018, a Federal District Court judge dismissed the suit, arguing that while the Michigan state constitution requires the legislature to "maintain and support a system of free public elementary and secondary schools," the state has no requirement to ensure that students in that system learn how to read (United States District Court Eastern District of Michigan Southern Division, 2016: 45).[1]

Detroit's public schools are among the worst in the nation, which suggests that the city is providing exactly what the court decried: schools, but not necessarily learning. In 2017, only 4 percent of Detroit's fourth graders were proficient in mathematics and only 5 percent were proficient in reading. Not unrelatedly, research has found that a significant percentage of *adults* in the City of Detroit are functionally illiterate, even though they might have a high school diploma or a GED (Detroit Regional Workforce Fund, 2011).[2]

Detroit, it could be argued, is part of a worldwide phenomenon that has been christened the "Global Learning Crisis," in relation to the city's low learning outcomes, as well as how they have been explained. Education researchers, practitioners, and policymakers have come to realize that attending school does not necessarily translate into literacy and numeracy.

---

[1] In early 2020, the Federal Appeals Court overturned this decision, ruling, for the first time in US history, that the constitution guarantees a right to literacy. The plaintiffs were able to reach a settlement, but the court's decision was later challenged by the Sixth Circuit Court, which thereby nullified the earlier ruling. This case will inform future efforts to define students' constitutional rights, but there is still no legal precedent for the right to read in the United States.

[2] A 2011 report from the Detroit Regional Workforce Fund stated that a third of adults in the City of Detroit were functionally illiterate, and half of this functionally illiterate population had either a high school diploma or a GED. These figures have been critiqued for being outdated, as they are from 1998. However, no current and rigorous adult literacy estimates exist for the City of Detroit, and other data suggest that the estimate might not be inaccurate. The most recently completed National Assessment of Adult Literacy (NAAL) found that 14% of Americans demonstrated a below-basic-literacy level in 2003, indicating that they cannot read paragraphs or connected sentences. This assessment has also found no significant changes in prose and document literacy between 1992 and 2003. https://nces.ed.gov/naal/kf_demographics.asp, accessed February 18, 2021.

A typical summation of the Global Learning Crisis is "In many parts of both East and West Africa, and almost all of South Asia, school enrollment has grown rapidly, with primary school enrollment now exceeding 90% in many areas… The problem is that the children are in school, but they are not learning" (Banerjee & Duflo, 2011: 38).

The "in school but not learning" refrain is present throughout the international development education discourse and has inspired a wave of reforms intended to improve the quality of education. Many efforts are underway to improve what is happening in schools. According to the Global Partnership for Education (GPE), for example, "Getting children into the classroom is only half the battle. Now the challenge is to ensure that every child in that classroom is learning the basic skills they need in reading and mathematics" (Montoya & Mundy, 2017: para 2). The GPE argues that the Global Learning Crisis "is, in essence, a wake-up call for far greater—and urgent—investment in the quality of education" (Montoya & Mundy, 2017: para 12). At its Financing Conference in February 2018, the GPE raised US$1.3 billion to support its work (GPE, 2014).

It is absolutely critical that the quality of education be addressed, but will focusing exclusively on quality really lead to meaningful change in children's educational experiences and learning? In the case of Detroit, for example, can education quality ever truly be addressed if the most high-needs, low-income black and Latinx children are increasingly concentrated in the same underperforming schools? Are not many issues of quality influenced by issues of access?

Over the past two decades, the international education discourse has been defined by a shift in focus from access to quality. I have called the underlying narrative behind this shift the access vs. quality paradigm. It has four arguments: (1) Access to education and educational quality are either independent or competing concerns; (2) the current Global Learning Crisis is the result of an overemphasis on access to education that overlooked or undermined the quality of education; (3) issues of access have largely been solved; and (4) to fix the Global Learning Crisis, attention must now be directed toward quality.

This book asks whether the access vs. quality paradigm and the work that it has inspired are missing something fundamental. It is an undeniable fact that actual learning outcomes, the ability to read with comprehension and perform basic calculations, are critical and should be the core focus of any basic education program. It is also clear that learning has long been overlooked; until recently, many organizations and school systems did not even measure learning outcomes. But a near singular focus on the quality of education and often exclusively on test scores has the potential to be as myopic as the field's previous focus on access. In addition, it fails to recognize the many ways in which issues of access and quality are connected. In order to move beyond the access vs. quality paradigm and rethink the Global Learning Crisis, I focused on the idea of education as a system and turned to complexity theory.

The founding principle of complexity theory is connectivity, the idea that different actors and elements are interconnected and that together they comprise a system that exhibits its own properties and characteristics beyond those of its parts. Accordingly, my approach to the study of the Global Learning Crisis began with the premise that issues of access and issues of quality are interconnected. I conducted a case study of Ugandan primary education to explore these connections and develop a new understanding of access, quality, and the relationship between them. In a sample of Ugandan primary schools and communities, I analyzed three issues: grade repetition, private schools, and school fees, viewing each issue as an illustration of the connection between access and quality.

My research on grade repetition focused on the presumed connection between repetition and school dropout. Repetition, a practice believed to emphasize the quality of education, is widely assumed to be positively associated with school dropout, a clearly negative effect on access to education. The international education literature presents a simple negative linear association between repetition and school dropout. Citing both methodological and conceptual concerns, I argue against this understanding of repetition. I believe grade repetition is better understood in relation to the principle of nonlinearity. There is no linear correspondence between a repetition rate and dropout rate, as repetition has an inconstant and at times nonexistent association with dropout. A single point estimate of the association between repetition and dropout is an inaccurate representation of the functioning of an education system.

In my analysis, I did not find that there was an association between repeating first or second grade and later school dropout, but that there was a positive association between repeating third grade and later dropping out of school. In Uganda, third grade is the last grade in which local languages serve as the medium of instruction; in fourth grade, there is a dramatic and abrupt transition to English. Improving this language policy, making it more gradual and providing pupils with the support they need, could improve this important transition, decrease repetition, and potentially keep more children in school. Improving the quality of education, by improving language policy and practice, accordingly, has the potential to improve access to education and reduce dropout.

The idea that there could be a positive rather than negative association between education quality and access to education is also supported by a second conclusion from my research on grade repetition, that improving age of entry into primary school could improve children's learning. In my research on repetition, I found that the strongest predictor of school dropout was a child's age, even when controlling for grade repetition. One reason why a child's age is an important concern is that more than 50 percent of Ugandan children are overage by the time they begin primary school, missing an important developmental period and making them older than many of their peers. Uganda also has one of the lowest enrollment rates in early childhood education in sub-Saharan Africa, with research showing that many children struggle in their first years of school. Ensuring that children enroll in school on time could improve the quality of education. This would be an access-oriented intervention that would improve quality, again supporting a positive association between access and quality.

In my second topic of analysis, private primary schools, I also conclude by discussing a dynamic in which access and quality are positively associated. The issue of privatization is often considered within the framework of access vs. quality. Private schools are believed to offer a higher-quality education than public schools, but at the expense of access, in that such schools are only accessible to certain children, which deepens educational inequality. Much of the research on private schools investigates these claims—do private schools actually offer a higher quality education? Are certain children excluded from these schools? Research frequently focuses on comparing private and public schools. In my longitudinal data, I find that there is significant overlap between private and public schools and that this issue exhibits another principle of complexity theory: interdependence. The private sector is defined by the public sector and vice versa. Children frequently transfer between sectors and a single family will send children to both types of schools, the family's experience at one school influencing their engagement with another. In my sample, children with lower test scores were more likely to transfer to private schools than children with higher test scores. This existing dynamic could be encouraged, as I found that, after transferring, children had higher test scores than those who did not transfer.

Given the interconnectedness and overlap of the sectors, it could be helpful to consider private and public schools together, as part of one dynamic system. If they are intentionally working together and guided by policy and active regulation, it might be possible to encourage, for example, private schools to serve struggling students who might not be keeping up in public schools. Children could be sorted by ability, which would enable teachers to direct instruction at the appropriate level for their students. Acknowledging the interdependence between these sectors—from governance, community, individual household and student levels—could guide approaches to coordinating the private and public sector, another access-oriented intervention that could improve the quality of education for all children.

Finally, for my third topic of analysis, I investigated the issue of school fees in relation to access and quality. Much of the literature on school fees concerns access. Over the past two decades, particularly in sub-Saharan Africa, countries have made significant efforts to abolish school fees. This policy intervention is believed to have increased access exponentially. In Uganda, after fees were abolished, primary school enrollment nearly doubled in a single year. Such dramatic increases in access are believed to have undercut quality. The discussion of school fees is perhaps the clearest representation of the access vs. quality paradigm, but while it is widely recognized that the removal of fees improves access and as a result lowers quality, there has been little to no exploration of the reverse, whether fees might improve quality.

By analyzing the experimental impacts of a school savings program, I was able to investigate how emphasizing the payment of school fees might affect not just access, but also quality. The savings program began with an informational campaign, communicating to parents that, according to the government's policy, it was parents' responsibility to pay for their children's uniforms, books, lunches, and other basic user fees. Parents and children were then encouraged to save money to pay for these fees (importantly, there were no cash grants to families in this study). In different treatment variations, the intensity of outreach to parents and the form in which children received their savings varied. Previous research found that a combination of additional parent outreach and disbursing children's savings as cash improved children's test scores (Karlan & Linden, 2017). In my secondary analysis, I investigated mediation and moderation of this successful treatment variation's outcomes—mediation through school fee expenditure and moderation by socioeconomic status. I was able to confirm that the improvement in test scores came as a result of children spending their savings on school fees. I did not find evidence of moderation, the program seemed to work equally well for children of different socioeconomic status. These results indicate that encouraging user fee payments does not necessarily have to negatively impact access, even for the poorest children. Urging those who can afford fees to pay them, and possibly cover those who cannot, could be a dynamic in which improvements in quality and access are achieved in tandem.

In analyzing another treatment variation, though, I found that without sufficient parent outreach, the cash program actually increased dropout, which supported the prevailing understanding that an emphasis on fees decreases access. I believe this represents the principle of emergence, in that the issue of school fees is defined by system level properties and not just its own characteristics. With parent outreach, the program's emphasis on school fees was contextualized within an education system in which parents were aware of UPE policy and its delineation of responsibilities. Without parent outreach, school fees might interact with an environment in which parents are misinformed or unsure of different actors and children are working to earn money. The payment of school fees can be a positive expression of parents' support of education or a reason why children drop out of school, depending upon the larger system dynamics beyond either household or school finances considered in isolation.

To summarize, I analyzed grade repetition, privatization, and school fees in a sample of Ugandan primary schools and communities. These three issues illustrated complexity theory's principles of nonlinearity, interdependence, and emergence, respectively, further supporting my framing of primary education as a system defined by complexity. Rather than assuming a basic input-output design for education, it highlighted unintended consequences and chains of effects. In studying each of these issues, I found that there were dynamics where access and quality could be seen to be mutually reinforcing. There does not always have to be a trade-off between efforts to improve access to education and education quality.

I concluded my study of each of these topics by suggesting that a new direction for work in primary education could be to work to create an alliance between access to education and education quality. My case study of Ugandan primary education accordingly comes to three conclusions: (1) Primary education should be recognized as a system defined by complexity where issues of access and quality are interconnected; (2) it is possible for there to be a positive association between access to education and the quality of education; and (3) education actors should work to encourage dynamics where improvements in access and quality are mutually reinforcing.

This book accordingly results in concrete and specific policy recommendations for the Ugandan context, from improving the age of entry into primary school to more accurately communicating school fee policy (see Figure 8.1). These recommendations directly correspond to the three

Recommendations for Policy and Practice in the Ugandan Context

Encouraging Dynamics where Access and Quality can be Mutually Reinforcing

- Increase the number of children who enroll in primary school on time
- Increase opportunities for early childhood education
- Make the transition between languages of instruction more gradual
- Provide multiple forms of support for children who struggle with English in early grades
- Provide remedial education opportunities for children who are struggling with basic skills, grouping children by ability level and providing targeted instruction
- Improve payment systems for government teachers so that teachers receive a livable wage on time and consistently
- Improve regulation and monitoring of the private sector
- Improve commmunication of key policies – particlarly those concerning school fees, cost-sharing, and the division of roles and responsibility across different actors (local officials, schools, teachers, and parents)
- Encourage collective support from communities and the mobilization of avaiable resources, not just individualized school fee payments
- Encourage and support parents – particularly parents with limited educational experience

Figure 8.1 Recommendations for policy and practice in the Ugandan context

specific issues I investigate, grade repetition, private schools, and school fees. But what more universal conclusions might be drawn from this work? In this final chapter, I consider broader applications of my research in relation to both primary education and complexity theory.

What Have We Learned about Education?

While my book focuses on two fundamental dimensions of any education system, access and quality, and the belief that they are connected, it is also important to take a step back and consider the issue of connectedness on a less theoretical level in relation to students, teachers, and textbooks, in other words, to examine the idea of an education system. A system can be defined as "a regularly interacting or interdependent group of items forming a unified whole" (Merriam-Webster, 2018, s.v. system). An education system, accordingly, could be considered to be any regularly interacting items related to a specific practice of education, in which case, items could include stakeholders such as teachers, students, parents, and policymakers, as well as curriculum, school buildings, laws, and policy.

The idea of an education system should not to be taken for granted. On September 12, 2017, US Secretary of Education Betsy DeVos, speaking to a school in Wyoming, stated, "Today, there is a whole industry of naysayers who loudly defend something they like to call the education 'system.' What's an education 'system'? There is no such thing! Are you a system? No, you're individual students, parents, and teachers" (US Department of Education, 2017).

While my book specifically argues that access and quality are interconnected, this idea is predicated on the belief that all elements of an education system are connected. Throughout the book there are many instances in which I show that stakeholders, policies, and practices in either Ugandan or American primary education are connected. In Chapter 5 on grade repetition, language policy, grade repetition, and school dropout are all linked. In my discussion of private schools, fathers' education level is the strongest predictor of a child's transfer to private school, which illustrates that schools are defined not just by their students, but also by those students' parents. The intervention I analyze in Chapter 7 on school fees shows the link between financial services, basic supplies such as books and pencils, and students' learning.

If we recognize that, for the majority of the world's children, education takes place in a system comprised of interconnected components, then our attempts to solve the problems of education systems must also move beyond focusing on single components or functions of the system in order target broader, more far-reaching objectives. Our policies and interventions should be intentionally linked. We must expect that interventions will have unintended consequences beyond their specific targets and encourage the flexibility to address them. Instead of looking for a discrete, clearly defined, single policy solution, it would be helpful for education officials to explore the connections between different issues and interventions. As Robert Jervis writes in his book *System Effects: Complexity in Political and Social Life*, if we are to embrace the complexity of certain problems, "Multiple policies must then be applied sequentially and actors must be ready to alter their behavior to cope with unintended consequences and the novel strategies that others employ" (Jervis, 1998: 293). A clear illustration of this perspective is the fact that I identified the issue of age of entry into primary education by studying children in fourth–seventh grade; issues and interventions in education have myriad long-term consequences. Improving early childhood education and age of entry might necessitate changes to grade repetition policies, early grade instruction, and other related concerns.

In fact, all of the recommendations for policy and practice that I present in this book are, in essence, a recommendation to consider primary education from a larger systems perspective and to link multiple issues and interventions. In order to address grade repetition, policy must also consider early childhood education and the transition between languages of instruction. To respond to a growing private sector, private schools could be incentivized to focus on struggling students and offer remediation classes to those coming from the public sector. School fee policy must be coupled with community outreach and engagement. The work to integrate student populations across schools must also explicitly include policy to integrate teachers as well.

A final key inference to draw from my analysis is to consider issues outside of the classroom and, in particular, the role of parents. To address grade repetition and school dropout, my recommendation to improve age of entry into primary education will depend upon engaging with parents and families to understand and support the transition into school. My analysis of transfer to private schools found fathers' education was a strong predictor of transfer, which indicated that parent outreach and communication will need to be an important part of equalizing access. And analysis of school fees also directly supports this hypothesis, as the school savings program only worked when coupled with parent outreach.

Schools do not exist in a vacuum. Education policy and practice must consider society at large, and one clear and concrete way in which to address that is to work intensively with parents. Outreach to families and communities can address some of the clear linkages between what happens in and outside of the classroom. As education systems coevolve with many other aspects of society—child labor, residential segregation, socioeconomic inequality, geographic differences, it might also be an important direction for future work to consider linking policy and practice across different sectors, such as health, housing, and welfare.

It is important to note that many of these conclusions reflect the existing ideas and perspectives of stakeholders in Ugandan primary education highlighted by my qualitative data. Teachers connected the issue of grade repetition to children's lives outside of the classroom, discussing poverty and the lack of community support as the key reasons why children repeat classes. In relation to privatization, parents already view private and public schools as part of the same system of primary education and have their own strategies for navigating the complexity of that system. The savings program only worked when combined with a parent outreach program that deliberately engaged parents in the discussion of education policy. Future work should continue to engage parents, guardians, and other community stakeholders, both to learn from their perspective and to fully involve them as a key stakeholder in primary education.

The broader education conclusions of this book are, accordingly, (1) primary education must be seen not as independent individual actors and issues, but as a complex system of interconnected elements, and (2) that in order to address the challenges present in such systems, intervention must be multiple, sequential, and interconnected as well, considering not just issues within a classroom or school, but in surrounding communities and society as well.

What Have We Learned about Complexity?

Throughout this book, I applied the principles of complex systems to the study of education, but it could also be useful to apply insight from education to the study of complexity. How might the concepts of access and quality contribute to our understanding of complexity, for example? As I described in Chapter 2, complexity theory highlights the interrelationship, interaction, and interconnectivity between the elements within a system and between a system and its environment (Chan, 2001). To put this in the terms of the educational discourse and the key concepts of this book, the concept of "access" could be defined as the factors that that determine membership in a system, and "quality" could be used to refer to the dynamics and relationships of elements within the system. When access and quality are positively associated, the factors that determine membership in a system are positively reinforced by the relationships and characteristics of the system. To illustrate, an education system that actively supports girls' education recognizes the challenges girls face and the potential stereotypes and biases that define their lives outside of school, and works to address them—thus making school accessible to girls and then providing a high-quality educational experience that meets the needs of girls. In this way, the education system also interacts with the larger context in which it is situated.

To briefly expand on this idea, "access" could define not just membership in a system, but also the relationship between a system and its environment. Access determines any particular element's engagement with a system, whether it is in or outside of the system, at what points, and why. "Quality" relates to the nature of the connections within a system. Together, access and quality determine the output of the system.

The key conclusions of my book, that access and quality are connected and can sometimes defined by a positive association, accordingly suggest that the relationships within a system and the relationships between a system and its environment are connected and can be defined by a positive association. In this final section of the book, I propose that this could be considered the definition of an enabling environment.

Though the term "enabling environment" is used throughout many different fields, there does not appear to be any single clear definition of the concept. For example, in describing the "ubiquity of the term" in discussion of the Millennium Development Goals, Brinkerhoff (2004) states:

> In some formulations, the enabling environment is defined so expansively that it becomes nearly synonymous with socio-economic development itself. In others, it is treated so narrowly as to be clearly inadequate to stimulate sufficient response absent the presence of additional factors; for example, considering the enabling environment as consisting primarily of an appropriate regulatory framework.   (Brinkerhoff, 2004: 1)

In light of the ambiguity of the term, I believe education systems can offer a unique perspective on enabling environments and, accordingly, complexity. I investigate the concept here to suggest how the study of education can contribute to our understanding of complex adaptive systems.

Across all conceptions of the enabling environment, one idea seems particularly widespread: An enabling environment is defined in relation to a single focal entity. An enabling environment describes the broader setting in which the focal entity is located. The focal entity could be an individual or type of individual, as in this definition, for an enabling environment for adolescent health: "An enabling environment reflects a set of interrelated conditions legal, political, social, and cultural, among others that affect the capacity of young people to lead healthy lives and access relevant and necessary services, information, and products" (Svanemyr et al., 2015: 58). The focal entity could also be an organization, as in this definition of a business-enabling environment: "The business-enabling environment (BEE) is the set of policy, institutional, regulatory, infrastructure, and cultural conditions that govern formal and informal business activities" (Goodpaster, 2011: 4). Or the focal entity could be an entire sector or trend—such as nutrition ("How Senegal Created an Enabling Environment for Nutrition: A Story of Change" (Kampman et al., 2017)) or privatization (*Creating an Enabling Environment for Private Sector Development in Sub-Saharan Africa* (UNIDO, 2008) In each case there is the focal item and then the entirety of the environment that surrounds it.

In international development education, an enabling environment is often understood in relation to an intervention and its potential for scale. The focal entity is the intervention, and the environment includes all factors of the context in which that intervention is located—political, economic, cultural, etc. An enabling environment supports successful implementation and scaling of the intervention.

As their name suggests, enabling environments place special emphasis on the environment, as opposed to the focal entity, in relation to the issues they affect. For example, in the Brookings *Millions Learning* Report (Perlman Robinson & Winthrop, 2016: 116), a chapter on enabling environments quotes Patrick McCarthy, the CEO of the Anne E. Casey Foundation, "A bad system will trump a good program every time." This idea is echoed throughout the report, for instance in the idea that "Successful scaling efforts are more often about creating an enabling environment for innovation to flourish than specific action required for an individual program to grow" (Perlman Robinson & Winthrop, 2016: 116).

However, given the fundamental principles of connectivity and interdependence, should we focus on either an intervention or an environment in isolation? Is a program a "good program" if it does not fit in the environment in which it is located? Conversely, can an enabling environment be developed or enhanced without any information on individual programs?

To return to two of the previous examples, an enabling environment for adolescent health depends upon and is defined by the characteristics and behavior of adolescents. The factors that determine whether, when, and how adolescents access information and services will determine how that information or service is received. Similarly, who a business employs, serves, and interacts with will determine how it operates and interacts with its environment. The concept of an enabling environment, like all of complexity theory, should emphasize interrelationship, interaction, and interconnectivity, not just within either the environment or the focal entity, but between them.

Three features of education systems underscore this perspective on enabling environments: the hierarchical nature of education systems, the indefinite quality of the outcomes of education systems, and the reciprocal relationship between education and society at large. In relation to the first, an education system is defined by systems nested within systems. Any particular actor can be an entity in an environment and also a feature of that environment. A teacher could be considered part of the enabling environment for a student, but is also an actor operating in a greater school and system context. Any intervention must consider the perspective of multiple stakeholders, as education is not a simple dichotomy between a single entity and then the environment in which that entity operates. A headmaster has to balance competing objectives between parents, children, teachers, district officials, donors, and national policymakers. The distinction between entity and environment is not clear. To return to the idea of "level-jumping" introduced in Chapter 3, education must consider multiple stakeholders and levels of the system.

Second, the output of an education system depends upon the environment in which it takes place. As compared with health, agriculture, or other systems, the definition of learning and education may vary by community or nation in response to variation in language, culture, and context. The goal of any education system, accordingly, cannot be determined by a single entity. The purpose of education must be defined through interaction between the education system and society at large, which leads to the third feature of education systems that influences our understanding of enabling environments and, accordingly, complexity: the connection between education and greater society.

Education is at once a force for change in society and a reflection of society. An enabling environment for education could be defined as a society which prioritizes education, fully funding its structures and honoring and recognizing its participants. On the other hand, an unequal society might be successfully replicating itself through an inadequate education system. The goals and objectives of society and the education system that reproduces it are aligned. Determining an enabling environment for education, accordingly, introduces interesting issues in relation to defining objectives, goals, and outputs.

These three features of education systems advance our understanding of enabling environments beyond a dichotomy between a focal entity and the entirety of the environment that surrounds it. Instead, enabling environments can be considered the positive dynamics that occur when the relationships within a system are positively reinforced by the relationships between a system and its environment, and vice versa.

Conclusion

The stakes for improving education could not be higher. Understanding education systems is critical, as education supports all other efforts for sustainable development, from population growth to peace and security to the management of the material resources of the planet. In the first section of this conclusion chapter, I suggested that the field of international education should move away from single policy solutions and toward sequential, interconnected, and responsive policies. In the second section, I argued that we should move away from interventions that focus on a single element or actor, seen as apart from the broader environment, and instead consider multifaceted interventions that engage with various levels and dimensions of the environment.

Such an approach will be critical as different actors and stakeholders around the world work together to improve primary education. Our goal will be to answer the question "Are our children learning?" with a resounding *yes*.

Technical Appendix

Grade Repetition (Chapter 4)

To determine whether repeating a grade increased the likelihood that a child would drop out of school, I use logistic regression to predict school dropout, covarying child demographic characteristics, and baseline achievement. I report the results of this regression in **Table A.1**. I test three different measures of repetition: in the first two columns, I predict dropout using whether or not a child repeated (measured at the baseline) as a predictor variable. In the third and fourth columns, I use the number of times a child repeated, also measured at baseline. And in the final three columns, I separate repetition into a series of indicator variables of whether or not a respondent repeated each of grades 1 through 6, using data from the endline. As each of these indicator variables is included in the same model, the odds ratios represent the additive nature of repeating a specific grade; for example, the association between repeating second grade and dropping out of school, holding constant repetition of first, third, fourth, fifth, and sixth grade.

Repeating a grade, measured either as ever repeating a grade or the number of times a child repeated grades, was not associated with dropping out of school. The first four rows of the table have no statistically significant odds ratios.

It is possible that repetition of early grades might be different from the repetition of later grades. To investigate potential variation by grade and possible covariation between grades, I conduct Pearson Pairwise correlations between repeating specific grades, reported in **Table A.2**.

I find a statistically significant and positive correlation between repeating first and second grade, suggesting that, in some cases, students who repeat first grade also repeat second grade. This finding aligns with research on the repetition of early grades and the concern that some children, without any early childhood education, "churn" by repeating multiple early grades as they adjust to the environment of the school (Crouch, Olefir, & Saeki, 2020: 15). Conversely, there are statistically significant negative correlations between repeating grades 5 and 6 and repeating earlier grades. This indicates that children who repeat either first, second, or third grade are not the same children who repeat fifth or sixth grade.

To allow for the covariation between grades, I isolated each indicator variable of the specific grade repeated in separate models and again predicted dropout (**Table A.3**). The odds ratios in these models thus represent the association between repeating a specific grade and school dropout, without controlling for repetition of other grades.

When I isolate the repetition of individual grades, a few specific grades appear to have an association with later school dropout. Repetition of grades 5 and 6 is negatively associated with dropout, but this is most likely a result of the timing of the study. All children in the sample were enrolled in grades 4 and 5 at baseline. During the two-year course of the study, if a child was observed repeating 5th or 6th grade, they could not have been observed dropping out of school at the same time. What these results do suggest is that the association between repeating and dropping out appears to vary by grade. As can be seen in the last rows of the table, both the magnitude and statistical significance of the odds ratios vary by grade.

Table A.1 Logistic regression predicting dropout from repetition as a dichotomous variable, ordinal variable, and by the grade repeated

	Dichotomous Variable yes/no repeat		Ordinal Variable no. times repeated		Indicator Variable which grade repeated		
	N = 3,753	N = 3,082	N = 2,776	N = 2,310	N = 3,778	N = 3,103	N = 3,103
	$R^2 = 0.15$	$R^2 = 0.18$	$R^2 = 0.15$	$R^2 = 0.18$	$R^2 = 0.17$	$R^2 = 0.20$	$R^2 = 0.19$
Repeated yes	0.937 (0.167)	0.973 (0.196)					
Repeated times			0.896 (0.077)	0.877 (0.083)			
Female	1.305* (0.189)	1.225 (0.197)	1.305* (0.213)	1.211 (0.218)	1.338** (0.196)	1.282 (0.209)	1.241 (0.200)
Urban	0.588* (0.183)	0.692 (0.257)	0.408** (0.171)	0.561 (0.257)	0.549* (0.172)	0.661 (0.246)	0.680 (0.254)
Socioeconomic status	0.964 (0.049)	1.024 (0.058)	0.979 (0.056)	1.025 (0.065)	0.959 (0.049)	1.020 (0.058)	1.028 (0.059)
Age	2.245*** (0.126)	2.204*** (0.136)	2.348*** (0.159)	2.325*** (0.172)	2.241*** (0.127)	2.224*** (0.138)	2.204*** (.135)
Child works	1.388** (0.200)	1.232 (0.198)	1.431** (0.231)	1.248 (0.224)	1.390** (0.202)	1.230 (0.200)	1.216 (0.196)
P5 at baseline	0.630** (0.092)	0.709** (0.115)	0.543*** (0.089)	0.626** (0.114)	0.859 (0.138)	0.964 (0.177)	0.735* (0.121)
Test score math		0.750*** (0.070)		0.791** (0.080)		0.754*** (0.071)	0.750*** (0.070)
Test score grammar	0.826* (0.099)	0.826* (0.099)		0.865 (0.115)		0.803* (0.097)	0.826 (0.099)

Test score reading	1.143	1.098	1.118	1.134
	(0.128)	(0.139)	(0.127)	(0.127)
Absence	1.539***	1.483***	1.553***	1.545***
	(0.146)	(0.157)	(0.149)	(0.147)
Transfer (endline)	1.028	1.056	1.006	1.011
	(0.176)	(0.200)	(0.174)	(0.173)
Treatment	1.108	1.141	1.102	1.120
	(0.172)	(0.195)	(0.172)	(0.173)
Repeated Grade 1		0.987	0.741	0.772
		(0.270)	(0.250)	(0.260)
Repeated Grade 2		1.069	1.097	1.208
		(0.256)	(0.292)	(0.318)
Repeated Grade 3		1.206	1.186	1.361*
		(0.188)	(0.208)	(0.230)
Repeated Grade 4		1.128	0.950	
		(0.169)	(0.162)	
Repeated Grade 5		0.663***	0.564***	
		(0.109)	(0.105)	
Repeated Grade 6		0.423***	0.466***	
		(0.123)	(0.141)	

Note: Odds ratios with standard errors in parentheses. R^2 values are pseudo R^2 from logistic regression.

* p < 0.10, ** p < 0.05, *** p < 0.01

Table A.2 Pairwise correlation table-repetition of specific grades

	Repeated P1	Repeated P2	Repeated P3	Repeated P4	Repeated P5
Repeated P1					
Repeated P2	0.1082***				
Repeated P3	−0.0087	0.0250			
Repeated P4	−0.0308*	0.0109	−0.0518***		
Repeated P5	−0.0657***	−0.0898***	−0.1409***	−0.2596***	
Repeated P6	−0.0483***	−0.0781***	−0.0876***	−0.1502***	−0.0924***

Table A.3 Logistic regression predicting dropout from repetition as grade repeated

	N = 3,103	N= 3,103	N = 3,103	N = 3,103	N = 3,103	N = 3,103
	$R^2 = 0.18$	$R^2 = 0.18$	$R^2 = 0.19$	$R^2 = 0.18$	$R^2 = 0.19$	$R^2 = 0.19$
Repeated Class 1	0.819 (0.271)					
Repeated Class 2		1.199 (0.311)				
Repeated Class 3			1.361** (0.229)			
Repeated Class 4				1.110 (0.178)		
Repeated Class 5					0.618*** (0.105)	
Repeated Class 6						0.561** (0.162)
Female	1.225 (0.197)	1.222 (0.197)	1.242 (0.200)	1.226 (0.197)	1.254 (0.203)	1.233 (0.199)
Urban	0.695 (0.258)	0.696 (0.258)	0.680 (0.254)	0.697 (0.259)	0.676 (0.252)	0.694 (0.258)
Socioeconomic status	1.025 (0.058)	1.027 (0.058)	1.029 (0.059)	1.026 (0.058)	1.025 (0.058)	1.022 (0.058)
Age	2.201*** (0.134)	2.211*** (0.135)	2.208*** (0.135)	2.198*** (0.135)	2.227*** (0.137)	2.205*** (0.134)
Child works	1.231 (0.198)	1.231 (0.198)	1.220 (0.197)	1.228 (0.198)	1.245 (0.201)	1.224 (0.197)
Test score math	0.751*** (0.070)	0.751*** (0.070)	0.750*** (0.070)	0.753*** (0.071)	0.748*** (0.070)	0.756*** (0.071)
Test score grammar	0.829 (0.100)	0.829 (0.100)	0.826 (0.099)	0.829 (0.100)	0.821* (0.099)	0.819* (0.099)
Test score reading	1.138 (0.127)	1.139 (0.127)	1.134 (0.127)	1.143 (0.128)	1.119 (0.126)	1.144 (0.128)
Absence	1.539*** (0.146)	1.546*** (0.147)	1.544*** (0.147)	1.541*** (0.146)	1.541*** (0.147)	1.553*** (0.148)
Transferred	1.027 (0.176)	1.023 (0.172)	1.015 (0.174)	1.022 (0.175)	1.026 (0.176)	1.018 (0.174)

	N = 3,103	N = 3,103	N = 3,103	N = 3,103	N = 3,103	N = 3,103
	$R^2 = 0.18$	$R^2 = 0.18$	$R^2 = 0.19$	$R^2 = 0.18$	$R^2 = 0.19$	$R^2 = 0.19$
Intervention	1.110	1.109	1.122	1.114	1.098	1.113
	(0.172)	(0.172)	(0.174)	(0.173)	(0.171)	(0.173)
P5 at baseline	0.704**	0.711**	0.730*	0.728*	0.808	0.782
	(0.115)	(0.116)	(0.120)	(0.124)	(0.137)	(0.132)

Note: Odds ratios with standard errors in parentheses. R^2 values are pseudo R^2 from logistic regression.
* $p < 0.10$, ** $p < 0.05$, *** $p < 0.01$

Table A.4 Odds ratio from logistic regression on dropout, excluding age

	Dichotomous Variable yes/no repeat		Ordinal Variable no. times repeated	
	N = 3,756	N = 3,085	N = 2,778	N = 2,312
	$R^2 = 0.02$	$R^2 = 0.06$	$R^2 = 0.02$	$R^2 = 0.05$
Repetition yes/no	1.532***	1.518**		
	(0.258)	(0.287)		
Repetition times			1.284***	1.279***
			(0.095)	(0.103)
Female	0.939	0.916	0.915	0.909
	(0.127)	(0.137)	(0.137)	(0.150)
Urban	0.553**	0.771	0.427**	0.672
	(0.166)	(0.272)	(0.170)	(0.288)
Socioeconomic status	0.982	1.036	0.986	1.025
	(0.047)	(0.055)	(0.052)	(0.061)
Child works	1.369***	1.449**	1.565***	1.370*
	(0.230)	(0.219)	(0.238)	(0.230)
Test score math		0.777***		0.825**
		(0.069)		(0.080)
Test score grammar		0.773**		0.819
		(0.088)		(0.104)
Test score reading		1.066		1.019
		(0.113)		(0.120)
Absence		1.640***		1.599***
		(0.143)		(0.157)
Transfer		1.157		1.167
		(0.186)		(0.208)
Intervention		1.069		1.064
		(0.156)		(0.171)
P5 at baseline		1.418**		1.341*
		(0.208)		(0.216)

Note: Standard errors in parenthesis. R^2 values are pseudo R^2 values from logistic regression.
* $p < 0.10$, ** $p < 0.05$, *** $p < 0.01$

Table A.5 Logistic regression predicting dropout from repetition including second hand reports of children's schooling

	Dichotomous Variable yes/no repeat		Ordinal Variable no. times repeated	
	N = 4,202	N = 3,082	N = 3,127	N = 2,310
	R² = 0.15	R² = 0.18	R² = 0.14	R² = 0.18
Female	1.902***	1.251	1.919***	1.217
	(0.215)	(0.200)	(0.063)	(0.218)
Urban	0.541***	0.772	0.397***	0.550
	(0.131)	(0.277)	(0.128)	(0.252)
Socioeconomic status	0.963	1.023	0.979	1.031
	(0.038)	(0.058)	(0.044)	(0.065)
Child works	1.369***	1.244*	1.436***	1.230
	(0.230)	(0.199)	(0.179)	(0.220)
Age	2.089***	2.178***	2.133***	2.294***
	(0.089)	(0.133)	(0.108)	(0.168)
Repetition yes/no	0.881	0.958		
	(0.119)	(0.190)		
Repetition times			0.902	0.886
			(0.063)	(0.084)
Test score math		0.820***		0.789**
		(0.098)		(0.080)
Test score grammar		0.820*		0.858
		(0.098)		(0.114)
Test score reading		1.141		1.105
		(0.127)		(0.140)
Absence		1.533***		1.493***
		(0.145)		(0.158)
Transfer		1.042		1.067
		(0.177)		(0.202)
Intervention		1.101		1.120
		(0.169)		(0.191)
P5 at baseline		0.732**		0.640**
		(0.118)		(0.116)

Note: Standard errors in parenthesis. R^2 values are pseudo R^2 values from logistic regression.
* $p < 0.10$, ** $p < 0.05$, *** $p < 0.01$

As I mention in the main text, I test my hypothesis that age might be a confounding variable in the association between grade repetition and school dropout. In **Table A.4**, I drop age as a coefficient in my equations and see a statistically significant association between repetition and dropout, which supports my hypothesis. Research that does not control for age, accordingly, might be mistakenly identifying an association between repetition and dropout.

And finally, in **Table A.5**, I include secondhand reports of children's schooling status as a robustness check. After rerunning some of my analysis using this additional information and accordingly a larger sample, there were no substantial changes in relation to the main findings on repetition and dropout. As before, it seems that female pupils might be more likely to drop out than males, and that children with lower test scores are more likely to drop out than children with higher test scores.

Private Primary Schools (Chapter 5)

To investigate what might predict transfer to a private school, I use logistic regression to compare students' likelihood of being enrolled in a private school as compared with a government school at the second time point, the endline survey. As I described in Chapter 3, when first surveyed, all students in my sample were originally enrolled in either fourth or fifth grade of a government primary school. The follow up survey was conducted two years later, so my analysis captures transfer to private schools among this cohort of students for this particular point in time.

In **Table A.6**, I report odds ratios from a logistic regression predicting students' transfer to private schools between the original and follow-up surveys. As many children did not

Table A.6 Odds ratios from logistic regression predicting transfer to private schools

	N = 3758	N = 3758	N = 2077	N = 2077	N = 3758	N = 3758
	$R^2 = 0.01$	$R^2 = 0.01$	$R^2 = 0.03$	$R^2 = 0.03$	RVI = 0.04	RVI = 0.05
Female	0.961	0.967	1.051	1.067	0.963	0.969
	(0.107)	(0.107)	(0.155)	(0.157)	(0.107)	(0.107)
Class 4	0.928	0.928	0.917	0.910	0.951	0.951
	(0.111)	(0.108)	(0.144)	(0.142)	(0.114)	(0.114)
Age	0.842***	0.841***	0.825***	0.819***	0.848***	0.847***
	(0.035)	(0.034)	(0.046)	(0.046)	(0.035)	(0.035)
Child's assets	1.078*	1.078*	1.030	1.033	1.069*	1.070*
	(0.044)	(0.044)	(0.056)	(0.057)	(0.044)	(0.044)
Intervention	0.843	0.847	0.839	0.850	0.842	0.846
	(0.092)	(0.092)	(0.122)	(0.123)	(0.092)	(0.093)
Urban	0.808	0.820	0.817	0.865	0.778	0.789
	(0.178)	(0.178)	(0.242)	(0.253)	(0.172)	(0.172)
Math	0.931		0.839*		0.931	
	(0.063)		(0.077)		(0.063)	
Grammar	1.000		1.043		0.997	
	(0.081)		(0.113)		(0.081)	
Reading comprehension	0.890		0.913		0.891	
	(0.069)		(0.095)		(0.069)	
Total mean score		0.854***		0.835**		0.852***
		(0.054)		(0.071)		(0.054)
Class size	1.002*	1.002*	1.002	1.002	1.002*	1.002*
	(0.001)	(0.001)	(0.002)	(0.001)	(0.001)	(0.001)
Mother completed primary			1.043	1.038		
			(0.174)	(0.173)		
Father completed primary			2.032***	2.039***		
			(0.441)	(0.442)		

(continued)

Table A.6 Continued

	N = 3758	N = 3758	N = 2077	N = 2077	N = 3758	N = 3758
	$R^2 = 0.01$	$R^2 = 0.01$	$R^2 = 0.03$	$R^2 = 0.03$	RVI = 0.04	RVI = 0.05
Mother's education imputed					0.957 (0.128)	0.956 (0.128)
Father's education imputed					1.490** (0.248)	1.492** (0.248)

Notes: Standard errors are in parenthesis. R^2 values are pseudo R^2 from logistic regression, RVI.
The third and fourth columns use listwise deletion for the missing data on parents' education; the fifth and sixth use multiple imputation. "Intervention" refers to the randomized controlled trial for which data were originally collected.

* p<0.10, ** p < 0.05, *** p< 0.01

know the education level of their parents, I begin with models that do not include those variables (Columns 1 and 2). When these are included, the sample size decreases significantly. Columns 3 and 4 use listwise deletion for these missing data. In Columns 5 and 6, I use multiple imputation to address the missing data of parents' education level and find similar results.

In **Table A.7** I use multinomial logistic regression to account for children who have dropped out of school and report relative risk ratios. Between the original and follow-up

Table A.7 Relative risk ratios from multinomial logistic regression predicting both transfer to private schools and school dropout

	Model without Parents' Education		Model with Parents' Education	
	N = 3,759		N = 2,078	
	$R^2 = 0.076$		$R^2 = 0.073$	
	Dropout	Private	Dropout	Private
Female	1.214 (0.172)	0.978 (0.109)	1.374* (0.264)	1.086 (0.161)
Class 4	1.554*** (0.229)	0.961 (0.115)	1.646*** (0.327)	0.943 (0.148)
Age	2.214*** (0.124)	0.823*** (0.037)	2.083*** (0.156)	0.856*** (0.049)
Child's assets	1.002 (0.051)	1.079* (0.044)	0.970 (0.069)	1.032 (0.057)

	Model without Parents' Education		Model with Parents' Education	
	N = 3,759		N = 2,078	
	$R^2 = 0.076$		$R^2 = 0.073$	
	Dropout	Private	Dropout	Private
Intervention	1.250	0.856	1.206	0.856
	(0.178)	(0.094)	(0.231)	(0.124)
Urban	0.803	0.824	1.078	0.880
	(0.263)	(0.179)	(0.466)	(0.258)
Class size	1.001	1.002*	1.001	1.002
	(0.001)	(0.001)	(0.002)	(0.001)
Total mean score	0.697***	0.838***	0.731***	0.823**
	(0.061)	(0.054)	(0.086)	(0.070)
Mother completed primary			0.873	1.031
			(0.174)	(0.172)
Father completed primary			0.776	2.010***
			(0.164)	(0.436)

Notes: Reference group is children who remained in public school. Standard errors are in parentheses. R^2 values are pseudo R^2 from logistic regression. "Intervention" refers to the randomized controlled trial for which data were originally collected.

* $p < 0.10$, ** $p < 0.05$, *** $p < 0.01$

survey, 259 children reported that they had dropped out of school. In the dichotomous logistic regression, I am predicting children's transfer to private schools as compared with all other children, grouping together children who dropped out of school with those who remained in public school. In the multinomial logistic regression, dropping out of school is included as an additional outcome, with the comparison group as only the children who remained in public school. Results do not vary significantly between these two different approaches.

A child's age and mean test score appear to predict private school enrollment. As these two odds ratios are each less than one, they indicate that older children and children with a higher mean test score were less likely to have transferred to a private school. The strongest predictor of transfer to private school is father's education level. A child with a father who had completed primary school is 1.5 to 2 times more likely to transfer to a private school than a child whose father had not completed primary school.

In **Table A.8** I report the results of a regression predicting endline test scores. The strongest predictor of endline test scores was a child's baseline test score, followed by location in an urban municipality. For example, children who were originally located in the urban municipality score almost half a standard deviation higher on the grammar section than those located in the rural sub-counties. Across all sections and as a mean score, enrollment in a private school had a statistically significant and positive association with test scores.

Table A.8 Predicting endline test scores

	Mean Score			Math	Grammar	Reading
	N = 3,446	N = 1,912	N = 3,446	N = 3,449	N = 3,449	N = 3,446
	$R^2 = 0.53$	$R^2 = 0.53$	RVI=0.07	RVI=0.05	RVI=0.07	RVI=0.08
Female	−0.062***	−0.105***	−0.061***	−0.198***	0.023***	−0.019
	(0.024)	(0.032)	(0.024)	(0.028)	(0.026)	(0.026)
Class 4	−0.008	0.005	−0.005	0.019	−0.021	−0.007
	(0.025)	(0.034)	(0.025)	(0.030)	(0.027)	(0.028)
Age	−0.092***	−0.096***	−0.092***	−0.041***	−0.101***	−0.093***
	(0.009)	(0.012)	(0.009)	(0.011)	(0.010)	(0.010)
Child's assets	0.030***	0.034***	0.030***	0.009	0.037***	0.031***
	(0.009)	(0.012)	(0.009)	(0.010)	(0.009)	(0.010)
Intervention	0.020	0.076**	0.019	−0.028	0.053**	0.019
	(0.023)	(0.032)	(0.023)	(0.027)	(0.025)	(0.026)
Urban	0.282***	0.294***	0.278***	−0.028	0.451***	0.265***
	(0.043)	(0.061)	(0.043)	(0.051)	(0.047)	(0.047)
Class size	0.001**	0.001	0.001**	0.000	0.001**	0.001**
	(0.000)	(0.000)	(0.000)	(0.000)	(0.000)	(0.000)
Baseline mean score	0.641***	0.640***	0.642***	0.523***	0.592***	0.582***
	(0.013)	(0.018)	(0.013)	(0.016)	(0.025)	(0.015)
Private school	0.106***	0.085*	0.104***	0.140***	0.106***	0.047
	(0.038)	(0.051)	(0.038)	(0.044)	(0.041)	(0.041)
Mother completed primary		−0.043				
		(0.036)				
Father completed primary		0.055***				
		(0.040)				
Mother completed primary Imputed			−0.015	−0.022	−0.007	−0.012
			(0.030)	(0.034)	(0.034)	(0.034)
Father completed primary Imputed			0.041	0.021	0.044	0.037
			(0.034)	(0.040)	(0.036)	(0.038)

Notes: Standard errors are in parenthesis. R^2 values are pseudo R^2 from logistic regression, RVI. "Intervention" refers to the randomized controlled trial for which data were originally collected

School Fees (Chapter 6)

Analytic Plan

Given the unique research design and more complicated analysis in this chapter, I describe my analytic plan and use it to organize my results.

Research Question 1:   Was the cash + parent program's positive impact on test scores moderated by children's socioeconomic status?

I investigate whether the cash + parent intervention's positive impact on test scores was moderated by children's socioeconomic status using two different measures of socioeconomic status: whether or not a child was reported to be working and the basic assets index. As I am interested in the observed effect for just this treatment variation, I drop the other treatment groups in order to focus on the comparison between the cash + parent schools and the control schools. My equation is

$$Test\ Score_{ik} = b_0 + \tau cash\_parent_k + \delta'X_{ik} + \alpha interaction + \zeta_{0k} + \varepsilon_{ik} \qquad 1$$

with $\zeta_{0k} \sim N(0, \sigma_\zeta^2)$ and $\varepsilon_{ik} \sim (0, \sigma_\varepsilon^2)$ representing school level and child level error terms, respectively, and independent of one another; where $cash + parent_k$ represents enrollment in a school that received both the cash and parent programs, and X_{ik} represents a vector containing six covariates (child's gender, age, baseline test score, the assets index, and whether or not the child reported working and whether or not the school in which the child was originally enrolled was considered urban). *Interaction* represents an interaction between cash + parent and either the working covariate or the assets index covariate or both. The intercept is b_0. The k subscript represents schools and the i subscript represents individual children. My multilevel model accounts for the fact that sample children were nested within schools and randomization occurred at the school level.

One major concern for this moderation analysis is that by focusing exclusively on the one treatment variation that exhibited impact, I significantly reduce my sample size. Limited statistical power will, accordingly, be a limitation of my moderation analysis. Using the "Power Up!" power analysis tool for hierarchical linear models put forth by Dong et al. (2016), I calculate my statistical power for moderation analysis. I find that I have statistical power of 0.32 for an effect size of 0.12, indicating that I have a 68 percent probability of a Type II error and will only be able to detect extreme differences in impact between children of high and low socioeconomic status. Given this limited power, I consider my moderation analysis to be exploratory and not resulting in any definitive conclusions.

Research Question 2:   Was the proposed mediation pathway, that the impact of the cash + parent program on test scores was mediated by an increase in scholastic materials, experienced by children of high and low socioeconomic status?

Continuing my work to explore the program's impact on test scores, I turn to my mediation analysis. In the original RCT study, observing an impact on both the presence of scholastic materials in the classroom and test scores, Karlan and Linden (2017) hypothesize that the improvement in test scores was caused by the increase in scholastic materials. I test this theory as a mediation pathway and also whether it was experienced by children of high and low socioeconomic status. As previously stated, I have limited power for any subgroup analysis and, accordingly, consider the moderation of the mediation pathway to be exploratory analysis.

Karlan and Linden (2017) use classroom-level data to observe the increase in scholastic materials. As I am interested in tracing how the intervention affected test scores, I explore the theory that children used their savings to purchase scholastic materials (which would explain the increase of materials in the classroom), which accordingly improved test scores. As I describe in the upcoming measures section, I code any reported educational spending from the endline survey question *What do you **usually** do with **most** of the money that you have saved?* This question applies to all children as whether or not a child saved money did not vary by treatment status (approximately 80 percent of children in both treatment and control schools reported saving some money) - only the use of savings varied by treatment. First, I use logistic regression to determine whether the cash + parent treatment intervention affected children's use of their savings for education. If I find a causal impact on children's savings use, I can then proceed with instrumental variable (IV) analysis.

For my instrumental-variables analysis (Imbens & Rosenbaum, 2005), I use two-stage least squares equations to determine whether the impact on test scores was mediated entirely by children's educational use of savings. The random assignment of the cash + parent treatment variation serves as the instrument. For the first-stage equation, children's savings for educational use is the outcome with the cash_parent treatment assignment as a predictor. In the second-stage equation, I predict mean endline test scores from the predicted values of savings from the first equation question (i.e. based on the estimated impact of the cash_parent intervention on that variable), and utilize the same vector of six covariates, 'X_{ik}. As before, I focus exclusively on the cash + parent treatment group and the control group.

$$Savings\_Use_{ik} = b_0 + b_1 cash\_parent_k + \varepsilon_{ik} \tag{2}$$

$$Test\ Score_{ik} = \gamma_0 + \gamma_1 Savings\_Use_{jk} + \delta'X_i + \upsilon_{ik} \tag{3}$$

I conduct this instrumental variable analysis with four different subgroups: children who worked and those who did not, and children with fewer than two assets and children with two or more assets.

Research Question 3:   Did any variation of the savings program impact children's dropout from school, and, if so, did the impact differ by socioeconomic status?

Finally, I consider an alternate outcome: dropping out of school. For this analysis, I use all treatment variations to test whether any of them affected school dropout.

$$logit(p(y)) = log\left(\frac{p(x)}{1-p^{(x)}}\right) = b_0 + \tau'treatment_k + \delta X_i + \varepsilon_{ik} \tag{4}$$

In this equation, '*treatment$_k$* is a vector of the four different treatment variations and δX_i is the same vector of covariates from previous equations; b_0 is the intercept and ε_i is the error term. I then include interaction terms for working and the assets index, investigating moderation as I did for the mean test score outcome.

$$logit(p(y)) = log\left(\frac{p(x)}{1-p^{(x)}}\right) = b_0 + \tau'treatment_k + \delta X_i + \alpha interaction + \varepsilon_i \tag{5}$$

As I described in the measures section, I repeat this analysis with the second measure of dropout—the larger endline sample, including secondhand reports of children's dropout or schooling. As before, I investigate possible moderation by including interaction terms.

Measures: Chapter 3 includes a complete description of the sample and data, but I repeat and provide some additional details relevant for this specific analysis here. The endline exam serves as the primary outcome. The exam included the same content and number of questions as the baseline exam, but was edited slightly so that children did not take the same exam twice. For example, the baseline exam included the math items 17*3 and 375 + 250; on the endline these questions were edited to 15*2 and 343 + 108. The exams included three sections: basic math, grammar, and reading comprehension. Children who were enrolled in P4 at baseline took the P4-level exam at both baseline and endline, and children who were enrolled in P5 at baseline took the P5-level exam at both baseline and endline. The test score variable I use in my analysis is the number of questions answered correctly averaged across the tests' three sections and normalized. Karlan and Linden (2017) also use this variable for their analysis.

In order to investigate whether the impact on test scores was moderated by children's socioeconomic status, I used two different measures of socioeconomic status: whether a child reported working and an index of basic assets. In the baseline survey, children were asked whether they ever worked to earn money. From this survey response, I created a binary variable to represent answers to this question. At baseline, 42 percent of children reported that they worked to earn money.

For children's basic assets, I create an index from the responses to three different questions from the baseline survey: whether or not the child was wearing shoes and/or school uniform (which were both observed by the enumerator interviewing the child) and whether or not the child reported sleeping on a mattress, (as compared with sleeping on the floor). Summing the responses to these questions created an index variable with values from 0 to 3.

To investigate the mediation pathway, whether test scores improved through the increase in scholastic materials, I create a variable to indicate how children used their savings. In the endline survey, children were asked, "What do you *usually* do with *most* of the money that you have saved?" The question was open-ended and responses were coded into different options. I coded any use related to education as a 1 and any unrelated use as a 0. This results in a binary mediator.

For my third research question, I investigate an alternative outcome: whether or not a child dropped out of school. During the endline survey, children were asked which primary school they were currently attending. If a child responded to this question by saying that they had dropped out of school, they were coded as having dropped out. To conduct a robustness check of this analysis, I use a second measure of dropout: secondhand reports of children's schooling from family, teachers, and neighbors.

As previously mentioned, the endline sample comprises 83 percent of the original baseline sample. Karlan and Linden (2017) analyzed attrition rates and concluded that rates of attrition did not differ across the four treatment groups or the control, and also that, for a range of different measures, there were not any compositional effects due to differential attrition. For this reason, attrition is not a very significant concern for my analyses. I still conduct a robustness check for my analysis of dropout using secondhand reports of children's schooling, as I did in Chapter 5 on grade repetition.

Results

Research Question 1:   Was the cash + parent treatment impact on test scores moderated by children's socioeconomic status?

In **Table A.9**, I report the results of my analysis exploring whether the impact on test scores observed by Karlan and Linden (2017) was moderated by children's socioeconomic status.

Table A.9 Moderation in impact on normalized endline test scores

	N = 2,124	N = 2,124	N = 2,124
Baseline test score	0.621***	0.621***	0.621***
	(0.018)	(0.018)	(0.018)
Female	−0.043	−0.043*	−0.043
	(0.032)	(0.032)	(0.032)
Age	−0.098***	−0.098***	−0.098***
	(0.011)	(0.011)	(0.011)
Urban	0.216***	0.215***	0.216***
	(0.079)	(0.079)	(0.079)
Socioeconomic status index	0.055***	0.057***	0.057***
	(0.019)	(0.022)	(0.022)
Works	−0.063*	−0.069*	−0.062*
	(0.037)	(0.032)	(0.037)
Cash + Parent	0.122**	0.121*	0.134
	(0.061)	(0.077)	(0.085)
Work interaction	−0.025		−0.026
	(0.072)		(0.072)
Assets interaction		−0.008	−0.009
		(0.043)	(0.043)

* p < 0.1, ** p < 0.05, *** p < 0.01

I do not find any evidence to suggest that the impact of the cash + parent treatment intervention was moderated by either a child working or their assets. As previously mentioned, I am underpowered for this analysis and so interpret these results not as definitive conclusions, but as exploration to inform future research.

The interaction term of working and treatment status is negative, which would suggest that the impact of the program might be lower for children who work than for those who do not. The coefficient for the socioeconomic status index interaction, though, is negative, which would indicate that children with more resources experienced less of an improvement in test scores than children with fewer resources. A possible interpretation is that children who already had basic supplies would not benefit from the program simply because they already had the materials which the program would supposedly enable them to buy. In this respect it seems that the program might be more effective for children of lower socioeconomic status, as the practice of savings could enable them to purchase supplies that more affluent children already have. This coefficient is small, about a third the size of the coefficient for the work interaction. Given that the average treatment effect on normalized test scores was 0.11, this effect would be 7 percent higher for children of low socioeconomic status than for those of high socioeconomic status, and 23 percent lower for children who work than for those who do not.

Research Question 2:   Was the proposed mediation pathway (the impact on test scores was mediated by an increase in scholastic materials) experienced by children of high and low socioeconomic status?

Karlan and Linden (2017) hypothesize that the improvement in test scores for the cash + parent intervention was mediated by the increased presence of scholastic materials in the classroom. The savings program and parent outreach combination enabled children and families to purchase basic supplies such as pens and exercise books, which led to the improvement in learning. To test this hypothesis, I first investigate how children used their savings. In the endline survey, children were asked, "What do you *usually* do with *most* of the money that you have saved?" The question was open-ended and all responses were coded into one of nine options. The question was intended to include all savings, not just the money that was included in the program, and could therefore be asked of children in both treatment and control schools. These are illustrated in **Figure A.1**.

From these responses I created a binary variable to reflect whether or not the child used their savings for some education-related purchase. Combining "scholastic materials" and "school fees" into one response results in a binary variable in which 28.07 percent of children spent their savings on education-related expenses and the remaining 71.93 percent of students did not.[1] I then run a logistic regression to see whether children in schools with the cash + parent treatment variation were more likely to spend their savings on education-related expenses than children in control schools.

I report the results of this regression in **Table A.10**. I find that the cash + parent intervention had a positive effect on children's use of savings. Children in schools that received this intervention were 1.9 times more likely to use their savings to make some education-related purchase than children who did not receive the intervention.

Given this result, which indicates a causal impact of the cash + parent intervention on children's use of savings, I move forward with my IV analysis. In my second stage, I regress student test scores outcomes on the predicted values of spending on education from the first-stage equation. Due to the exclusion restriction of instrumental variable analysis, this analytic strategy tests for complete mediation, determining whether the entirety of the impact on test scores was mediated by the purchasing of scholastic materials.

The results of my IV analysis support the hypothesis that the impact of the cash + parent treatment was mediated by the purchasing of scholastic materials (**Table A.11**). In a simple OLS regression predicting endline test scores (not using IV analysis), the coefficient for the use_of_savings variable is 0.261, which indicates that students who spent their savings on some education-related purchased scored 0.261 standard deviations higher on the endline

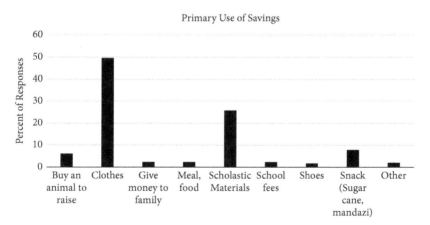

Figure A.1 Reponses to survey question "What do you usually do with most of your savings?"

---

[1] Uniforms were coded as scholastic materials, not as clothes.

Table A.10 Logistic regression predicting use of savings to purchase scholastic materials or school fees from experimental condition, N=1,702, Pseudo R^2 = 0.16

Baseline test score	1.230***
	(0.079)
Female	0.937
	(0.111)
Age	0.973
	(0.038)
Urban	1.270
	(0.258)
Socioeconomic index	0.959
	(0.068)
Works	0.702***
	(0.086)
Cash + Parent	1.891***
	(0.236)

* $p < 0.1$, ** $p < 0.05$, *** $p < 0.01$

Table A.11 Estimated effect of the use of savings on endline test scores

	(1)	(2)	(3)	(4)	(5)	(6)
	OLS	IV	IV	IV	IV	IV
		Total sample	Few assets	Many assets	Working	Not working
Coefficient	0.261***	0.919***	0.826*	0.932*	0.706*	1.251*
	(0.037)	(0.347)	(0.479)	(0.491)	(0.382)	(0.696)
F		206.31	95.76	89.46	84.51	124.73
R^2		0.41	0.34	0.46	0.37	0.34
N		1,662	1,037	625	760	902

* $p < 0.1$, ** $p < 0.05$, *** $p < 0.01$.
Controlling for age, baseline test scores, gender, socioeconomic status, urban, working

exam than those who did not use their savings for education-related purchases (for example, buying a chicken to raise or extra clothes). In the results of the second-stage equation for the IV analysis, the coefficient on use_of_savings was 0.919, which indicates that the test scores of students who used their savings to pay for education-related expenses as a result of receiving the cash + parent treatment intervention were higher than students in the control group by 0.919 standard deviations.

I conduct this same IV analysis among various subsamples to answer my second research question: whether the mediation pathway was experienced by children of varying socioeconomic status. I divide the sample into children of few (0–1) assets and many assets (2–3) and children who work and those who do not, aiming to investigate whether the mediation is present for all groups of children.

I find that, across all of my subgroups, there is a significant effect of the cash + parent treatment intervention through children's use of savings on mean test scores. This finding supports both the mediation hypothesis concerning how the program worked and also the findings of my moderation analysis that the program did not seem to privilege children of high or low socioeconomic status. Both the main impact on test scores and the mediation pathway seem to have been experienced equally by children who worked and those who did not, and by children with different assets.

The largest coefficient is for the subgroup of children who reported during the baseline that they were not working to earn any money. At 1.251, this coefficient is almost double the coefficient for children who reported that they were working, 0.706. Although both of these coefficients are positive, statistically significant, and large in achievement test units, this suggests that the program worked best for children who were not working. Children who did not work experienced an improvement in test scores as a result of the savings program almost twice as large as those children who reported working.

Research Question 3:   Did any variation of the savings program affect children's dropout from school, and, if so, did that impact vary by socioeconomic status?

In the two years between baseline and endline, 254 children reported that they had dropped out of school, representing 6.62 percent of the endline sample. Using logistic regression to predict dropout, I find that the cash savings variation without the parent intervention increased the likelihood that a child would drop out of school. Children in schools that received the cash program without the parent intervention were 1.47 times more likely to drop out of school than children in control schools (**Table A.12**). No other treatment variation had a statistically significant associated with dropout, and all other coefficients were also smaller in magnitude.

To see whether the impact of the cash w/o parent treatment intervention was moderated by children's socioeconomic status, I include interaction terms between the cash w/o parent term and a child's working and basic assets. As before, when investigating the interaction, I drop the other treatment variations so as to focus on the observed impact, but this time I am focused on a different treatment group and keep the cash w/o parent group to compare with the control group.

The coefficient on work as a main effect is statistically significant, which indicates that children who reported working to earn money in the baseline survey were 1.3 times more likely to drop out than children who did not. In the presence of either interaction (assets or work), the coefficient on the work variable is not statistically significant, which indicates that for different comparison groups (children who worked vs. those who did not and children with no assets vs. children with some assets) the association between work and dropout might differ. Coefficients on the working interaction are greater than one, which suggests that children who work were more likely to drop out as a result of the intervention than children who did not work (**Table A.12**). Conversely, coefficients on the socioeconomic status interaction are less than one, which indicates that children with more assets are less likely to drop out as a result of the intervention than children with fewer assets. None of the coefficients is statistically significant, likely due to the limited statistical power of this secondary analysis.

Statistical power is an important concern for my moderation analysis of both test scores and dropout. Comparing the results of these two outcomes highlights some differences. As previously reported, the coefficients for interaction terms in the test score models (Table A.9) are both low in magnitude and not significant. For example, the coefficient on the assets interaction term in the test score model is 0.0085 with a p value of 0.898. In the dropout

Table A.12 Odds ratios from logistic regression on dropout

N = 3,799		N = 2,151	N = 2,151	N = 2,151
Pseudo R^2 = 0.16		= 0.153	=0.154	=0.154
Baseline test score	0.714***	0.786**	0.790**	0.788**
	(0.063)	(0.091)	(0.091)	(0.091)
Female	1.317*	1.293	1.288	1.289
	(0.190)	(0.251)	(0.250)	(0.250)
Age	2.123***	2.046***	2.057***	2.053***
	(0.114)	(0.138)	(0.140)	(0.139)
Urban	0.932	1.009	1.009	1.003
	(0.309)	(0.421)	(0.421)	(0.418)
Asset index	0.940	0.942	0.910	0.936
	(0.082)	(0.129)	(0.104)	(0.128)
Works	1.335**	1.320	1.188	1.195
	(0.194)	(0.254)	(0.274)	(0.276)
Cash + Parent	1.239			
	(0.269)			
Cash w/o Parent	1.466**	1.633	1.229	1.368
	(0.292)	(0.547)	(0.361)	(0.558)
Voucher + Parent	1.100			
	(0.240)			
Voucher w/o Parent	1.254			
	(0.254)			
Interaction assets		0.905		0.914
		(0.213)		(0.217)
Interaction work			1.372	1.361
			(0.546)	(0.543)

* p < 0.1, ** p < 0.05, *** p < 0.01

models (**Table A.12**), the coefficients on the basic asset interaction are also relatively small in magnitude and statistically insignificant. The coefficient on the work interaction, though, is somewhat larger, an odds ratio of 1.37, and has a smaller p value of 0.427, suggesting that a child's working is a more relevant concern than the assets index.

As a robustness check, I use the same analytic technique I used in Chapter 5 on grade repetition. I conduct my analysis of dropout including the secondhand reports of children's schooling (cf. Chapter 4). Findings are very similar (**Table A.13**). The cash without parent treatment intervention led to an increase in school dropout. No other treatment variation appeared to affect dropout. The most notable difference emerging from this new analysis appears to be related to gender. When these additional data are included, female pupils appear far more likely to drop out of school. Though rates of attrition and the composition of attrition across treatment groups were statistically equal, it is likely that attrition from the study and school dropout are related. Missing data might, accordingly, be masking important variation. The addition of these secondhand reports draws attention to the issue of gender.

In relation to the research questions of the present study, with the inclusion of secondhand reports, the coefficient on the cash w/o parent treatment indicator increased from 1.466 to 1.511, and the coefficient on the work interaction term increased from 1.37 to 1.56. With this

Table A.13 Odds ratios from logistic regression on dropout using additional data on dropout

N = 4,255		N = 2,425	N = 2,425	N = 2,425
Pseudo R^2 = 0.16		= 0.171	=0.172	=0.172
Baseline test score	0.666***	0.723***	0.726**	0.725***
	(0.046)	(0.065)	(0.065)	(0.065)
Female	1.917***	1.989***	1.988***	1.989***
	(0.219)	(0.298)	(0.298)	(0.299)
Age	2.062***	2.101***	2.112***	2.109***
	(0.087)	(0.116)	(0.116)	(0.116)
Urban	0.905	0.713	0.716	0.710
	(0.234)	(0.252)	(0.253)	(0.251)
Asset index	0.972	1.066	1.020	1.055
	(0.066)	(0.113)	(0.091)	(0.112)
Works	1.285**	1.285*	1.119	1.127
	(0.144)	(0.187)	(0.194)	(0.196)
Cash + Parent	1.128			
	(0.190)			
Cash w/o Parent	1.511***	1.766**	1.197	1.381
	(0.230)	(0.480)	(0.265)	(0.451)
Voucher + Parent	1.087			
	(0.179)			
Voucher w/o Parent	0.905			
	(0.234)			
Interaction assets		0.875		0.895
		(0.162)		(0.168)
Interaction work			1.557	1.533
			(0.477)	(0.471)

* $p < 0.1$, ** $p < 0.05$, *** $p < 0.01$

larger sample of children, the p value of the coefficient on the interaction term also decreased from 0.427 to 0.148.

To help interpret these differences, I provide the number of children who reported that they had dropped of school for all experimental conditions, with both the traditional sample and the extended sample that includes secondhand reports of children's schooling status. This information is reported in **Table A.14**. As a quick reminder, the control group was the largest, with fifty-eight schools; each treatment variation included thirty-nine schools. For this reason, it is helpful to look at the rates of dropout, not just the raw numbers.

To illustrate the interaction, for the cash only and control treatment groups, I further divide children's reports of dropout by whether or not children reported working at baseline, as illustrated in **Table A.15**.

These tables give a sense of the magnitude of the effects of my interaction analysis. Children who reported during the baseline that they were working to earn money were more likely to drop out of school than the children who were not working. In the control group, the difference in dropout rate between children who worked and who did not work was about 2–3 percent.

Table A.14 Dropouts by experimental condition

Experimental Condition	Traditional Sample		Including Secondhand Reports	
	Number of children who dropped out	Percentage of total children	Number of children who dropped out	Percentage of total children
Cash	46	8.50%	84	13.64%
Cash + parent	35	6.43%	61	10.13%
Voucher	42	7.22%	61	9.47%
Voucher + parent	33	6.09%	63	10.41%
Control	98	6.02%	184	10.05%
Total	254	6.62%	453	10.54%

Table A.15 Dropouts by experimental condition and child work

Experimental Condition	Work	Traditional Sample		Including Secondhand Reports	
		Number of children who dropped out	Percentage of total children	Number of children who dropped out	Percentage of total children
Cash	No	20	6.37%	37	10.36%
Cash	Yes	25	11.31%	46	18.18%
Control	No	43	4.74%	89	8.69%
Control	Yes	55	7.66%	95	11.86%

In the cash only treatment group, the difference in dropout rate between children who worked and children who did not work was about 5–8 percent.

To further investigate the impact of the cash only savings program on dropout, I consider the same mediator that I used in my analysis of the positive effects of the cash + parent program: children's use of their savings. If a child's work is a key predictor of dropout, and other research on youth savings programs has found that these programs can increase child labor (Berry, Karlan, & Pradhan, 2016), I wonder whether children in the cash only treatment group might have used the money they had saved for work activities, which might possibly have drawn them out of the classroom. Of the nine responses to the question, *What do you usually do with most of your savings?* it seems that "buy an animal to raise" is the clearest example of an income-generating activity. In these communities, children will often purchase chicks or a goat in order to raise and then later sell. It is a relatively common economic activity for young people. Overall, 6.15 percent of children in the endline sample who said that they had saved money reported that the primary use of their savings was to buy an animal to raise.

Using logistic regression to predict whether or not a child used their savings primary to buy an animal to raise, I find that none of the cash only, voucher only, or voucher + parent treatments had a statistically significant association with buying an animal to raise. The cash + parent treatment group, however, seemed to reduce the number of children who used their savings in this way. Children in the cash + parent treatment group were half as likely as children in the control group to use their savings to purchase an animal to raise ($p = 0.019$).

Table A.16 The distribution of children's responses to the question, *What do you usually do with most of your savings?* by treatment group (in percentage points)

Primary Use of Savings	Cash + parent	Cash	Voucher + parent	Voucher	Control
Buy an animal to raise	**3.72**	**6.94**	5.62	5.39	7.15
Scholastic materials	**30.70**	**28.47**	48.54	30.56	19.43
School fees	**3.49**	**2.08**	1.35	2.47	1.71
Clothes	43.26	43.75	48.54	48.54	55.48
Give money to family	2.09	1.85	1.12	2.70	2.87
Meal, food	1.63	3.94	1.57	1.80	2.02
Shoes	2.09	2.08	1.35	0.90	1.48
Snack	10.47	9.03	5.84	6.52	8.16

My previous mediation analysis supports the hypothesis that the improvement in children's test scores was mediated by their use of their savings to purchase scholastic materials and pay school fees; my analysis of dropout seems to suggest that what the cash + parent treatment did was to inspire a key group of children to use their money to purchase scholastic materials and pay school fees who otherwise would have used their savings to buy an animal to raise. The difference in primary use of savings between the cash + parent treatment group and all other treatment groups appears to be the percentage of children who buy an animal to raise, as opposed to purchasing scholastic materials. I summarize how children respond to the question *What do you usually do with most of your savings?* by treatment group in **Table A.16**. I highlight in a box in the upper left corner a key set of comparisons, showing that in the cash only treatment group, the percentage of children who used their savings to buy an animal to raise is double that of the cash + parent treatment group. In that treatment, those children seemed to have purchased scholastic materials and paid school fees. As noted throughout, a key concern for all of this analysis is limited statistical power. But as an exploration into how school fees and in particular the purchasing of scholastic materials might relate to themes of access and quality, this work suggests that there can be ways to improve quality without undermining access.

References

Adams, A., & van der Gaag, A. (2010). *Where is the Learning? Measuring Schooling Efforts in Developing Countries*. Brookings, https://www.brookings.edu/research/where-is-the-learning-measuring-schooling-efforts-in-developing-countries/, accessed February 20, 2021.

Africa Progress Panel. (2012). *Africa Progress Report 2012: Jobs, Justice and Equity*, https://reliefweb.int/sites/reliefweb.int/files/resources/00031701-14b51160c4c3c4a100e8a69324d-aca79.pdf.

Ahimbisibwe, P. (2019). "Poor Funding Killing UPE: Report," *Daily Monitor* (October 15, 2019), https://www.monitor.co.ug/uganda/news/national/poor-funding-killing-upe-report-1855458.

Akaguri, L. (2014). "Fee-Free Public or Low-Fee Private Basic Education in Rural Ghana: How Does the Cost Influence the Choice of the Poor?," *Compare: A Journal of Comparative and International Education*, 44(2): 140–61.

Akmal, M., Crawfurd, L., Hares, S. (2019). *Low-Cost Private Schools: What Have We Learned in the Five Years Since the DFID Rigorous Review*. Center for Global Development. Retrieved from: https://www.cgdev.org/blog/low-cost-private-schools-what-have-we-learned-five-years-dfid-rigorous-review.

Alcott, B., & Rose, P. (2016). "Does Private Schooling Narrow Wealth Inequalities in Learning Outcomes? Evidence from East Africa," *Oxford Review of Education*, 42: 495–510.

Alesina, A., Devleeschauwer, A., Easterly, W., Kurlat, S., & Wacziarg, R. (2003). "Fractionalization," *Journal of Economic Growth*, 8(2): 155–94.

Alexander, K., Entwisle, D., & Dauber, S. (2003). *On the Success of Failure: A Reassessment of the Effects of Retention in the Primary Grades*. Cambridge: Cambridge University Press.

Al-Samarrai, S. (2003). *Financing Primary Education for All: Public Expenditure and Education Outcomes in Africa*. Brighton, United Kingdom: Institute of Development Studies, University of Sussex.

Amakyi, M., & Ampah-Mensah, A. (2016). "Dilemma of Access and Provision of Quality Basic Education in Central Region," *Ghana Journal of Education and Practice*, 7(11): 61–5, https://files.eric.ed.gov/fulltext/EJ1099489.pdf, accessed February 19, 2021.

Amoussouga, F. G., Cuenin, S., & Rakotomalala, R. (2002). "Le system educatif Béninois: Performance et espaces d'amélioration pour la politique educative," in *Africa Region Human Development Series*. Washington, DC: World Bank.

Analysis. (2017). In *Merriam-Webster.com*. Retrieved April 19, 2017 from: https://www.merriam-webster.com/dictionary/analysis.

Anderson, G., Jimerson, S., & Whipple, A. (2005). "Student Ratings of Stressful Experiences at Home and School," *Journal of Applied School Psychology*, 21(1): 1–20.

Andrabi, T., Das, J., & Khwaja, A. I. (2008). "A Dime a Day: The Possibilities and Limits of Private Schooling in Pakistan," *Comparative Education Review*, 52(3): 329–55.

ASER. (2013). *Annual Status of Education Report (ASER) (Rural) 2012*. New Delhi: ASER Centre, http://img.asercentre.org/docs/Publications/ASER%20Reports/ASER_2012/fullaser2012report.pdf, accessed February 22, 2021.

Aslam, M. (2009). "The Relative Effectiveness of Government and Private Schools in Pakistan: Are Girls Worse Off?," *Education Economics*, 17(3): 329–54.

Avenstrup, R., Liang, X., & Nellemann, S. (2004). *Kenya, Lesotho, Malawi and Uganda: Universal Primary Education and Poverty Reduction.* Washington, DC: World Bank, http://documents1.worldbank.org/curated/en/126191468779365715/pdf/307650East0Afr10ed01see0also0307591.pdf.

Baird, S., McIntosh, C., & Özler, B. (2011). "Cash or Condition? Evidence from a Cash Transfer Experiment," *The Quarterly Journal of Economics*, 126(4): 1709–53.

Baker, E. L., Barton, P.E., Darling-Hammond, L., Haertel, E., Ladd, H. F., Linn, R. L., Ravitch, D., Rothstein, R., Shavelson, R. J., & Shepard, L. A. (2010). *Problems with the Use of Student Test Scores to Evaluate Teachers*, Economic Policy Institute Briefing Paper 278. Washington, DC: Economic Policy Institute (EPI).

Banerjee, A., Banerji, R., Berry, J., Duflo, E., Kannan, H., Mukherji, S., Shotland, M., & Walton, M. (2016). *Mainstreaming an Effective Intervention: Evidence from Randomized Evaluations of "Teaching at the Right Level" in India*, Working Paper 22746. Cambridge, Massachusetts : National Bureau of Economic Research.

Banerjee, A. & Duflo, E. (2011). "Why Aren't Children Learning." *Development Outreach*, https://openknowledge.worldbank.org/handle/10986/6100, accessed February 19, 2021.

Banerji, R., Bhattacharjea, S., & Wadhwa, W. (2013). "The Annual Status of Education Report (ASER)," *Research in Comparative and International Education*, 8(3): 387–96, https://journals.sagepub.com/doi/pdf/10.2304/rcie.2013.8.3.387, accessed February 19, 2021.

Barber, M. (2015). '"Forward" to Tooley, James and David Longfield, 2015,' in *The Role and Impact of Private Schools in Developing Countries: A Response to the DFID-Commissioned 'Rigorous Literature Review'*. London: Pearson. https://research.pearson.com/content/plc/prkc/uk/open-ideas/en/articles/role-and-impact-of-private-schools/_jcr_content/par/articledownloadcompo/file.res/150330_Tooley_Longfield.pdf.

Barder, O. (2012). *The Implications of Complexity for Development.* Center for Global Development, https://www.cgdev.org/media/implications-complexity-development-owen-barder.

Bategeka, L. & Okurut, N. (2006). *Universal Primary Education: Uganda.* Overseas Development Institute (Policy Brief No. 10).

Baum, D. R., & Riley, I. (2019). "The Relative Effectiveness of Private and Public Schools: Evidence from Kenya," *School Effectiveness and School Improvement*, 30(2): 104–30.

Beatty, A. (2015). In J. Sandefur & Mari Oye, eds. (2015, June 16). RISE: A call to arms for education researchers. Center for Global Development. Oxford, UK: Research on Improving Systems of Education (RISE), https://riseprogramme.org/node/191.

Behrman, J. R., Parker, S. W., & Todd, P. E. (2011). "Do Conditional Cash Transfers for Schooling Generate Lasting Benefits? A Five-Year Followup of PROGRESA/Oportunidades," *Journal of Human Resources*, 46(1): 93–122.

Bekunda C. and Walubiri, M. (2011). "Ministry to Look into Teacher's Salaries," *New Vision* (July 19, 2011), https://www.newvision.co.ug/new_vision/news/1008005/ministry-look-teachers-eur-salaries.

Berete, H., Diawara, B., Sow, S., Yattara, A. S., Amelewonou, K., Brossard, M., et al. (2005). Le système educatif Guinéen: Diagnostic et persepctives pour la politique educative dans un contexte de contraintes macro-économiques fortes et de réduction de la pauvreté. *Africa Region Human Development Working Paper Series.* Washington, DC: World Bank.

Bernal, P., Mittag, N., & Qureshi, J. A. (2016). "Estimating Effects of School Quality Using Multiple Proxies," *Labour Economics*, 39: 1–10.

Berry, J., Karlan, D., & Pradhan, M. (2018). "The Impact of Financial Education for Youth in Ghana." *World Development*, 102: 71–89.

Bertoncino, C., Murphy, P., & Wang, L. (2002). *Achieving Universal Primary Education in Uganda : The 'Big Bang' Approach. Education Notes.* Washington, DC: World Bank. https://openknowledge.worldbank.org/handle/10986/10412.

Bernard, J-M., Simon, O., and Vianou, K. (2005). *Le Redoublement: Mirage de l'école africaine?* Dakar, Senegal: Programme d'annalyse des systemes éducatifs de la CONFEMEN.

Berry, C., Barnett, E., & Hinton, R. (2015). "What Does Learning for All Mean for DFID's Global Education Work?" *International Journal of Educational Development*, 40: 323–9.

Bertoncino, C, Murphy, P, & Wang, L. (2002). *Achieving Universal Primary Education in Uganda: The "Big Bang" Approach*, Education Notes. Washington, DC: World Bank.

Birdsall, N. (2013). "Preface," in L. Pritchett, *The Rebirth of Education: Schooling Ain't Learning*, xi. Washington, DC: Brookings Institution Press CGD Books.

Biryabarema, Elias. (2013). "Ugandan Teachers Go on Strike to Demand 20 Percent Pay Rise," *Reuters* (September 16, 2013), https://www.reuters.com/article/uganda-strike/ugandan-teachers-go-on-strike-to-demand-20-percent-pay-rise-idUSL5N0HC17L20130916, accessed February 19, 2021.

Bold, T., Kimenyi M., Mwabu G., & Sandefur J. (2010). *Does Abolishing Fees Reduce School Quality? Evidence from Kenya*, CSAE Working Paper WPS/2011–04. Oxford, UK: Center for the Study of African Economies (CSAE).

Brinkerhoff, D. W. (2004). "The Enabling Environment for Implementing the Millennium Development Goals: Government Actions to Support NGOs." Paper Presented at. George Washington University Conference: "The Role of NGOs in Implementing the Millennium Development Goals," Washington, DC, May 12–13, 2004, https://citeseerx.ist.psu.edu/viewdoc/download?doi=10.1.1.465.4500&rep=rep1&type=pdf, accessed February 19, 2021.

Brophy, J. (2006). *Grade Repetition*. Retrieved from: http://unesdoc.unesco.org/images/0015/001520/152038e.pdf.

Bundy, D., Burbano, C., Grosh, M., Gelli, A., Jukes, M., & Drake, L. (2009). *Rethinking School Feeding: Social Safety Nets, Child Development, and the Education Sector*. Washington, DC: World Bank.

Businge, C. (2007). *"Automatic Promotion: Quality or Numbers" New Vision*. Kampala, Uganda. Retrieved from: https://allafrica.com/stories/200711280062.html.

Caucutt, E. M., & Kumar, K. B. (2007). "Education for All. A Welfare-Improving Course for Africa?," *Review of Economic Dynamics*, 10(2): 294–326.

Chan, S. (2001). "Complex Adaptive Systems," ESD.83 Research Seminar in Engineering Systems, http://web.mit.edu/esd.83/www/notebook/Complex%20Adaptive%20Systems.pdf, accessed February 19, 2021.

Chapman, C., Laird, J., & Kewal Ramani, A. (2010). *Trends in High School Dropout and Completion Rates in the United States: 1972–2008*. Compendium Report. NCES 2011–012. Washington, DC: National Center for Education Statistics.

Chetty, R. Friedman, J., & Rockoff, J. (2014). "Measuring the Impacts of Teachers I: Evaluating Bias in Teacher Value-Added Estimates," *American Economic Review*, 104(9): 2593–632. doi: 10.1257/aer.104.9.2593.

Chohan, B. I., & Qadir, S. A. (2011). "Automatic Promotion Policy at Primary Level and MDG-2," *Journal of Research and Reflections in Education*, 5(1): 1–20.

Chudgar, A., & Quin, E. (2012). "Relationship between Private Schooling and Achievement: Results from Rural and Urban India," *Economics of Education Review*, 31(4): 376–90.

CIA. (2016). *World Factbook: Uganda*. Retrieved from: https://www.cia.gov/the-world-factbook/countries/uganda/#geography.

Clinton, W. (1998). *Address Before a Joint Session of the Congress on the State of the Union*. Government Publishing Office. Retrieved from: https://www.govinfo.gov/content/pkg/WCPD-1998-02-02/html/WCPD-1998-02-02-Pg129-2.htm.

Colclough, C., Kingdon, G., & Patrinos, H. (2009). *The Pattern of Returns to Education and Its Implications*. RECOUP Policy Brief, 4. Cambridge: University of Cambridge, Faculty of Education, Research Consortium on Educational Outcomes and Poverty (RECOUP). https://nbn-resolving.org/urn:nbn:de:0168-ssoar-69182, accessed February 19, 2021.

Commission of Inquiry (Mismanagement of Funds under Universal Primary Education (UPE) and Universal Secondary Education (USE)). (2012, August). Justice Ezekiel Muhanguzi – Chairperson, Dr. Rose Nassali Lukwago - Deputy Chairperson, Eng. Patrick Batumbya – Member, Prof. Lawrence Mukiibi – Member. Kampala, Uganda: Commission of Inquiry.

Corbin, J., & Strauss, A. (2012). "Strategies for Qualitative Data Analysis," in *Basics of Qualitative Research. Techniques and Procedures for Developing Grounded Theory*. 3rd ed. SAGE Publications.

Crouch, L., Olefir, A., Saeki, H. et al. (2020). "Déjà vu all over again? Recent evidence on early childhood and early grade repetition in developing countries," *Prospects*: 1–8. doi: 10.1007/s11125-020-09473-2.

Datta, S., & Kingdon, G. G. (2019). Gender Bias in Intra-Household Allocation of Education in India: Has It Fallen over Time? (No. 12671). IZA Discussion Papers.

Davidson, M., & Hobbs, J. (2013). "Delivering Reading Intervention to the Poorest Children: The Case of Liberia and EGRA-Plus, a Primary Grade Reading Assessment and Intervention," *International Journal of Educational Development*, 33(3): 283–93.

Davis, B., and Sumara, D. (2006). *Complexity and Education: Inquiries into Learning, Teaching, and Research*. Mahwah, NJ: Lawrence Erlbaum Associates.

Day Ashley, L., Mcloughlin, C., Aslam, M., Engel, J., Wales, J., Rawal, S., Batley, R., Kingdon, G., Nicolai, S., Rose, P. (2014). *The Role and Impact of Private Schools in Developing Countries: A Rigorous Review of the Evidence. Final Report. Education Rigorous Literature Review*. Department for International Development.

Deininger K. (2003). "Does Cost of Schooling Affect Enrollment by the Poor? Universal Primary Education in Uganda," *Economics of Education Review*, 22 (3): 291–305.

Desai, S., Dubey, A., Vanneman, R., & Banerji, R. (2008). Private Schooling in India: A New Educational Landscape. In *India Policy Forum (Vol. 5, No. 1, pp. 1-58). Global Economy and Development Program*. The Brookings Institution.

Descartes, René. (1637). "Discourse on Method" in *Discourse on Method and Related Writings*, 16(AT VI 20).

DeStefano, J. (2012). Opportunity to learn. *EQUIP2: Educational Policy, Systems*. Quoting Adelman, Schuh Moore and Shanti, (2011) referenced pg. 2. https://www.epdc.org/sites/default/files/documents/EQUIP2%20OTL%20Book.pdf?

Detroit Regional Workforce Fund. (2011). *Addressing Detroit's Basic Skills Crisis*. Detroit Regional Workforce Fund. Retrieved from: https://skilledwork.org/wp-content/uploads/2014/01/BasicSkillsReport.pdf.

DFID (Department for International Development). (2013). *Education Position Paper: Improving Learning, Expanding Opportunities*. London, UK: DFID https://assets.publishing.service.gov.uk/government/uploads/system/uploads/attachment_data/file/225715/Education_Position_Paper_July_2013.pdf, accessed February 19, 2021.

Dong, N., Kelcey, B., Spybrook, J., & Maynard, R. A. (2016). PowerUp!—Moderator: A tool for calculating statistical power and minimum detectable effect size of the moderator effects in cluster randomized trials (Version 1.07), http://www.causalevaluation.org, accessed February 19, 2021.

Dorit, R. L. (2011). "Marginalia: The Humpty-Dumpty Problem," *American Scientist*, 99(4): 293–5.

Duraisamy, P., James, E., Lane, J I., and Tan, J. (1997). "Is There a Quantity-Quality Tradeoff as Enrollments Increase? Evidence from Tamil Nadu, India. World Bank, https://ssrn.com/abstract=604926, accessed February 19, 2021.

Eberhard, D. M., Simons, G. F., & Fennig, C. D. (eds.). (2017). *Ethnologue: Languages of the World*. Twenty-fourth edition. Dallas, Texas: SIL International, http://www.ethnologue.com.

Education for All: Fast-Track Initiative. (2007). "Removing Barriers to Accessing Quality Basic Education." Draft. Summary Report of an Online Discussion Held January 16–February 2, 2007, https://inee.org/system/files/resources/e2-SF-SummaryOnlineDiscussion.pdf, accessed February 19, 2021.

Education Policy and Data Center. (2012). *Uganda Core USAID Education Profile.* FHI 360. Washington, DC: Education Policy and Data Center.

Education Population and Data Center. (2010). "Tanzania Data Profile." FHI 360, https://www.epdc.org/sites/default/files/documents/Tanzania_coreusaid.pdf, accessed February 19, 2021.

Eide, E. & Showaler, M. (2001). "The Effect of Grade Retention on Educational and Labor Market Outcomes," *Economics of Education Review*, 20(6): 563–76.

Eisemon, T. O. (1997). *Reducing Repetition: Issues and Strategies.* Paris: UNESCO IIEP.

Eremu, J. (2003). "Can Automatic Promotion Work?," *The New Vision.* Retrieved from: https://www.newvision.co.ug/new_vision/news/1255034/automatic-promotion.

Eurydice. (2011). *Grade Retention during Compulsory Education in Europe: Regulations and Statistics.* Brussels: European Commission.

Evans, D., Kremer, M., & Ngatia, M. (2008). *The Impact of Distributing School Uniforms on Children's Education in Kenya.* World Bank.

Feierman, S. (1985). "Struggles for Control: The Social Roots of Health and Healing in Modern Africa," *African Studies Review*, 28 (2/3): 73–147.

Ferguson, J. (1990). *The Anti-Politics Machine: 'Development', Depoliticization and Bureaucratic Power in Lesotho.* CUP Archive.

Filmer, D., Rogers, H., Angrist, N., & Sabarwal, S. (2020). "Learning-Adjusted Years of Schooling (LAYS): Defining a New Macro Measure of Education," *Economics of Education Review*, 77: 101971.

Franks N. R. (1989). "Army Ants: A Collective Intelligence," *American Scientist* 77: 139–45.

French, R., & Kingdon, G. (2010). *The Relative Effectiveness of Private and Government Schools in Rural India: Evidence from ASER Data.* London: Institute of Education.

Ganimian, A. J., & Murnane, R. J. (2016). "Improving Education in Developing Countries: Lessons from Rigorous Impact Evaluations," *Review of Educational Research*, 86(3): 719–55.

Ghana Information Service. (1960). P. 10 found in Tettey, W. J., Puplampu, K. P., & Berman, B. J. (Eds.). (2003). *Critical Perspectives in Politics and Socio-Economic Development in Ghana* (Vol. 6). Brill.

Glewwe, P., Kremer, M., & Moulin, S. (2009). "Many Children Left Behind? Textbooks and Test Scores in Kenya," *American Economic Journal: Applied Economics*, 1(1): 112–35.

Glewwe, P., & Muralidharan, K. (2016). "Improving Education Outcomes in Developing Countries: Evidence, Knowledge Gaps, and Policy Implications," in E. A. Hanushek, S. J. Machin, & L. Woessmann, eds., *Handbook of the Economics of Education*, vol. 5, 653–743. Elsevier.

Glick, P., & Sahn, D. (2010). "Early Academic Performance, Grade Repetition, and School Attainment in Senegal" *World Bank Economic Review*, 24: 93–120.

Goodpaster, G. (2011). *Business Enabling Environment Measure Plus: Indonesia.* Business Growth Initiative. USAID Office of Economic Growth. EEM-C-00-06-00022-00, C:\Users\DMW\Downloads\business_enabling_environment_indonesia_-_usaid:2011.pdf, accessed February 19, 2021.

Gomes-Neto, J. B., & Hanushek, E. A. (1994). "Causes and Consequences of Grade Repetition: Evidence from Brazil," *Economic Development and Cultural Change*, 43(1): 117–48.

Goyal, S. (2009). "Inside the House of Learning: The Relative Performance of Public and Private Schools in Orissa," *Education Economics*, 17(3): 315–27.

Goyal, S., & Pandey, P. (2012). "How Do Government and Private Schools Differ?," *Economic and Political Weekly*: 67–76.

Goyal, S., & Pandey, P. (2013). "Contract Teachers in India," *Education Economics*, 21(5), 464–84.

GPE (Global Partnership for Education) Secretariat. (2014). "Final Pledge Report Second Replenishment Pledging Conference," https://www.globalpartnership.org/sites/default/files/2014-07-GPE-Replenishment-Pledge-Report.pdf, accessed February 22, 2021.

Green, E. C., Halperin, D. T., Nantulya, V., & Hogle, J. A. (2006). "Uganda's HIV Prevention Success: The Role of Sexual Behavior Change and the National Response," *AIDS and Behavior*, 10(4), 335–46. doi: 10.1007/s10461-006-9073-y.

Green, A. (2016). "Uganda Discovered the Zika Virus. And the Solution for It." *Foreign Policy*. https://foreignpolicy.com/2016/02/10/uganda-discovered-the-zika-virus-and-the-solution-for-it/.

Hanson, H. E. (2010). Indigenous Adaptation: Uganda's Village Schools, ca. 1880–1937. *Comparative Education Review*, 54(2): 155–74.

Hanushek, E. A. (2003). "The Failure of Input-Based Schooling Policies," *The Economic Journal*, 113(485): F64–F98.

Hardesty, L. (2010). "Explained: Linear and Nonlinear Systems," *MIT News* (February 26, 2010), http://news.mit.edu/2010/explained-linear-0226, accessed February 19, 2021.

Harding, R., & Stasavage, D. (2014). "What Democracy Does (and Doesn't Do) for Basic Services: School Fees, School Inputs, and African Elections," *The Journal of Politics*, 76(1): 229–45.

Härma, J. (2011). "Low Cost Private Schooling in India: Is it Pro Poor and Equitable?," *International Journal of Educational Development*, 31(4): 350–6.

Härmä, J. (2015). *Comment on The Role and Impact of Private Schools in Developing Countries: A Response to the DFID – Commissioned 'Rigorous Literature Review'.* Available at: https://research.pearson.com/articles/role-and-impact-of-private-schools.html.

Härmä, J. (2016). "School Choice in Rural Nigeria? The Limits of Low-Fee Private Schooling in Kwara State," *Comparative Education*, 52(2): 246–66.

Härmä, J. and Adefisayo, F. (2013). "Scaling Up: Challenges Facing Low-Fee Private Schools in the Slums of Lagos, Nigeria," in *Low-Fee Private Schooling: Aggravating Equity or Mitigating Disadvantage*, 129–51.

Hauser, R. M. (2001). "Should We End Social Promotion?" in G. Orfield & M. L. Kornhaber, eds., *Raising Standards or Raising Barriers*, 151–78. New York: Century Foundation.

Hirschman, A. O. (1970). *Exit, Voice, and Loyalty: Responses to Decline in firms, Organizations, and States* (Vol. 25). Boston: Harvard University Press.

Hirschman, A. O. (2014). *Development Projects Observed.* Washington, DC: Brookings Institution Press.

House, E. (1989). "Is Retaining Students in the Early Grades Self-Defeating?" Brookings CCF Brief No. 45.

115th Congress (2017–18). "H.R.4049—Equal Access to Quality Education Act of 2017," https://www.congress.gov/bill/115th-congress/house-bill/4049/text?format=txt, accessed February 19, 2021.

Hungi, N. (2011). *Characteristics of Grade 6 Pupils, Their Homes and Learning Environments.* SACMEQ Working paper No. 1 September 2011. Gabarone, Botswana: SAQMEC.

Huylebroeck, L., & Titeca, K. (2008). "Universal Secondary Education in Uganda: Blessing or Curse? The Impact of USE on Educational Attainment and Performance," *Journal of Educational Development*, 28: 161–175.

Imbens G, & Rosenbaum P. (2005). "Randomization Inference with an Instrumental Variable," *Journal of the Royal Statistical Society*, Series A, 168 (1):109–26.

İşcan, T., Rosenblum, D., & Tinker, K. (2015). "School Fees and Access to Primary Education: Assessing Four Decades of Policy in Sub-Saharan Africa," *Journal of African Economics*, 24 (4): 559–92.

Istance, D., Paniagua, A., Winthrop, R., & Zielger, L. (2019). "Learning to Leapfrog: Innovative Pedagogies to Transform Education," Brookings, https://www.brookings.edu/research/learning-to-leapfrog/, accessed February 20, 2021.

Jacob, B. A., & Lefgren, L. (2004). "Remedial Education and Student Achievement: A Regression-Discontinuity Analysis," *Review of Economics and Statistics*, 86(1): 226–44.

Jacob, B. & Lefgren, L. (2009). "The Effect of Grade Retention on High School Completion," *American Economic Journal: Applied Economics*, 1(3): 33–58.

Jacobs, J. (1961). *The Death and Life of Great American Cities*. New York: Vintage Books.

Javaid, K., Musaddiq, T., & Sultan, A. (2012). *Prying the Private School Effect: An Empirical Analysis of Learning Outcomes of Public and Private Schools in Pakistan*. Lahore: LUMS, Department of Economics.

Jervis, R. (1998). *System Effects: Complexity in Political and Social Life*. Princeton, NJ: Princeton University Press.

Jimerson, S. R., Anderson, G. E., & Whipple, A. (2002). "Winning the Battle and Losing the War: Examining the Relation between Grade Retention and Dropping out of High School," *Psychology in the Schools*, 39(4): 441–57.

Jones, S., & Schipper, Y. (2015). Does Family Background Matter for Learning in East Africa?," *Africa Education Review*, 12(1): 7–27.

JPAL. (2018). *Teaching at the Right Level to Improve Learning*. JPAL. Retrieved from: https://www.povertyactionlab.org/case-study/teaching-right-level-improve-learning.

Kalibala, E. B. (1934). *Education for the Villages in Uganda, East Africa*. MA thesis, Ithaca, NY: Teachers College, Columbia University.

Kampman, H., Zongrone, A., Rawat, R., & Becquey, E. (2017). "How Senegal Created an Enabling Environment for Nutrition: A Story of Change," *Global Food Security*, 13: 57–65.

Karlan, D., & Linden, L. (2017). *Loose Knots: Strong versus Weak Commitments to Save for Education in Uganda*. NBER Working Paper. Cambridge, Massachusetts: NBER National Bureau of Economic Research.

Kasozi, A. B. K., with Nakanyike Musisi and James Mukooza Sejjengo. (1994). *The Social Origins of Violence in Uganda, 1964–1985*. Kampala: Fountain Publishers.

Kattan, R. B., & and Burnett, L. (2004). "User Fees in Primary Education." World Bank 30108. World Bank, http://documents.worldbank.org/curated/en/584751468779390222/pdf/301080PAPER0EFAcase1userfees.pdf, accessed February 20, 2021.

Kerwin, J. T., & Thornton, R. L. (2020). "Making the Grade: The Sensitivity of Education Program Effectiveness to Input Choices and Outcome Measures," *Review of Economics and Statistics*, 102: 1–45. doi: 10.1162/rest_a_00911.

Khiddu Makubuya, H. E. Dr. Edward, Minister of Education and Sports of Uganda (2002). "Education and Development in Uganda," in S. Khan, ed., *Human Development, Health and Education: Dialogues at the Economic and Social Council*, 172–7. New York: United Nations Department of Economic and Social Affairs. https://www.un.org/en/ecosoc/docs/health&educ.pdf, accessed February 20, 2021.

Kim, J. Y. (2015). "The New Horizon in Education: From Access to Quality." World Education Forum Incheon Korea. World Bank, https://www.worldbank.org/en/news/speech/2015/05/19/speech-new-horizon-education-access-quality, accessed February 20, 2021.

King, E. M., Orazem P. F., & Paterno E. M. (1999). Promotion with and without Learning: Effects on Student Dropout. World Bank Development Research Group. Working Paper Series on Impact Evaluation of Education Reforms, 18. doi: 10.1596/1813-9450-4722.

Kingdon, G., & Banerji, R. (2009). "Addressing School Quality: Some Policy Pointers from Rural North India," *RECOUP Policy Brief*: 5.

Kirunda, R. (2015). "Iganga Bans Automatic Promotion in Schools," *Daily Monitor*. Kampala, Uganda. https://www.monitor.co.ug/News/National/Iganga-bans--automatic--promotion-schools/-/688334/2620770/-/ivxgda/-/index.html?fbclid=IwAR0UBgQt3zxVSuBIKPbD_7UQNei7Dds9CgrDolD4IBKDyznuMU2bnq25GGE.

Kisira, S. (2008). "Uganda," in Phillipson, B. (ed.). *Low-Cost Private Education: Impacts on Achieving Universal Primary Education*. London, UK: Commonwealth Secretariat, 131–71.

Knudsen, E. I., Heckman, J. J., Cameron, J. L., & Shonkoff, J. P. (2006). "Economic, Neurobiological, and Behavioral Perspectives on Building America's Future Workforce," *Proceedings of the National Academy of Sciences*, 103(27): 10155–62.

Koppensteiner, M. F. (2014). "Automatic Grade Promotion and Student Performance: Evidence from Brazil," *Journal of Development Economics*, 107: 277–90. doi: 10.1016/j.jdeveco.2013.12.007.

Kremer M., & Holla A. (2009). "Improving Education in the Developing World: What Have We Learned from Randomized Evaluations?," *Annual Review of Economics*, 1: 513–42.

Ladd, H., & Loeb, S. (2013). "The Challenges of Measuring School Quality," *Education, Justice, and Democracy*, 19: 19–42.

Lederer, E. M. (2014). "250 Million Primary School Age Children Can't Read, Write or Do Basic Math: UN Report" *Global News* Associated Press (January 30, 2014). https://globalnews.ca/news/1117609/250-million-primary-school-age-children-cant-read-write-or-do-basic-math-un-report/#:~:text=Education-, 250 percent20million%20primary%20school%20age%20children%20can't%20read%2C%20write,do%20basic%20math%3A%20UN%20report&text=link%20Copy%20link-,At%20least%20250 percent20million%20of%20the%20world's%20650 percent20million%20primary,by%20the%20U.N.%20education%20agency, accessed February 20, 2021.

Levy, M. (1971). "Determinants of Primary School Dropouts in Developing Countries," *Comparative Education Review*, 15(1): 44–58.

Lewin, K. M. (2007). "Improving Access, Equity and Transitions in Education: Creating a Research Agenda." Consortium for Research on Educational Access, Transitions and Equity. Research Monograph No 1. University of Sussex Centre for International Education, https://files.eric.ed.gov/fulltext/ED508613.pdf, accessed February 20, 2021.

Lewin, K. M. (2009). "Access to Education in Sub-Saharan Africa: Patterns, Problems and Possibilities," *Comparative Education*, 45(2): 151–74.

Lincove, J. (2012). "The Influence of Price on School Enrollment under Uganda's Policy of Free Primary Education," *Economics of Education Review*. 31(5): 799–811.

Mashburn, A. J., Pianta, R. C., Hamre, B. K., Downer, J. T., Barbarin, O. A., Bryant, D., Burchinal, M., Early, D. M., & Howes, C. (2008). "Measures of Classroom Quality in Prekindergarten and Children's Development of Academic, Language, and Social Skills," *Child Development*, 79(3), 732–49.

Masset, E., Mascagni, G., Acharya, A., Egger, E.-M., & Saha, A. (2018) "The Cost-Effectiveness of Complex Projects: A Systematic Review of Methodologies," *IDS Bulletin-Institute of Development Studies*, 49 (4): 33–51. doi: 10.19088/1968-2018.160.

Mbogo, S., Ssenkabirwa, A., & Kutamba, W. (2019). "Mpigi Residents Pull Down Houses for Expressway," *Daily Monitor* (February 28, 2019), https://www.monitor.co.ug/uganda/news/national/mpigi-residents-pull-down-houses-for-expressway-1810190, accessed February 20, 2021.

Mbonye, A. K., Wamala, J. F., Nanyunja, M., Opio, A., Makumbi, I., & Aceng, J. R. (2014). Ebola viral hemorrhagic disease outbreak in West Africa-lessons from Uganda. *African Health Sciences*, 14(3), 495–501.

McEwan, P. J. (2015). "Improving Learning in Primary Schools of Developing Countries: A Meta-Analysis of Randomized Experiments," *Review of Educational Research*, 85(3): 353–94.

Michaelowa, K. (2001). "Primary Education Quality in Francophone Sub-Saharan Africa: Determinants of Learning Achievement and Efficiency Considerations," *World Development*, 29(10): 1699–716.

Michaelowa, K. (2003). Determinants of Primary Education Quality: What Can We Learn from PASEC for Francophone Sub-Saharan Africa? Background Paper Prepared for ADEA Biennale Meeting in Mauritius. Paris: ADEA.

Mihaly, K., McCaffrey, D., Sass, T. R., & Lockwood, J. R. (2013). "Where You Come from or Where You Go? Distinguishing between School Quality and the Effectiveness of Teacher Preparation Program Graduates," *Education Finance and Policy*, 8(4): 459–93.

Mingat, A. (2002). *Deux Études pour la scolarisation primaire universelle dans les pays du Sahel en 2015*. Africa Region Human Development Working Paper Series, No. 18. Washington, DC: World Bank.

Mingat, A., Rakotomalala, R., & Tan, J. P. (2002). *Financing Education for All by 2015: Simulations for 33 African Countries (No. 26535, pp. 1-79)*. Washington, DC: The World Bank.

Ministry of Education, (2016). *Liberia Education Sector Analysis*. Monrovia: Ministry of Education, http://documents1.worldbank.org/curated/en/481011575583469840/pdf/Liberia-Education-Sector-Analysis.pdf, accessed February 20, 2021.

Mitchell, M. (2009). *Complexity: A Guided Tour*. Oxford: Oxford University Press.

Mitleton-Kelly, E. (2003). *Complex Systems and Evolutionary Perspectives on Organisations: The Application of Complexity Theory to Organisations*. Oxford, UK: Elsevier Science Ltd.

Mitleton-Kelly, E. (2008). "The Practical Application of Complexity Theory in the Public and Private Sector: Exploring the Science of Complexity in Aid Policy and Practice at ODI on 8th July 2008," https://www.powershow.com/view/7c9a6-ZmI4Z/The_Practical_Application_of_Complexity_Theory_in_the_Public_and_Private_Sector_Exploring_the_Science_of_Complexity_in_Aid_Policy_and_Practice_at_ODI_on_8th_July_2008_powerpoint_ppt_presentation, accessed February 20, 2021.

Mitleton-Kelly E., & Puszczynski L.R. (2006). "An Integrated Methodology to Facilitate the Emergence of New Ways of Organising," in Y. Bar-Yam and A. Minai, eds., *Unifying Themes in Complex Systems*. Proceedings of the Fifth International Conference on Complex Systems, vol. 5, Paper #659. Berlin, Germany: Springer, http://emk-complexity.s3.amazonaws.com/projects/ICoSS/AnIntegratedMethodology.pdf, accessed February 20, 2021.

MoES (Ministry of Education and Sports). (1998). *Guidelines on Policy, Roles and Responsibilities of Stakeholders in the Implementation of Universal Primary Education (UPE)*. Kampala, Uganda: Center for Applied Research in Development.

MoES (Ministry of Education and Sports). (2001). "The Development of Education in Uganda in the Last Ten Years." Report on the Development of Education for the 46th Session of (Ice). Geneva: UNESCO. http://www.ibe.unesco.org/International/ICE/natrap/Uganda.pdf.

MoES (Ministry of Education and Sports). (2011). *The Ugandan Experience of Universal Primary Education*. Uganda: Government of the Republic of Uganda.

MoES (Ministry of Education and Sports). (2013). *Education and Sports Sector Fact Sheet: Education Management Information System*. Uganda: Ministry of Education and Sports.

Ministry of Education and Sports (MoES). (2015). *Education and Sports Sector Fact Sheet. Education Management Information System*. Uganda: Ministry of Education and Sports.

Montoya, S. and Mundy, K. (2017). "New Data Reveal a Learning Crisis That Threatens Development around the World." UNESCO, http://uis.unesco.org/en/blog/new-data-reveal-learning-crisis-threatens-development-around-world, accessed February 20, 2021.

Mufumba, Issac. (2018). "Pupils Wait for Museveni's Books, Pens Two Years Later," *Daily Monitor* (March 27, 2018), http://www.monitor.co.ug/SpecialReports/Pupils-Musevenis-books-pens-two-years-NRM-manifesto/688342-4360842-f99edhz/index.html, accessed February 20, 2021.

Muralidharan, K., & Kremer, M. (2007). *Public and Private Schools in Rural India*. Retrieved from: https://citeseerx.ist.psu.edu/viewdoc/download?doi=10.1.1.716.22&rep=rep1&type=pdf.

Musisi, N. B., Kasente, D. & Balihuta, A. M. (2008). *Attendance Patterns and Causes of Dropout in Primary Schools in Uganda: A Case Study of 16 Schools*. Makerere Institute of Social Research (MISR) Collections. Kampala: Makerere University.

Nangonzi, Y. (2017). "Uganda: MPs Want UPE, USE Automatic Promotion Scrapped." *The Observer*. Kampala: Uganda. Retrieved from: http://allafrica.com/stories/201706060133.html.

National University of Educational Planning and Administration. (2014). Education for All: Towards Quality with Equity India. Government of India Section 3 of the UGC Act, 1956. New Delhi, India: Government of India.

Ndaruhutse, S. (2008). *Grade Repetition in Primary Schools in Sub-Saharan Africa: An Evidence Base for Change*. UK: CfBT Education Trust.

Nellemann, S., Van Uythem, B., Bashir, S., Higgins, C., Mambo, M., Galloway, R., et al. (2004). "Cost, Financing and School Effectiveness of Education in Malawi: A Future of Limited Choices and Endless Opportunities," in *Africa Region Human Development Working Paper Series*. Washington, DC: World Bank.

New Vision. (2015). "Museveni Pledges Free Exercise Book, Geometry Set," http://www.elections.co.ug/new-vision/election/1408205/museveni-pledges-free-exercise-book-geometry-set, accessed February 20, 2021.

Nishimura, M., & Yamano, T. (2013). "Emerging Private Education in Africa: Determinants of School Choice in Rural Kenya," *World Development*, 43: 266–75.

Nishimura, M., Yamano, T., Sasaoka, Y. (2008) "Impacts of the Universal Primary Education Policy on Educational Attainment and Private Costs in Rural Uganda," *International Journal of Educational Development*, 28: 161–75.

N'tchougan-Sonou, C. (2001). "Automatic Promotion or Large-Scale Repetition: Which Path to Quality?," *International Journal of Educational Development*, 21: 149–62.

Odongo, R. (2017). "Over 50 People Sue Soroti University for Compensation," *Uganda Radio Network* (September 28, 2017), https://ugandaradionetwork.net/story/over-50-families-sue-soroti-university-over-compensation, accessed February 20, 2021.

OECD. (2012). *Equity and Quality in Education: Supporting Disadvantaged Students and Schools*. Paris, France: OECD Publishing. doi: 10.1787/9789264130852-en.

Oketch, M., Mutisya, M., Ngware, M., & Ezeh, A. C. (2010). "Why are there Proportionately More Poor Pupils Enrolled in Non-State Schools in Urban Kenya in Spite of FPE Policy?," *International Journal of Educational Development*, 30: 23–32.

Okurut, J. M. (2015). "Examining the Effect of Automatic Promotion on Students' Learning Achievements in Uganda's Primary Education," *World Journal of Education*, 5(5): 85–100. doi: 10.5430/wje.v5n5p85.

Okurut, H. E. (2016). "Uganda Second in World with Pupils Who Can't Count – Study," *Daily Monitor*. http://www.monitor.co.ug/OpEd/Commentary/let-it-be-planned-universal-pre-primary-education/689364-3382740-af8w9m/index.html.

Oxfam, (2011). "Land and Power: The Growing Scandal Surrounding the New Wave of Investments in Land." 151 Oxfam Briefing Paper, https://s3.amazonaws.com/oxfam-us/www/static/media/files/land-and-power-220911-en.pdf, accessed February 20, 2021.

Pal, S. (2010). "Public Infrastructure, Location of Private Schools and Primary School Attainment in an Emerging Economy," *Economics of Education Review*, 29(5): 783–94.

Parliament of the Republic of Uganda. (2017). December 14th, 2017. Kampala. Retrieved from: https://www.parliament.go.ug/cmis/views/17a4a9ef-f3bc-41b9-a341-b812de9c0ce0%253B1.0.

Pawlikova, V. (2006). "Biblical Translations of Early Missionaries in East and Central Africa. I. Translations into Swahili," *Asian and African Studies*, 15(1): 80–9.

Perlman Robinson, J., & Winthrop, R. (2016). *Millions Learning: Scaling Up Quality Education in Developing Countries*. Brookings Center for Universal Education, https://www.brookings.edu/wp-content/uploads/2016/04/final-millions-learning-report.pdf, accessed February 20, 2021.

Phillipson, B. (2008). *Low-Cost Private Education: Impacts on Achieving Universal Primary Education*. London, UK: Commonwealth Secretariat.

Piper, B. (2010). *Uganda Early Grade Reading Assessment Findings Report: Literacy Acquisition and Mother Tongue*. Kampala: RTI International and Makerere Institute of Social Research.

Piper, B., Destefano, J., Kinyanjui, E. M., & Ong'ele, S. (2018). "Scaling Up Successfully: Lessons from Kenya's Tusome National Literacy Program," *Journal of Educational Change*, 19(3): 293–321.

Pritchett, L. (2013). *The Rebirth of Education: Schooling Ain't Learning*. Washington, DC: Center for Global Development.

Pritchett, L. (2015). "Creating Education Systems Coherent for Learning Outcomes: Making the Transition from Schooling to Learning." Working Paper 15/005, https://riseprogramme. org/publications/creating-education-systems-coherent-learning-outcomes,   accessed February 20, 2021.

Pritchett, L., and Banerji, R., eds. (2013). *Schooling Is Not Education! Using Assessment to Change the Politics of Non-Learning: A Report of the Center for Global Development Study Group on Measuring Learning Outcomes*. Washington, DC: Center for Global Development.

Pritchett, L., & Viarengo, M. (2015). "The State, Socialisation, and Private Schooling: When Will Governments Support Alternative Producers?," *The Journal of Development Studies*, 51(7): 784–807.

MoES. (2017). *Education and Sports Sector Fact Sheet 2002–2016*. Ministry of Education and Sports, Republic of Uganda. http://www.education.go.ug/fact-booklet/.

National Planning Authority. (2015). *Uganda Vision 2040 Pre-primary and Primary Education in Uganda: Access, Cost, Quality and Relevance*. http://www.npa.go.ug/wp-content/uploads/2020/08/NDPF5-Primary-Education.pdf.

Ramalingam, B. (2013). *Aid on the Edge of Chaos: Rethinking International Cooperation in a Complex World*. Oxford: Oxford University Press.

Ranger, T. (1965). "African Attempts to Control Education in East and Central Africa, 1900–1939," *Past & Present* 32: 57–85.

Republic of Uganda Ministry of Finance, Planning and Economic Development. (2010). Uganda National Report. United Nations Office of the High Representative for the Least Developed Countries and Small Island Developing States (UNOHRLLS) https://www.un.org/en/conf/ldc/pdf/uganda.pdf.

Robinson, J. P., & Winthrop, R. (2016). *Millions Learning: Scaling up Quality Education in Developing Countries*. Center for Universal Education at The Brookings Institution.

Roderick, M., Jacob, B. A., & Bryk, A. S. (2002). "The Impact of High-Stakes Testing in Chicago on Student Achievement in Promotional Gate Grades." *Educational Evaluation and Policy Analysis*, 24(4): 333–57. doi: 10.3102/01623737024004333.

Romero, M., & Sandefur, J. (2020) "The Impact of Outsourcing Schools in Liberia to Bridge International Academies after Three Years." Center for Global Development, https://www.cgdev.org/sites/default/files/impact-outsourcing-schools-liberia-after-three-years-bridge.pdf, accessed February 20, 2021.

Rothstein, J. (2009). "Student Sorting and Bias in Value-Added Estimation: Selection on Observables and Unobservables," *Education Finance and Policy* 4 (4): 537–71.

Rothstein, J. (2010). "Teacher Quality in Educational Production: Tracking, Decay, and Student Achievement," *Quarterly Journal of Economics* 125 (1): 175–214.

Rothstein, J. (2017a). "Measuring the Impacts of Teachers: Comment," *American Economic Review*, 107 (6): 1656–84.

Rothstein, J. (2017b). "Documentation for 'Revisiting the Impacts of Teachers,'" https://eml.berkeley.edu/~jrothst/CFR/, accessed February 16, 2021.

Rubin, H. J. and Rubin, I. S. (2005). *Qualitative Interviewing: The Art of Hearing Data*. 2nd ed. Thousand Oaks, CA: Sage.

Rumanzi, Peter. (2016). "Pack Pupils' Food in Flasks to Keep It Warm—Ms. Museveni," *Daily Monitor* (December 8, 2016), http://www.monitor.co.ug/News/National/Pack-pupils--food-flasks-keep-warm--Ms-Museveni/688334-3479112-wgp37w/index.html, accessed February 20, 2021.

Sandefur, J., & Oye, M. (2015). "RISE: A Call to Arms for Education Research." Center for Global Development. https://www.cgdev.org/blog/rise-call-arms-education-researchers, accessed February 20, 2021.

Sarangapani, P. M., & Winch, C. (2010). "Tooley, Dixon and Gomathi on Private Education in Hyderabad: A Reply," *Oxford Review of Education*, 36(4): 499–515.

Scott, J. C. (2020). *Seeing Like a State: How Certain Schemes to Improve the Human Condition Have Failed*. New Haven, Connecticut: Yale University Press.

Sebano, J. (2015) "Museveni Warns UPE Schools on Charging Fees." *Daily Monitor* (September 6, 2015), http://www.monitor.co.ug/News/National/Museveni-warns-UPE-schools-charging-fees/688334-2860488-juouu5/index.html, accessed February 20, 2021.

Seidman, E., Kim, S., Raza, M., Ishihara, M., & Halpin, P. F. (2018). "Assessment of Pedagogical Practices and Processes in Low and Middle Income Countries: Findings from Secondary School Classrooms in Uganda," *Teaching and Teacher Education*, 71: 283–96.

Shonkoff, J., & Phillips, D. eds. (2000). *From Neurons to Neighborhoods: The Science of Early Childhood Development*. Washington, DC: National Academy Press.

Sifuna, D. N. (2007). "The Challenge of Increasing Access and Improving Quality: An Analysis of Universal Primary Education Interventions in Kenya and Tanzania since the 1970s," *International Review of Education*, 53(5/6): 687–99.

Singh, A. (2013). "Size and Sources of the Private School Premium in Test Scores in India," in *Young Lives*. Oxford, UK, https://ora.ox.ac.uk/objects/uuid:4edff2cf-5534-473f-b01d-f21e10f1a34d.

Singh, R., & Sarkar, S. (2015). "Does Teaching Quality Matter? Students Learning Outcome Related to Teaching Quality in Public and Private Primary Schools in India," *International Journal of Educational Development*, 41: 153–63.

Somerset, A. (2011). "Access, Cost and Quality: Tensions in the Development of Primary Education in Kenya," *Journal of Education Policy*, 26(4): 483–97.

Srivastava, P. (ed.) (2013). "Low-Fee Private Schooling: Issues and Evidence," in *Low-Fee Private Schooling: Aggravating Equity or Mitigating Disadvantage*. Symposium Books Ltd., 7–35.

Ssekamwa, J. (1997). *History and Development of Education in Uganda*. Kampala: Fountain Publishers.

Ssenkabirwa, A., & Miti, J. (2010). "Government Defends Automatic Promotion of UPE Pupils," *Daily Monitor*. Kampala, Uganda. Retrieved from: http://www.monitor.co.ug/News/Education/688336-928770-lh7smo/index.html.

Steer, L. (2014). "Seven Facts about Global Education Financing." Brookings, https://www.brookings.edu/blog/education-plus-development/2014/02/20/seven-facts-about-global-education-financing/, accessed February 20, 2021.

Stewart, D. W., Shamdasani, P. N., & Rook, D. W. (2007). "Analyzing Focus Group Data," *Focus Groups: Theory and Practice*, 20: 102.

Svanemyr, J., Amin, A., Robles, O. J., & Greene, M. E. (2015). "Creating an Enabling Environment for Adolescent Sexual and Reproductive Health: A Framework and Promising Approaches," *Journal of Adolescent Health*, 56(1): S7–S14.

Sylva, K. (2010). "Quality in Early Childhood Settings," in K. Sylva, E. Melhuish, P. Sammons, I. Siraj-Blatchford, & B. Taggart, *Early Childhood Matters: Evidence from the Effective Pre-school and Primary Education Project*, 70–91. Abingdon: Routledge.

System. (2018). In *Merriam-Webster.com*. Retrieved April 19, 2016 from: https://www.merriam-webster.com/dictionary/system.

Talemwa, M. (2014). "Headteachers Resist Automatic Promotion" in *The Observer*. Retrieved from: https://www.observer.ug/component/content/article?id=30693:-head-teachers-resist-automatic-promotion.

Taniguchi, K. (2015). "Determinants of Grade Repetition in Primary School in Sub-Saharan Africa: An Event History Analysis for Rural Malawi," *International Journal of Educational Development*, 45: 98–111.

Taylor, S. & Spaull, N. (2013). "The effects of rapidly expanding primary school access on effective learning: The case of Southern and Eastern Africa since 2000." Stellenbosch Economic Working Papers: 1/13. Department of Economics and the Bureau for Economic Research at the University of Stellenbosch, https://resep.sun.ac.za/wp-content/uploads/2017/10/wp-01-2013.pdf.

Taylor, S., & Spaull, N. (2015). Measuring Access to *Learning* over a Period of Increased Access to *Schooling*: The Case of Southern and Eastern Africa since 2000," *International Journal of Educational Development* 41: 47–59, https://nicspaull.files.wordpress.com/2011/04/taylor-and-spaull-2015-ijed-access-to-quality-over-time.pdf, accessed February 20, 2021.

Thomas, D., Witoelar, F., Frankenberg, E., Sikoki, B., Strauss, J., Sumantri, C., & Suriastini, W. (2012). "Cutting the Costs of Attrition: Results from the Indonesia Family Life Survey," *Journal of Development Economics*, 98(1): 108–23.

Tiberondwa, A. K. (1998). *Missionary Teachers as Agents of Colonialism: A Study of Their Activities in Uganda, 1877–1925*. 2nd ed. Kampala: Fountain Publishers.

Tooley, J., Dixon, P., & Stanfield, J. (2008). "Impact of Free Primary Education in Kenya: A Case Study of Private Schools in Kibera," *Educational Management Administration & Leadership*, 36(4): 449–69.

Tooley, J., & Longfield, D. (2015). *The Role and Impact of Private Schools in Developing Countries: A Response to the DFID-Commissioned 'Rigorous Literature Review'*. Pearson. https://research.pearson.com/content/plc/prkc/uk/open-ideas/en/articles/role-and-impact-of-private-schools/_jcr_content/par/articledownloadcompo/file.res/150330_Tooley_Longfield.pdf.

Tooley J., Dixon P., Shamsan Y., & Schagen I. (2010). "The Relative Quality and Cost-Effectiveness of Private and Public Schools for Low-Income Families: A Case Study in a Developing Country," *School Effectiveness and School Improvement*, 21 (2): 117–44.

Tooley, J., Bao, Y., Dixon, P., & Merrifield, J. (2011). "School Choice and Academic Performance: Some Evidence from Developing Countries," *Journal of School Choice*, 5(1): 1–39.

Uganda Bureau of Statistics (UBOS). (2016). *The National Population and Housing Census 2014 – Main Report*. Kampala, Uganda.

Uganda Bureau of Statistics (UBOS). (2018). *Uganda National Household Survey 2016/2017*. Kampala, Uganda: UBOS, https://ubos.org/wp-content/uploads/publications/03_20182016_UNHS_FINAL_REPORT.pdf.

UBOS (Uganda Bureau of Statistics) and ICF. 2017. 2016 Uganda Demographic and Health Survey Key Findings. Kampala, Uganda, and Rockville, Maryland, USA. UBOS and ICF.

UN. (2016). SDG-Education 2030 Steering Committee. Sustainable Development Goals Knowledge Platform, https://sustainabledevelopment.un.org/index.php?page=view&type=30022&nr=100&menu=3170.

UN Millennium Project. (2005). *Investing in Development: A Practical Plan to Achieve the Millennium Development Goals. Overview*, https://www.who.int/hdp/publications/4b.pdf.

UNDP. (2020). *President Endorses New UN Cooperation Framework for Uganda 2021-2025*. Uganda: UNDP. Retrieved from https://www.ug.undp.org/content/uganda/en/home/presscenter/articles/2020/president-endorses-new-un-cooperation-framework-for-uganda-2021-.html#:~:text=%E2%80%9CUganda%20has%20the%20second%20 youngest%20population%20in%20the,their%20efforts%20to%20skill%20the%20 youth%20of%20Uganda.%E2%80%9D.

United Nations Population Fund. (2020). *World Population Dashboard*. Uganda. https://www. unfpa.org/data/world-population/UG.

United Nations, Department of Economic and Social Affairs, Population Division. (2017). *World Population Prospects 2017 – Data Booklet (ST/ESA/SER.A/401).*

UNESCO. (2004). *Education for All: The Quality Imperative*. EFA Global Monitoring Report 2005. Paris: UNESCO.

UNESCO. (2011a). "Eleventh Meeting of the Working Group on EFA (Paris, 2–3 February 2011): Key points/policy recommendations," http://www.unesco.org/new/fileadmin/ MULTIMEDIA/HQ/ED/ED_new/pdf/Key%20point_policy%20recommendationsEN.pdf, accessed February 20, 2021.

UNESCO. (2011b) The Hidden Crisis: Armed Conflict and Education. EFA Global Monitoring Report 2011. Paris: UNESCO.

UNESCO. (2012). *Opportunities Lost: The Impact of Grade Repetition and Early School Leaving*. Global Education Digest. Montreal, Quebec, Canada: UNESCO Institute for Statistics.

UNESCO. (2013). *The Global Learning Crisis: Why Every Child Deserves a Quality Education*. Paris: UNESCO, https://unesdoc.unesco.org/ark:/48223/pf0000223826, accessed February 20, 2021.

UNESCO. (2014). *Teaching and Learning: Achieving Quality Education for All*. EFA Global Monitoring Report. Paris: UNESCO.

UNESCO. (2015). *Education for All 2000–2015: Achievements and Challenges*. EFA Global Monitoring Report. Paris: UNESCO.

UNESCO Institute for Statistics (UIS). (n.d.) "International Observatory on Equity and Inclusion in Education." Equity in Education, http://uis.unesco.org/en/topic/equity-education, accessed February 20, 2021.

UNESCO Institute for Statistics (UIS) & Brookings. (2013). *Learning Metrics Task Force: Recommendations for Universal Learning*. Center for Universal Learning Brookings. Washington, DC: Brookings.

UNESCO Institute for Statistics (UIS). FHI 360 EPDC, Oxford Policy Management, & REAL Centre at the University of Cambridge. (2018). *Handbook on Measuring Equity in Education*. Paris: UNESCO UIS, http://www.educationequity2030.org/resources-2/2018/4/18/ handbook-on-measuring-equity-in-education, accessed February 20, 2021.

UNICEF. (n.d.). "Uganda Country Profile," https://data.unicef.org/country/uga/, accessed February 20, 2021.

United Nations Industrial Development Organization (UNIDO). (2008). *Creating an Enabling Environment for Private Sector Development in Sub-Saharan Africa*. Vienna: United Nations Industrial Development Organization (UNIDO) and the Deutsche Gesellschaft für Technische Zusammenarbeit (GTZ) https://www.unido.org/sites/default/files/2008-06/ creating_an_enabling_environment_for_private_sector_development_in_subSaharan_ Africa_01_0.pdf, accessed February 20, 2021.

United States District Court Eastern District of Michigan Southern Division. (2016). "Civil Action No.: 16-CV-13292. Class Action Complaint," https://www.detroit-accesstoliteracy. org/wp-content/uploads/2016/09/2016-09-13-Complaint.pdf, accessed February 20, 2021.

US Department of Education. (2017). "Prepared Remarks by Secretary DeVos to Students and Faculty at Woods Learning Center: September 12, 2017," https://www.ed.gov/news/ speeches/prepared-remarks-secretary-devos-students-and-faculty-woods-learning-center, accessed February 20, 2021.

Uwezo. (2010). *Are Our Children Learning? Annual. Learning Assessment Report Uganda 2010.* uwezo.net.

Uwezo. (2011). *Are our Children Learning? Annual Learning Assessment Report*. Kampala: Uwezo. http://www.uwezo.net/wp-content/uploads/2012/08/UG_2011_AnnualAssessment Report.pdf, accessed February 20, 2021.

Uwezo, U. (2015). *Are Our Children Learning? Literacy and Numeracy Across East Africa 2013*. Uganda, Kampala.

Uwezo. (2016). *Are Our Children Learning? Uwezo Uganda 6th Learning Assessment Report*. Kampala: Twaweza, East Africa.

Uwezo. (2019). *Are our Children Learning? Uwezo Uganda Eighth Learning Assessment Report*. Kampala: Twaweza, East Africa. https://twaweza.org/uploads/files/UWEZO%20REPORT% 202019%20FINAL-42.pdf, accessed February 20, 2021.

van Fleet, J. (2012, September 12). "Africa's Education Crisis: In School but Not Learning." Brookings, https://www.brookings.edu/blog/up-front/2012/09/17/africas-education-crisis-in-school-but-not-learning/, accessed February 20, 2021.

Varcoe, K. P., Martin, A., Devitto, Z., & Go, C. (2005). "Using a Financial Education Curriculum for Teens," *Journal of Financial Counseling and Planning* 16 (1): 63–71.

Wadhwa, W. (2009). Are Private Schools Really Performing Better Than Government Schools. *Annual Status of Education Report (Rural)*. New Delhi. Retrieved from: http://img.asercentre. org/docs/Publications/ASER%20Reports/ASER_2009/Articles/WW2009.pdf.

Wagner, D. (2012). "Addressing the Global Learning Crisis: Some Comments: Brookings Washington, DC: Jan 27, 2012," https://www.brookings.edu/wp-content/uploads/2012/ 04/0127_wagner.pdf, accessed February 20, 2021.

Walford, G. (2011). "Low-Fee Private Schools in England and in Less Economically Developed Countries: What Can Be Learned from a Comparison?," *Compare*, 41(3): 401–13.

Walford, G. (2013) "Low-Fee Private Schools: A Methodological and Political Debate," in Srivastava, P., ed., *Low-Fee Private Schooling: Aggravating Equity or Mitigating Disadvantage*, 199–212. Oxford: Symposium Books.

Walker, J., Pearce, C., Boe, K., & Lawson, M. (2019). *The Power of Education to Fight Inequality: How increasing educational equality and quality is crucial to fighting economic and gender inequality*. Oxford: Oxfam International.

Watkins, K. (2013). "Too Little Access, Not Enough Learning: Africa's Twin Deficit in Education." Brookings, https://www.brookings.edu/opinions/too-little-access-not-enough-learning-africas-twin-deficit-in-education/, accessed February 20, 2021.

Weatherholt, T., Crouch, L., Merseth, K., Dick, A., Cummisky, C., Pressley, J., Nabacwa, R., & Jordan, R. (2017). "Examination of Over-Enrollment, Repetition, and ECD Access in Uganda." Presentation at Comparative International Education Society (CIES) Conference. RTI International, https://shared.rti.org/content/examination-over-enrollment-repetition-and-ecd-access-uganda-presentation, accessed February 20, 2021.

Weatherholt, T., Jordan, R., Crouch, L., Barnett, E., & Pressley, J. (2019). "Challenge and drivers of over-enrollment in the early years of primary school in Uganda," *International Journal of Early Childhood*, 51(1): 23–40.

Weaver, W. (1948). "Science and Complexity," *Scientific American*, 36: 536–44.

West, M., (2012, August 16). *Is Retaining Students in the Early Grades Self-Defeating?* Brookings CCF Brief No. 45. Washington, DC: Brookings.

Woodhead, M., Ames, P., Vennam, U., Abebe, W., & Streuli, N. (2009). *Equity and Quality? Challenges for Early Childhood and Primary Education in Ethiopia, India and Peru*. The Netherlands: Bernard van Leer Foundation.

fortes et de réduction de la pauvreté. Africa Region Human Development Working Paper Series, No. 90. Washington, DC: World Bank.

http://documents.worldbank.org/curated/en/370901468154169343/pdf/372650Schooling0 Access01PUBLIC1.pdf, accessed February 20, 2021.

World Bank. (2004). User Fees in Primary Education. Education Sector Human Development Network, http://documents1.worldbank.org/curated/en/584751468779390222/text/301080P APER0EFAcase1userfees.txt.

World Bank. (2006). United Nations Girls' Education Initiative, "The School Fee Abolition Initiative." Quoted in Institute for Domestic and International Affairs. p. 8. UNICEF Access to Education. Philadelphia, PA: World Bank, https://issuu.com/idialibrary/docs/p07-unicef-accesstoeducation.

World Bank. (2009). *Abolishing School Fees in Africa: Lessons from Ethiopia, Ghana, Kenya, Malawi, and Mozambique*. Washington, DC: World Bank/UNICEF, https://openknowledge. worldbank.org/bitstream/handle/10986/2617/482370PUB0AFR0101OFFICIAL0USE0 ONLY1.pdf?sequence=1&isAllowed=y.

World Bank. (2011). *Fertility Rate, Total (Births Per Woman) - Uganda*. World Bank. Retrieved from: https://data.worldbank.org/indicator/SP.DYN.TFRT.IN?locations=UG.

World Bank. (2016). *Poverty headcount ratio at $1.90 a day (2011 PPP) (% of population) – Uganda*. World Bank, https://data.worldbank.org/indicator/SI.POV.DDAY?locations=UG.

World Bank. (2018). *Atlas of Sustainable Development Goals 2018: From World Development Indicators*. Washington, DC: World Bank, https://openknowledge.worldbank.org/handle/ 10986/29788, accessed February 22, 2021.

World Bank. (2020). "Fertility Rate, Total (Births per Woman): Uganda," https://data.worldbank. org/indicator/SP.DYN.TFRT.IN?locations=UG, accessed February 20, 2021.

World Bank & UNICEF. (2009). *Abolishing School Fees in Africa: Lessons from Ethiopia, Ghana, Kenya, Malawi, and Mozambique*. Washington, DC: World Bank/UNICEF.

Yuki, T., & Kameyama, Y. (2013). *Improving the Quality of Basic Education for the Future Youth of Yemen post Arab Spring*. Washington, DC: Brookings Institution.

Zittel, C., Nanni, R., Engel, G., & Karafyllis, N. (2008). *Philosophies of Technology: Francis Bacon and his Contemporaries (2 vols)*. Brill. p. 349.

Zuilkowski, S.S., Piper, B., Ong'ele, S., & Kiminza, O. (2018). "Parents, Quality, and School Choice: Why Parents in Nairobi Choose Low-Cost Private Schools over Public Schools in Kenya's Free Primary Education Era," *Oxford Review of Education*, 44(2): 258–74.

Zuilkowski, S. S., Piper, B., & Ong'ele, S. (2020). "Are Low-Cost Private Schools Worth the Investment?: Evidence on Literacy and Mathematics Gains in Nairobi Primary Schools," *Teachers College Record*, 122(1): n1.

Zuze, T. L. (2008). "Equity and Effectiveness in East African Primary Schools." PhD dissertation, University of Cape Town. Cape Town.

Index